Fostering transformation and growth in Niger's agricultural sector

Fostering transformation and growth in Niger's agricultural sector

edited by:

Fleur Wouterse

Ousmane Badiane

Wageningen Academic Publishers

EAN: 9789086863273
e-EAN: 9789086868735
ISBN: 978-90-8686-327-3
e-ISBN: 978-90-8686-873-5
DOI: 10.3920/978-90-8686-873-5

Cover photo:
Le Niger, Agadez, marché quotidien,
by Guiziou Franck (https://www.hemis.fr)

First published, 2018

© **Wageningen Academic Publishers**
The Netherlands, 2018

Table of contents

Acknowledgements

The editors gratefully acknowledge the invaluable assistance of the following people in reviewing the chapters: Margaret McMillan, Alisher Mirzabaev, Marrit van den Berg, Melinda Smale, Amber Peterman, Arjun Bedi, Nicholas Minot, Mansoob Murshed, Nicholas Magnan, Aslihan Arslan, Peter van Bergeijk and Mohamed Chemingui.

Introduction

Fleur Wouterse* and Ousmane Badiane
IFPRI c/o ISS, Kortenaerkade 12, 2518 AX, The Hague, the Netherlands; f.wouterse@cgiar.org

Niger, like many other African countries, experienced high rates of economic growth since the middle of the 1990s coupled with a rapid pace of urbanisation. Between 2000 and 2015, the country tripled its gross domestic product (GDP) but its growth path is still unstable (Figure 1). The mining sector's share of GDP increased from an average of 6.1% in 2009-2011 to 28% in 2012, reflecting the start of petroleum oil production, then collapsed to 10% in 2013, following a terrorist attack that damaged the largest uranium mine of the country in May 2013 (World Bank, 2013).

Growth outside of agriculture has been concentrated in the low productivity informal services sector. As in other African countries, the longstanding neglect of agriculture played a key role in this outcome, as more and more labour moved out of a stagnating rural economy and a declining agricultural sector into a rapidly expanding informal sector around the urban centres (Badiane and McMillan, 2016). This pattern of growth offers limited possibilities for more rapid and sustained growth of per capita incomes (Badiane, 2014; Hazell, 2017). In Niger, most people in rural areas tend to be low-income farmers and over 80% of the labour force works in agriculture (World Bank, 2013). Faster productivity growth in the sector must therefore be part of any strategy to address much of the remaining poverty in the country. For instance, it is estimated that a 1% increase in crop productivity reduces the number of poor people by 0.72% among African countries (Thirtle *et al.*, 2003). Studies that compare growth-poverty elasticities across sectors typically find much higher elasticities for agriculture than for non-agriculture (Christiaensen and Demery, 2007; World Bank, 2007).

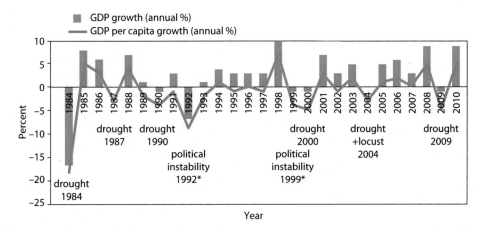

Figure 1. Annual gross domestic product (GDP) growth (%) and GDP per capita (%) (1984-2010) (World Bank, 2013).

Fleur Wouterse and Ousmane Badiane (eds.) **Fostering transformation and growth in Niger's agricultural sector**
DOI 10.3920/978-90-8686-873-5_0, © Wageningen Academic Publishers 2018

Despite two decades of sustained growth, there is still a lot to be done in terms of modernising the agriculture sector. For instance, Niger's agricultural growth, averaging about 3% per year since 2012, was driven more by expansion of the cropped area rather than by improvements in labour or land productivity. In fact, although the country's cereal yields did grow after 2000, they remained low compared to other countries in West Africa or the continental average and gaps are widening (Figure 2).

Given the predominance of rainfed crop production in the economy, rainfall variability has often had some direct bearing on the overall economic growth of Niger. A near-average level of rainfall as in 2008, 2010 and 2012, has always led to an acceleration in the real GDP growth rate while below average rainfall as in 2009, 2011 and 2013, generally triggered a deceleration in growth (Figure 1). In addition to strong dependence on rainfall, the recent growth performance of Niger's economy appears to be very sensitive to external shocks that affected the mining industry and foreign trade sectors, such as security threats in the northern part of the country, fluctuations in the world prices of uranium and crude oil and changes in Nigeria's economy.

The population of Niger, which stood at 19.8 million in 2016, combines the highest fertility rate in the world and the lowest human development index (HDI) with one of the lowest levels of income per capita (World Bank, 2018). Most of Niger's rural population is involved in agriculture, which contributed 42% of the country's gross domestic product on average between 2012 and 2014 (INS, 2017). Although more than 80% of working-age adults are employed in agriculture, this sector has the lowest level of productivity in the economy (World Bank, 2013). Almost all cultivated land is rain-fed and mainly devoted to drought-resistant cereals – millet and sorghum – and cowpeas and groundnuts. Rice and vegetables, mostly onions, are irrigated and grown mainly in the Niger river valley. Cassava, sweet potato, maize and wheat are cultivated on a small scale under rainfed and/or irrigated conditions. Livestock raising is based on extensive grazing and involves camels, cattle, goats, sheep, chickens and guinea fowl.

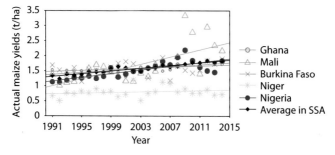

Figure 2. Maize yields in West African countries (1991-2015) (Van Ittersum et al., 2016).

Fostering transformation and growth in Niger's agricultural sector

The share of cultivated land has increased and competes severely with livestock keeping. Between 1980 and 2012, the ratio of arable land to agricultural worker shrank from 11.8 to 1.1 hectares per worker (INS, 2012). Clearing and wood-exploitation has considerably reduced the original vegetation and fallow periods are shortened with rotation having been brought down to 2-3 years further affecting soil fertility. Given that most of Niger's soils are *arenosol* (particularly prone to erosion and loss of nutrients), this increased pressure on land contributes to a rapid acceleration of land degradation. Due to soil degradation, shortening or disappearance of fallow periods, and increased pest pressure, cereal yields in Niger have decreased over the last decades and average yields are around 400 kg/ha for millet and around 190 kg/ha for sorghum. Food insecurity is a big concern for Niger. In 2006, more than 50% of Niger's population was estimated to be chronically food insecure, with 22% suffering from extreme chronic food insecurity. In addition, much of the population frequently suffers from seasonal and transitory food insecurity (World Bank, 2013). Annually, Niger's cereal production needs to be supplemented by thousands of tons of international aid to feed the country's fast-growing population.

Niger runs a structural trade deficit as well. Food and capital goods accounted on average for 51% of all imports between 2006 and 2014. Exports to world markets consist basically of mining products. The share of mining products in Niger's exports increased from an average of 49.1% between 2006 and 2008 to an average of 53.1% between 2009 and 2011, then decreased to an average of 43.8% between 2012 and 2014, in response to declining world commodity prices.

For Niger, the development of agriculture is thus essential to strategies to raise incomes and eradicate poverty in a sustainable manner, that is without further depleting its natural resource base. Since the great famines of the 70's and 80's challenges to the food security situation in the Sahel have been at the heart of research to develop policies on agriculture. The international attention devoted to famine and food shortages in Niger has culminated in a call for agricultural change involving Green Revolution plant varieties, chemical fertiliser, irrigation, mechanised equipment and fossil fuel energy (Stone *et al.*, 1990). However, reducing rural poverty across the board requires more than a green revolution. It also needs an agricultural and rural transformation (AGRA, 2017). Improving the competitiveness of locally produced commodities, such as cereals is likely to increase market capture in domestic, regional and international markets, which will result in increased incomes for smallholders.

The agricultural value chain perspective provides a reference point for improvements in supporting services and the business environment and can contribute to pro-poor initiatives and better linking of smallholders to markets. For example, a variety of market agents are involved in moving cereals from the farm to rural and urban consumers in Niger. These include farmers, who purchase inputs, produce and sell grains; traders, including retailers, intermediaries, semi-wholesalers, and wholesalers; and transporters. In Niger's cereal chain, farmers sell their production directly to intermediaries, who sell directly to wholesalers in local markets. Wholesalers are primarily responsible for inter-regional trade, selling the commodity to other wholesalers, retailers, or consumers. Increasing the efficiency of agricultural value chains is thought to be essential for the success of Niger's rural economy and to the growth of incomes of its rural population (World Bank, 2010).

The current publication intends to add to the understanding of the potential role that smallholders and the institutional and market environment play in a sustainable transformation of the agriculture sector in Niger. The first six chapters look at various innovations, factors promoting their adoption and related impacts on smallholders. Chapter 1 describes the farmer-managed natural regeneration (FMNR) in Niger as one of the most extensive agro-environmental transformations in Africa. Chapter 2 assesses the determinants and productivity outcomes of the adoption of zaï pits (a soil and water conservation measure) by smallholders. Chapter 3 explores the extent and severity of land degradation and the impact of rehabilitation on food and nutrition security. Chapter 4 analyses the relationship between gender parity, which exists in households where women are as empowered as men, and fertiliser use. Chapter 5 assesses the potential impacts of the development of small irrigation infrastructure on irrigated land allocation, agricultural production and agricultural income for farm households. Chapter 6 reviews the evidence of links between information and communication technologies (ICTs) and outcomes of farm households in Niger.

Chapters 7 to 10 analyse price formation and the integration of cereal markets, trade and the agreements governing trade. Chapter 7 uses spatial econometrics to study market integration of cereals in Niger with a special focus on the millet market. Chapter 8 assesses the structure, past trends and prospects of agricultural trade between Niger and the rest of the region and projects changes in traded quantities, both imports and exports, assuming a continuation of current trends in production, population and non-agricultural income. Chapter 9 gives an overview of the trade patterns in terms of commodities, geographical orientation and nature and provides a description of the institutional framework governing Niger's trade policy. Finally, Chapter 10 delves into one arrangement governing regional trade, the ECOWAS CET and assesses the benefits and costs of a successful implementation of the ECOWAS CET by its fifteen Member States, with a focus on Niger.

References

Alliance for a Green Revolution in Africa (AGRA), 2017. Africa agriculture status report: the business of smallholder agriculture in sub-Saharan Africa. AGRA, Nairobi, Kenya. Available at: https://tinyurl.com/y7cacb3g.

Badiane, O. and McMillan, M., 2016. Economic transformation in Africa: patterns, drivers, and implications for future growth strategies. In: Badiane, O. and Makombe, T. (eds.) Beyond a middle-income Africa: transforming African economies for sustained growth with rising employment and incomes. ReSAKSS Annual Trends and Outlook Report, International Food Policy Research Institute, Washington, DC, USA, pp. 107-132.

Badiane, O., 2014. Agriculture and structural transformation in Africa. In: Falcon, W.P. and Naylor, R.L. (eds.) Frontiers in food policy: perspectives on sub-Saharan Africa. The center on food security and the environment. Stanford University, Stanford, CA, USA, chapter 1.

Christiaensen, L. and Demery, L., 2007. Down to earth: agriculture and poverty reduction in Africa. World Bank, Washington, DC, USA.

Hazel, P.B.R., 2017. Why an inclusive agricultural transformation is Africa's way forward. In: AGRA (ed.) Africa agriculture status report: the business of smallholder agriculture in sub-Saharan Africa. AGRA, Nairobi, Kenya, pp 1-23.

Institut National de la Statistique du Niger (INS), 2012. Recensement Général de la Population et de l'Habitat. INS-Niger, Niamey, Niger.

Institut National de la Statistique du Niger (INS), 2017. Comptes Economiques de la Nation Institut National de Statistiques du Niger. Avril 2017. INS-Niger, Niamey, Niger.

Stone, G.D., Netting, R.M. and Stone, M.P., 1990. Seasonally, labor scheduling, and agricultural intensification in the Nigerian Savanna. American Anthropologist 92: 7-23.

Thirtle, C., Piesse, J. and Lin, L., 2003. The impact of research led productivity growth on poverty in Africa, Asia and Latin America. World Development 31: 1959-1975.

Van Ittersum, M.K., Van Bussel, L.G., Wolf, J., Grassini, P., Van Wart, J., Guilpart, N., Claessens, L., De Groot, H., Wiebe, K., Mason-D'Croz, D. and Yang, H., 2016. Can sub-Saharan Africa feed itself? Proceedings of the National Academy of Sciences of the USA 113: 14964-14969.

World Bank, 2007. World development report 2008: agriculture for development. World Bank, Washington, DC, USA.

World Bank, 2010. Competitiveness in Africa's agriculture: a guide to value chain concepts and applications. World Bank, Washington, DC, USA.

World Bank, 2013. Agricultural sector risk. Assessment in Niger: moving from crisis response to long-term risk management. Agriculture and Environmental Services (AES) Department and Agriculture, Rural Development, and Irrigation (AFTAI) Unit in the Africa Region. Report no. 74322-NE. World Bank, Washington, DC, USA.

World Bank, 2018. Country overview. Niger. Available at: http://www.worldbank.org/en/country/niger/overview.

Chapter 1.
Farmer-managed restoration of agroforestry parklands in Niger

Melinda Smale[1]*, Gray Tappan[2] and Chris Reij[3]
[1]*International Development, Department of Agricultural, Food and Resource Economics, Michigan State University, Justin S Morrill Hall of Agriculture, East Lansing, MI 48824-1039, USA;* [2]*U.S. Geological Survey, EROS Center, Sioux Falls, SD 57198, USA;* [3]*World Resources Institute, 10 G Street NE Suite 800, Washington, DC 20002, USA; msmale@msu.edu*

Abstract

Land rehabilitation enables sustainable intensification of agriculture and more resilient food production systems. Despite severe development challenges, Niger is the site of successful, farmer-managed efforts to counteract the global trend in land degradation that was supported by policy change. The vast majority of Niger's land is located in the Sahara. Following a series of severe droughts during the 1970s, it seemed as if the harmattan would blow drought-stricken Niger from the map. In 1993, an enabling policy change in government regulations transferred the ownership of trees from the state to farmers. Even before the policy was enacted, farmers had begun restoring agroforestry parklands on the heavily populated, agricultural plains of south-central Niger. By 2005, the sparse tree cover of the 1970s was replaced by young and fast-growing parklands, with a high density of trees, often in the inner fields around a village. Village sizes continued to swell, with fallow continuing to disappear. Yet, comparing 2005 to 2013, high resolution imagery in 2013 showed almost no change in most sample plots, increasing tree density on nearly a quarter of them, and decreasing density in less than 2%. In 2017, an estimated 7 million ha are affected by the process of farmer-managed natural regeneration (FMNR) – a scale and longevity that attests to the economic viability of the approach.

Keywords: Sahel, land rehabilitation, farmer-managed natural regeneration, Niger, agro-forestry

1.1 Introduction

An estimated 12 million hectares of agricultural lands are lost worldwide each year as a result of inadequate soil and water management practices – a loss borne especially by developing countries where farmers and their governments are too strapped for resources to adapt to changing conditions (Delgado *et al.*, 2015). Yet, despite severe development challenges, Niger is the site of successful, farmer-managed efforts to counteract the global trend in land degradation (Binam *et al.*, 2017; Reij *et al.*, 2009; WRI, 2008). In Niger, farmers' efforts have been supported by policy changes that are strongly associated with improvements in human welfare (Moussa *et al.*, 2016).

The vast majority of Niger's land is located in the Sahara. The nation's farms are concentrated in a strip of savanna that falls within the Sahelian climatic zone – an area with intense population pressure that has been devastated by recurring droughts. During the mid-1980s, farmers began restoring agroforestry parklands on the heavily populated, agricultural plains of south-central Niger. Twenty years later, large areas devoid of vegetation in 1980 were 'densely studded by trees, shrubs and crops' (WRI, 2008). 'Discovered' through application of aerial photography and satellite imagery, this process, termed farmer-managed natural regeneration (FMNR), may be one of the most extensive agro-environmental transformations in Africa.

In 2009, the area affected (home to 1.25 M households) was estimated at 5 million ha, involving at least a 10-fold increase since 1980 in tree and shrub cover on farms (approximately 200 M additional trees) (Reij et al., 2009). Today, 34 years after its introduction in the region of Maradi, FMNR is reported to cover 7 M ha (Rinaudo, 2017). The scale and longevity of use attests to the economic viability of FMNR.

The low-cost, simple technique of FMNR entails the protection of sprouting seedlings and the selection and pruning of stems regenerating from stumps of felled trees that are still living (Rinaudo, pers. comm., 2018). Application of this technique was complemented by the adoption of improved soil and water conservation methods, such as placing stone bunds along field contours and digging planting pits to control erosion and enhance moisture retention (Abdoulaye and Ibro, 2006). Compared to Asia's 'Green Revolution,' FMNR seemed like 'barefoot science' (Harrison, 1987). Like Asia's 'Green Revolution,' however, the sustained diffusion of FMNR depended on an evolving coalition of actors. Farmers themselves, as well as local and international civic associations, religious groups, and nongovernmental organisations (NGOs) bore a substantial share of total investment costs. For farmers, direct costs consist of labour time and knowledge acquisition through experience. In some instances, outsiders played pivotal roles by facilitating the exchange of knowledge, furnishing start-up capital, or removing technical constraints. Farmers' perceptions, reflecting evolving norms, appear to have begun changing during the 1980s – although the reasons for change are not entirely clear. Later, in 1993, a change in government regulations transferred the ownership of trees from the state to farmers, permitting them to capture the benefits of bark, branches, seeds and fruits for the first time. This change generated strong incentives for more widespread use of FMNR.

This chapter summarises some of the key attributes of this transformation, based largely on overviews by Reij et al. (2009) and WRI (2008), and oral presentations at a recent expert workshop (WRI, 2017). Section 1.2 briefly describes the agro-environmental situation in Niger around 1980. Section 1.3 defines the technical innovations that occurred, and why it was not recognised for so long. The actors involved in the diffusion of the technical innovations and their respective roles are profiled in Section 1.4. The scale of adoption and impacts are discussed in Sections 1.5 and 1.6. Lessons are drawn in Section 1.7.

1.2 The situation in Niger around 1980

The Sahel has long been plagued by droughts. The major droughts of the 20th century occurred during the periods 1910-14 (Aubréville, 1949), 1942-49, 1968-73, and 1982-84. This last 'signature' drought was followed by persistent dryness through 1993. The decade from 1994 to 2003 remained far drier than the period from 1930 to 1965 (Anyamba and Tucker, 2005).

The realities of climate change have been much more severe than indicated by decreased precipitation alone because of changing farming practices that resulted from a combination of government policies, rising rural populations, and the extensive conversion of natural landscapes to cropland (CILSS, 2016). Traditionally, when rural populations were sparser, farmers in Niger fallowed land, harvested tree products from woodlands that were interspersed with their fields, and regenerated trees and shrubs to supplement timber needs (WRI, 2008). Land clearing and felling of trees became more common in Niger after the colonial government encouraged farmers to grow export crops. In 1935, French law established the state as the owner of all trees, requiring that Nigerien farmers purchase permits to use trees. At first, the independent government strengthened its enforcement of forestry law, fining farmers who lopped branches from trees on their own farmland (WRI, 2008). At the same time, row planting and animal traction was encouraged by agricultural extension services. The almost total destruction of trees and shrubs in the agricultural zone of Niger between the 1950s and 1980s had devastating consequences (Rinaudo, 2007). Deforestation aggravated the adverse effects of recurring drought, strong winds, high temperatures, and inherently infertile soils.

Combined with rapid population growth and poverty, these problems contributed to chronic hunger and periodic acute famine. In Niger's Maradi Region, crop yields were declining while land under cultivation expanded in pace with population growth. The denuded landscape was exposed to severe wind erosion, leaving the agro-environment increasingly vulnerable to drought (Raynaut, 1987, 1997). The crisis in Niger was aggravated by the migration that followed above-average rainfall from 1950 to 1968, when Hausa farmers moved northward to settle in lands reserved for pastoral communities. Farmers spoke of 'fighting the Sahara' – the sand and dust storms that damaged their crops and their health (Larwanou *et al.,* 2006).

The 1968-73 drought caused many deaths, as well as the loss of large numbers of animals and trees. An acute human and environmental crisis ensued. The humanitarian crisis attracted global attention. During the 1970s and 1980s, donors (including USAID, the World Bank, CARE, CIDA, IFAD, GTZ)[1] invested in forestry training and established tree nurseries and plantations, but most of these efforts were not successful. Tougiani *et al.* (2009) reported that less than half of the 60 million trees planted over 12 years survived. The institutional paradigm of this period remained bureaucratic and top-down. In addition, tree species were exotic. Confronted with

---

[1] CARE International, Canadian International Development Agency, International Fund for Agricultural Development, German Organization for Technical Cooperation (Deutsche Gesellschaft für Internationale Zusammenarbeit).

failure, development agencies began to recognise the value of local tree species and simple, locally-adapted methods (WRI, 2008).

1.3 The technical innovation

In contrast to forestry plantations that had been promoted previously in the Sahel, farmer-managed natural regeneration 'adapts centuries-old methods of woodland management to produce continuous harvests of trees for fuel, building materials, food and fodder without the need for frequent, costly replanting' (WRI, 2008). The only technical innovation was that farmers, with the help of new techniques, were once again protecting and managing the regeneration of native trees and shrubs among their crops (Larwanou *et al.*, 2006).

Traditionally, Nigerien farmers cleared their fields of vegetation, leaving living stumps and roots. FMNR regenerates trees and shrubs from these systems. Farmers use several steps to produce agroforestry parklands. First, when they clear land to plant crops, they select tree stumps from among the mature root systems in the field, based on the usefulness of the species for food (nutritious fruits and leaves), fuel, or fodder. The products of most of these species also have commercial value, which means that what is not used by a family for their own needs can also be sold on the market. Next, they select the tallest and straightest stems to maintain and protect on each stump. Finally, they remove the unwanted stems and prune surplus side branches.

The technical innovation is to use this approach to manage the trees and shrubs as an integral part of the cropland and farm enterprise. The original model, developed by Tony Rinaudo of Serving in Mission (SIM, formerly the Society of International Ministries) in Niger during the 1970s and 1980s, involved harvesting one of five original stems on each stump every year, with a newly sprouting stem chosen as a replacement. Rinaudo (2005) referred to cleared fields as 'underground forests'. SIM then launched the Maradi Integrated Development Project with this component as a feature. Farmers were encouraged to adapt techniques to their own situation and objectives rather than follow a protocol. Some farmers created woodlands by regenerating many more stems per stump, sometimes allowing more than 200 stumps per ha to regenerate (WRI, 2008).

The most common species regenerating naturally and protected by farmers in Niger include *Faidherbia albida* (winter thorn, commonly known as *gao* in Niger), *Combretum glutinosum*, *Guiera senegalensis*, *Piliostigma reticulatum* (camel's foot) and *Bauhinia rufescens*. Depending on the location of the village, other species can be important, such as *Adansonia digitata* (baobab) and *Prosopis africana* (ironwood).

1.4 The innovators

Effective management of natural resources 'interrelates technical practices and social arrangements' (Tougiani *et al.*, 2009). Natural resource endowments are highly location-specific;

many people can benefit from their use simultaneously and one person's use may also affect another's. These characteristics imply that local society plays a fundamental role in protecting natural resources. Location specificity also means that identical practices cannot be widely diffused among communities, and must be adapted. Generalizing the approach requires support from broader institutional and organisational structures, including legal frameworks and social norms.

In the Maradi Integrated Rural Development Project, initial adoption of the FMNR practice was slow because farmers were reluctant to change their practices and Niger's forestry laws still stipulated that the state owned all trees (Rinaudo, 2005). Some adoption was spontaneous, and experiential (learning through doing). In the late 1980s, the Maradi Forestry Department suspended enforcement of forestry laws, and cooperation between NGOs and local government enabled FMNR to spread more rapidly, supported eventually by official reform of the tree ownership code. Other rural development programs recognised the value of FMNR practices and contributed to their diffusion. Observers were surprised to learn in 2006, however, that despite the suspension of donor assistance after the military coup d'état of 1996, farmers in the densely populated Zinder Region (adjacent to Maradi Region) had almost universally adopted the practice (Larwanou et al., 2006).

Charismatic leaders, including both farmers and development agents, have played key roles in diffusing innovative soil and water conservation practices in the West African Sahel (Reij et al., 2009). One such leader in the spread of FMNR in Niger is Rinaudo. In 1983, Rinaudo recognised that the stumps and roots in farmers' fields could be regenerated at a fraction of the cost of growing nursery tree stock. During the droughts of 1984 and 1985, he offered food to farmers in return for protecting on-farm natural regeneration. FMNR spread spontaneously as farmers heard about the technique. Successful replication resulted from a confluence of efforts by individual farmers, farmers' groups, local and national government, NGOs, and donors – an illustration of the 'bridging' capital that enables local communities to link to national and international institutions.

Today, in efforts to mainstream FMNR with World Vision, Rinaudo (2017) recalls the key role of FMNR 'champions' among adopters, who led by example, and established model sites in communities with continuous follow-up, exchange visits, and awareness-building. FMNR required social cooperation. Institutionally, FMNR needs to be built into the annual budgets of the NGOs that support its implementation, and linkages should be demonstrated between FMNR's sector and other sectors where investments are made.

The long-standing assumption that trees belong to the government rather than the farmer presented an initial obstacle to FMNR. Nevertheless, widespread diffusion of FMNR began to occur even before the enactment of property reforms, as farmers began to perceive that they owned the trees and tree products on their fields. The underlying reasons for changes in farmers' perceptions are not entirely clear. In 1985, the general perception was that all natural resources, including trees, belonged to the state; but after the state was weakened by a 15-year economic and political crisis, farmers began to consider the trees in their fields as their own (Larwanou *et al.*, 2006). The 'proof of concept' thus originated with farmers and technicians, in advance of policy change (Michael McGahuey, personal communication, September 22, 2009). National policy also provided incentives for change by involving rural people in more development activities and informing them about the ecological crisis. The combination of farmers' efforts, dedicated work by national and international scientists, and policy dialogue (supported by the Comité Permanent Inter-Etats de Lutte contre la Sécheresse dans le Sahel (CILSS)) eventually led to the official reform of forestry policy.

1.5 The scale of adoption

During the two decades following 1985, a number of studies estimated the scale of FMNR adoption. Taylor and Rands (1992) observed that thousands of farmers in the Maradi region protected and managed natural regeneration. Rands (1996) reported that farmer-managed natural regeneration was among the most widely spread natural resource management innovations in Niger, noting that USAID-funded projects that organised farmer visits to the Maradi region helped spread this practice. A 1999 SIM survey estimated that 88% of farmers practiced a form of FMNR within the Maradi Integrated Development Project (MIDP) zone, with an estimated 1.25 M trees added each year (cited by Larwanou *et al.*, 2006). Based on their own surveys and field inspection, Larwanou *et al.* (2006) estimated a total affected area of 1 M ha in just three districts of Zinder, with a density of 20-120 trees per hectare. Many villages had 10-20 times more trees than 20 years earlier. Farmers had literally 'constructed' new agroforestry parklands on a massive scale.

In 2005-2006, a team of Nigerien researchers confirmed that FMNR was a locally substantial, geographically extensive, on-farm phenomenon, well correlated with the sandy ferruginous soils of the south-central agricultural plain (Adam *et al.*, 2006).[2] More significantly, the highest tree densities were found in areas of high rural population density: farmers had been protecting and managing on-farm trees to an unanticipated extent, since the middle of the 1980s. The high correlation to the sandy ferruginous soils and areas of intensive cultivation suggests that the FMNR area can be roughly equated to the mapped boundaries of agricultural land use.

Field work and initial analysis of high-resolution satellite imagery indicated that FMNR was present across much of the agricultural plain that dominates the Maradi and Zinder regions in 2009 (Reij *et al.*, 2009). Of 6.9 M ha in these regions, not all soil types found in the region are conducive to rainfed agriculture and field trees. The authors gauged the area of FMNR at 5 million ha, and high resolution images from 2003 to 2008 showed an area of 4,828,500 ha. FMNR was also visible in other regions (locally present in Tahoua and Dosso regions and in the

---

[2] The study was funded by Swiss Development Cooperation, with complementary funding provided by the U.S. Agency for International Development (USAID) for remote sensing (U.S. Geological Survey, Earth Resources Observation and Science Center, South Dakota) and for specific research support by the International Resource Group.

northern part of the Niamey Region). Many of the trees were young, the hallmark of a recent and rapidly developing agricultural parkland still increasing in density and cover. Today, Rinaudo (2017) reports 7 M ha covered by FMNR in Niger.

There are several reasons why the geographic extent of landscape transformation in Niger was not detected earlier by remote sensing scientists. First, the predominant literature concerning agriculture and the environment in the Sahel is replete with narratives about severe population pressure on limited, fragile resources, resulting in natural resource degradation. Southern Niger, with its very high rural population, was assumed to be highly degraded, with far less tree cover than it had before the drought of the 1970s. Many authors cite evidence of negative rainfall trends, causing soil erosion and loss of vegetation cover. The counter-narratives – the body of literature devoted to environmental successes – were limited to local studies. Few thought to look for positive changes at a regional scale.

By the mid-2000s, however, several papers were published using the U.S. National Aeronautic and Space Administration's (NASA's) normalised difference vegetation index (NDVI), based on a long-term time-series archive of satellite imagery from the National Oceanic and Atmospheric Administration going back to 1982. These provided some indication of environmental improvements in the Sahel, including a recently observed greening trend (Eklundh and Olsson, 2003; Herrmann et al., 2005; Olsson et al., 2005). The Maradi-Zinder corridor did show an increasing greening trend, but did not stand out above many other areas in the Sahel that also showed a similar trend.

Remote sensing scientists at the U.S. Geological Survey EROS Center had been working with medium resolution Landsat imagery in a collaborative effort with the AGRHYMET Regional Center and Niger's Direction de l'Environnement to map the land use and land cover of Niger from 1975 to 2000. Their work culminated in land use/land cover maps of the country, showing among other trends the expansion of the agricultural area in the Maradi and Zinder Regions. However, change in within-class land cover was not one of the characteristics they mapped.

Perhaps the most significant reason that remote sensing scientists missed the nascent regreening of the region's agricultural landscapes was that medium-resolution satellite imagery, predominantly from the Landsat satellites (30 m resolution), does not provide enough detail to see the trees. Additionally, the predominant species, the winter thorn or *gao* tree (*F. albida*), is unique in that it sheds its leaves at the onset of rains. Even in the dry season, the *gao* tree presents a rather sparse canopy to the aerial observer or remote sensor, as shown in Figure 1.1. Even the Advanced Spaceborne Thermal Emission and Reflection Radiometer (ASTER) imagery, with twice the detail of Landsat, fails to reveal the widespread diffusion of on-farm trees. Thus, with the tools available, the scale of the transformation was largely 'invisible'.

Figure 1.1. An aerial view of gao (whitish canopies) and other trees in millet fields, Maradi Region, Niger (photo: G. Tappan/USGS EROS).

1.6 Impacts

Economic benefits of FMNR are numerous, including higher crop yields, edible leaves and fruits, cash income from sales of forest products, and rural markets for forest products (Abdoulaye and Ibro, 2006; Tougiani *et al.*, 2009). Using continuous propensity score matching and data from not only Niger, but also Burkina Faso, Mali, and Senegal, Binam *et al.* (2017) recently demonstrated that FMNR can serve as a safety net in times of income shortages or crop failure through provision of tree products. FMNR not only augmented crop yields (275 kg/ha across countries of study, but only 113 kg/ha in Niger), but also enhanced cash income from tree products (again, the effect was less in Niger), providing calories and micronutrients (a greater effect on food consumption scores in Niger). They found a sharp increase in income from marketing of tree products when the number of trees managed on the farm was under 40 per ha, and also more responsiveness to income changes among these farmers – suggesting a turning point, or optimum number of trees per farm.

Environmental benefits include reduced damage from wind and water, the return of more diverse tree species, and in some cases, nitrogen fixation. All of these enhance the resilience of farming families and their communities in this drought-prone environment. In addition to environmental and economic benefits, the diffusion of FMNR contributed to building social capital, including greater self-reliance of farming communities and improved social status of women, especially widows, and other marginalised people (WRI, 2008). Aggregate benefits are likely to be great for years to come – especially in relation to the level of donor and national government funding. Tree-based systems, such as FMNR can also enhance the productivity, profitably and sustainability of agro-pastoral systems in semi-arid zones, although they are a riskier investment in more arid zones (Place *et al.*, 2016).

Larwanou *et al.* (2006) interviewed about 400 farmers in the Zinder Region, both individually and in groups. According to the farmers interviewed, the trees they manage in their croplands generate multiple benefits. First, they reduce wind speed and evaporation. In the 1980s, crops had to be replanted three or four times because they were covered by wind-blown sand, but today farmers typically plant only once. Trees produce at least a six-month supply of fodder for on-farm livestock. Firewood, fruit, and medicinal products are supplied by trees for home consumption or cash sales.

In particular, *gao* canopies have a well-recognised impact on soil fertility, raising productivity and contributing directly to food security. Nitrogen content of soils planted with *gao* trees has been found to increase from 15 to 156%, with substantially greater levels of carbon, phosphorus, exchangeable potassium, calcium, and magnesium as well. Boffa (1999) reported increases in millet yields ranging from 49 to 153%; for sorghum, from 36 to 169% – an additional cereal yield of 400 to 500 kg/ha or more. This helps explain why farmers in parts of the densely populated southern Zinder Region have created a high-density monoculture of *gao*. Over a broader expanse of millet or sorghum area, and with other tree species included, Reij *et al.* (2009) estimated an average yield increase of 100 kg/ha. This increment appears small, but in 2006, Niger was able to produce 283 kg of cereal per capita, not far below the 1980 level of 285 kg – despite a near-doubling of the population over 25 years (Wentling, 2008; WRI, 2008). The average of 283 kg per capita represented a 40% surplus over the estimated average annual per capita cereal requirement of 200 kg.

By increasing tree crop products, FMNR has an indirect, but substantial impact on food security. More fodder and crop residues on farms allow farmers to keep more livestock closer to their fields, enhancing livestock production (Baoua, 2006; Larwanou and Adam, 2008). More livestock means more manure is available to improve soil fertility, especially as firewood from trees on farms has replaced manure as cooking fuel. In addition, tree products may be sold by young men (fuel, poles) and young women (leaves, fruits), reducing incentives for migration and creating multiplier effects in village economies. Small businesses have emerged to supply rural people with medicinal plants, fodder, and materials for construction (Larwanou *et al.*, 2006), and sustainable fuelwood (Tougiani *et al.*, 2009).

Farmers involved in FMNR, and research such as the quantitative analysis by Binam *et al.* (2017), both report a stronger economic position of women through additional sources of income and reduction of risks of food insecurity. Women now have free access to deadwood in the fields and to tree products, such as *gao* pods to feed livestock; they may own trees that produce edible products, such as baobab, through inheritance or purchase (Larwanou *et al.*, 2006). FMNR requires year-round tending, even though many men still migrate during the dry season. Women save cash by using their own firewood and they earn income by selling wood and baobab leaves; they then invest in goats and sheep, fed with *gao* pods and leaves of *G. senegalensis* (Tougiani *et al.*, 2009). Time previously spent on fuelwood collection by women can be reallocated to other activities, including food production and preparation, and childcare.

Women also have an improved capacity to feed their families a nutritious, diverse diet. In poor growing seasons and during the hungry period that typically precedes harvest, some tree fruits and leaves assume even greater significance in the local diet, serving as key sources of vitamins and micronutrients during those periods (Savy *et al.*, 2006). In July and August 2005, thousands of women and children filled nutrition centres in the Maradi and Zinder regions. Field visits later confirmed that villages practicing FMNR had been much less affected by the food shortages than other villages. Parklands help families survive through consumption and sale of tree products (Larwanou *et al.*, 2006). Farmers able to stockpile cereals during good years and supplement cereal production with tree products are better insulated against cyclical droughts, which are predicted to increase as a result of climate change (WRI, 2008). In the Maradi Region of Niger, Mortimore *et al.* (2001) and Mortimore and Turner (2005) concluded that despite population growth, agriculture had intensified, and the environment had improved, with positive consequences for the local economy.

Agro-environmental impacts are confirmed with remote-sensing. The approach involved (1) obtaining complete coverage of recent high-resolution satellite imagery across the Maradi-Zinder agricultural region to map the density and distribution of FMNR with accuracy, and (2), quantifying change in FMNR density between 2005 and 2014 to determine whether tree density has continued to increase in recent years. Figure 1.2 shows average tree cover calculated from sampled frames in the southern Zinder Region. The v-shaped trend shows the parkland in 1957, the loss of nearly half of the tree cover by 1975, and the impressive upward trajectory in tree cover from 2005 through 2013.

Contrary to common assumptions of increasing environmental degradation with denser human populations, time-series, high-quality aerial photos of landscapes in south-central Niger clearly reveal a pattern of 'more people, more trees'. The high-resolution images in Figure 1.3 show a series of changes in the agricultural landscape south of Zinder in 1957, 1975, 2005 and 2013. Natural wetlands (two dark areas in the 1957 and 1975 photos) have been converted to off-season farmland by 2005. The on-farm tree density, seen in black spots, rises over time. The low density in 1957 reflects colonial development recommendations of pure cropping. The number of trees appears lowest in the 1975 photo.

The 1957 aerial photographs open a window onto the landscape at the end of the colonial era: during a relatively wet period, the region was, as today, devoted to rainfed agricultural

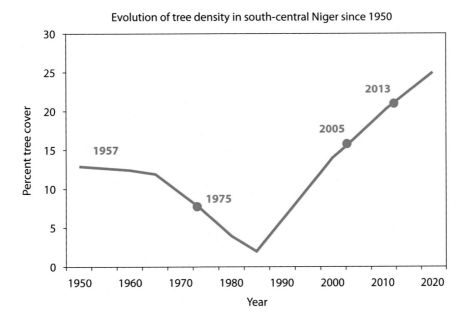

Figure 1.2. Average tree cover in southern Zinder region (CILSS, 2016).

production of cereal grains and peanuts – but with rural population at perhaps a third of the current level. The aerial views show the traditional bush fallow rotation system, with 30-50% of the land typically remaining in grassy fallow (medium gray surfaces). Fallow periods were apparently fairly short, perhaps 1-3 years, judging from the lack of dense bush growth. Farmers maintained cattle corridors of live hedges between village and pasture; and villages were much smaller and fewer. Natural depressions forming wetlands were much more pronounced, with aquatic and tall herbaceous vegetation. Trees were unevenly scattered throughout this ecosystem.

The 1975 aerial photographs provide a stark contrast. Niger was just recovering from perhaps the worst drought of the century (1968-73), with the government, international donors, and NGOs gearing up to improve food security. Numerous poorly designed projects attempted to combat desertification through tree plantations, windbreaks, and village woodlots (Rinaudo, 2001). The windbreaks of the Maggia Valley are a noteworthy exception (Rochette, 1989). The aerial views generally confirm the crisis. Much of the tree cover seen in the 1950s was gone, reflecting human and livestock pressure – including clearing for farming – as well as drought. Fallow land declined substantially, to between 0 and 20% of the land area. Rural populations had roughly doubled since 1957, as seen in the sizes of villages. The traditional agricultural parkland was considerably thinner. However, the natural wetlands (dark patches) appear relatively intact, providing sources of standing water and fresh grass during the early dry season.

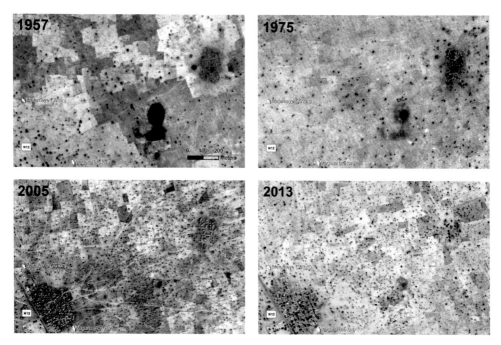

Figure 1.3. Aerial and satellite images showing changes in tree density on a typical heavily settled agricultural landscape south of Zinder, in 1957, 1975, 2005, and 2013. On-farm trees are seen as black spots (CILSS, 2016; Reij *et al.*, 2009).

In 1975, no one could have predicted the extent of the renaissance of the parkland today. By 2005, the sparse tree cover of the 1970s was replaced by young and fast-growing parkland, with high density of trees, often in the inner fields around a village. Village sizes have continued to swell, with numerous new settlements in the 2005 imagery, and the use of fallow has all but disappeared. The natural wetlands have been converted to off-season gardens, oriented toward market sales.

Recent trends in tree cover and density were studied using the same methodology to measure tree cover and density across the Zinder and Maradi Regions. Hundreds of sample plots on a 6-kilometer grid were used to compare on-farm tree cover and density using 2005 and 2013 high resolution imagery. Although most of the sample plots (73.3%) showed no change in FMNR density between the two periods, approximately 23.1% of the plots showed substantial increases in tree density. Less than 2% of the data indicate a decrease in on-farm tree density.

Earlier economic assessments of FMNR include a study by Abdoulaye and Ibro (2006), who calculated an internal rate of return of 31%, based on the value of firewood produced over 20 years and assuming an increase in cereal yields of 5% during the first five years. The analysis underestimated the benefits of FMNR by excluding its other impacts. Larwanou and Adam

(2008) made a useful first step to quantify other benefits. Average tree densities in villages in the Maradi and Zinder regions, measured by Saadou and Larwanou (2005) and by Larwanou and Adam (2008), were well above 40 trees/ha. Trees affect local climate, crop growth and yields, soil fertility, and the availability of fodder, fruit, and other nontimber forest products. Using their estimate that every tree produces an average value of $1.40 per year (in the form of improved soil fertility, fodder, fruit, firewood, and other produce), this would mean an additional value of at least $56/ha/year and a total annual production value of $280 million. On a current scale of 7 M ha, if FMNR has increased the number of trees (of all ages) by 40 trees/ha, it has added about 280 M new trees to Niger's total tree stock.

The longevity of this innovation process (two to three decades) attests to its social and political sustainability. In fact, the *process* of involving farmers in the development of these technologies may be more easily transferred than the technologies themselves (Haggblade and Hazell, 2010). The cross-country analysis by Binam *et al.* (2017) underscores the potential for legal frameworks and government policies to either encourage or impede success.

1.7 Conclusions

Land rehabilitation enables sustainable intensification of agriculture and more resilient food production systems. It contributes to maintaining socially and economically viable rural communities, stemming the tide of migration and reducing tensions among groups competing for scarce resources. Continued investments in soil, water, and agroforestry are essential to intensifying agriculture, securing livelihoods in this region, and mitigating the effects of global climate change. Much land remains to be rehabilitated; and on other cultivated land, agroforestry systems and soil fertility management can be improved.

In 1984, it seemed as if the *harmattan* would blow drought-stricken Niger from the map, generating a feeling of despair. No one could have imagined that farmers in densely populated parts of Niger would substantially increase on-farm tree densities with minimal external support – and on a scale that would not be recognised for many years, precisely because donors did not play a leading role. The agro-environmental transformation was invisible to governments and donors because it evolved largely from the grassroots, benefiting from occasional and well-timed input from outsiders – such as a change in forestry regulations. Farmer-managed natural regeneration is managed and maintained by land users and there are no recurring costs to governments or donor agencies, although it has produced multiple, long-term benefits. These stand in contrast to previous approaches that were 'top-down' and uniform. There is considerable scope for building on existing successes in Niger and other Sahelian countries.

The story of FMNR in Niger carries several important lessons about effective partnerships for agricultural development. From a technical perspective, both 'barefoot science' and cutting-edge science are important, particularly in difficult environments such as the West African Sahel. The most successful innovations are often low-cost technical improvements on local practices.

Second, a single technique or practice alone, while generally insufficient to achieve meaningful environmental and economic impacts alone, can act as a trigger for other innovations. When farmers undertook multiple innovations simultaneously, they accomplished more rapid environmental change through the synergies of soil, water, and vegetative regeneration. Third, a single 'menu' of technical options can be adopted on a large scale, but it must be flexible, adaptable, and testable by farmers under their own social, economic, and environmental conditions.

Organisational and institutional innovations were needed to attain widespread diffusion of the technical innovations. Tackling tough conservation problems needs strong village institutions and local leadership. Successful projects tended at first to be fairly small in scale and involved local farmers closely in the design of technical solutions.

FMNR is one example and component of agro-environmental restoration, or 'regreening,' although the determinants of success in this grassroots initiative are not entirely clear. 'Regreening may be driven by many factors, but it is almost always led by farmers (Reij and Winterbottom, 2015). Recognising the need to develop a practical framework to 'scale up' efforts such as FMNR, Reij and Winterbottom (2015) to identify six key steps for successful regreening. The first is to identify and analyse existing successes, improving recognition and understanding of process. The second is to build a grassroots movement to facilitate peer learning, support training, and promote the further development of community institutions. Third, policy and legal issues need to be addressed to create the enable conditions for agroforestry restoration. This aspect often involves analysis of legal frameworks and national policies, policy discussions and arranging visits by policymakers to field sites. Fourth, communication strategies, involving all types of media, help to gain widespread support. Fifth, developing and strengthening agroforestry value chains generates the economic incentives that contribute to sustainability. Sixth, research activities are fundamental to address knowledge gaps and impediments to long-term progress.

References

Abdoulaye, T. and Ibro, G., 2006. Analyse des impacts socio-économiques des investissements dans la gestion des ressources naturelles: Etude de cas dans les Régions de Maradi, Tahoua et Tillabéry (Niger). Centre Régional d'Enseignement Spécialisé en Agriculture, Université Abdou Moumouni, Niamey, Niger.

Adam, T., Abdoulaye, T., Larwanou, M., Yamba, B., Reij, C. and Tappan, G., 2006. Plus de gens, plus d'arbres: La transformation des systèmes de production au Niger et les impacts des investissements dans la gestion des ressources naturelles. Rapport de Synthèse Etude Sahel Niger. Comité Permanent Inter-Etats de Lutte contre la Sécheresse dans le Sahel and Université de Niamey, Niamey, Nigeria.

Anyamba, A. and Tucker, C.J., 2005. Analysis of Sahelian vegetation dynamics using NOAA-AVHRR NDVI data from 1981-2003. Journal of Arid Environments 63: 596-614.

Aubréville, A., 1949. Climats, forêts, et désertification de l'Afrique tropical. Société d'Editions Géographiques, Maritimes, et Coloniales, Paris, France.

Baoua, I., 2006. Analyse des impacts des investissements dans la gestion des ressources naturelles sur le secteur élevage dans les régions de Maradi, Tahoua et Tillabéry au Niger. Centre Régional d'Enseignement Spécialisé en Agriculture, Université de Niamey, Niamey, Niger.

Binam, J.N., Place, F., Djalal, A.A. and Kalinganire, A., 2017. Effects of local institutions on the adoption of agroforestry innovations: evidence of farmer managed natural regeneration and its implications for rural livelihoods in the Sahel. Agriculture and Food Economics 5: 2.

Boffa, J.-M., 1999. Agroforestry parklands in sub-Saharan Africa. FAO Conservation Guide 34. FAO, Rome, Italy.

Comité permanent inter-État de lutte contre la sécheresse au Sahel (CILSS), 2016. Landscapes of West Africa – a window on a changing world. US Geological Survey, Garretson, SD, USA.

Delgado, C., Wolosin, M. and Purvis, N., 2015. Restoring and protecting agricultural and forest landscapes and increasing agricultural productivity. Working Paper for seizing the global opportunity: partnerships for better growth and a better climate. New Climate Economy, London / Washington, UK / USA. Available at: https://tinyurl.com/ydfzkbh5.

Eklundh, L. and Olsson, L., 2003. Vegetation index trends for the African Sahel 1982-1999. Geophysical Research Letters 30: 1-4.

Haggblade, S. and Hazell, P., 2010. Successes in African agriculture: lessons for the future. Johns Hopkins University Press and International Food Policy Research Institute, Baltimore, MD, USA.

Harrison, P.B., 1987. The greening of Africa: breaking through in the battle for land and food. Paladin Grafton Books, London, UK.

Herrmann, S.M., Anyamba, A. and Tucker, C.J., 2005. Recent trends in vegetation dynamics in the Africa Sahel and their relationship to climate. Global Environmental Change 15: 394-404.

Larwanou, M. and Adam, T., 2008. Impacts de la régénération naturelle assistée au Niger: Etude de quelques cas dans les Régions de Maradi et Zinder. Synthèse de 11 mémoires d'étudiants de 3ème cycle de l'Université Abdou Moumouni de Niamey, Niamey, Niger.

Larwanou, M., Abdoulaye, M. and Reij, C., 2006. Etude de la régénération naturelle assistée dans la Région de Zinder (Niger): Une première exploration d'un phénomène spectaculaire. International Resources Group for the US Agency for International Development, Washington, DC, USA.

Mortimore, M. and Turner, B., 2005. Does the Sahelian smallholders' management of woodland, farm trees, rangeland support the hypothesis of human-induced desertification? Journal of Arid Environments 63: 567-595.

Mortimore, M., Tiffen, M., Boubacar, Y. and Nelson, J., 2001. Synthesis of long-term change in Maradi Department 1960-2000. Drylands Research Working Paper 39. Drylands Research, Crewkerne, UK.

Moussa, B., Nkonya, E., Meyer, S., Kato, E., Johnson, T. and Hawkins, J., 2016. Economics of land degradation and improvement in Niger. In: Nkonya, E., Mirzabaev, A. and Von Braun, I. (eds.) Economics of land degradation and improvement – a global assessment for sustainable development. Springer International Publishing, Dordrecht, the Netherlands, pp. 499-539.

Olsson, L., Eklundh, L. and Ardö, J., 2005. A recent greening of the Sahel – trends, patterns and potential causes. Journal of Arid Environments 63: 556-566.

Place, F., Garrity, D. and Agostini, P., 2016. Tree-based systems: multiple pathways to boosting resilience. In: Cervigni, R. and Morris, M. (eds.) Confronting drought in Africa's drylands: opportunities for enhancing resilience. World Bank, Washington, DC, USA, pp. 101-114.

Rands, B., 1996. Natural resources management in Niger: lessons learned. Agriculture Sector Development Grant, phase II. Report submitted to U.S. Agency for International Development by the International Resources Group. Available at: http://tinyurl.com/y6vu4so8.

Raynaut, C., 1987. L'agriculture nigérienne et la crise du Sahel. Politique Africaine 27: 97-107.

Raynaut, C., 1997. Sahels: diversité et dynamiques des relations sociétés-nature. Editions Karthala, Paris, France.

Reij, C. and Winterbottom, R., 2015. Scaling up regreening: six steps to success: a practical approach to forest and landscape restoration. World Resources Institute, Washington, DC, USA.

Reij, C., Tappan, G. and Smale, M., 2009. Agro-environmental transformation in the Sahel: another kind of 'Green Revolution.' IFPRI Discussion Paper. International Food Policy Research Institute, Washington, DC, USA.

Rinaudo, T., 2001. Utilizing the underground forest: farmer-managed natural regeneration of trees. In: Pasternak, D. and Schlissel, A. (ed.) Combating desertification with plants. Kluwer Academic/Plenum Publishers, New York, NY, USA.

Rinaudo, T., 2005. Uncovering the underground forest: a short history and description of farmer managed natural regeneration. World Vision, Melbourne, Australia.

Rinaudo, T., 2007. The development of farmer managed natural regeneration. LEISA Magazine 23: 32-34.

Rinaudo, T., 2017. Reflections on the roles and contributions of NGOS, farmer associations, church groups and civil society organizations in achieving successful restoration at scale. Webinar presented at Restoration Seminar – toward achieving greater success in restoring millions of hectares by 2020: an opportunity for knowledge transfer and idea sharing. World Resources Institute, Washington, DC, USA.

Rochette, R.M., 1989. Le Sahel en lutte contre la désertification: Leçons d'expérience. Josef Margraf Verlag, Weihersheim, Germany.

Saadou, M. and Larwanou, M., 2005. Evaluation de la flore et de la végétation dans certains sites traités et non-traités des Régions de Tahoua, Maradi et Tillabéri. Centre Régional d'Enseignement Spécialisé en Agriculture, Université de Niamey, Niamey, Niger.

Savy, M., Martin-Prevel, Y., Traissac, P., Emyard-Duvernay, S. and Delpeuch, F., 2006. Dietary diversity scores and nutritional status of women change during the seasonal food shortage in rural Burkina Faso. Journal of Nutrition 136: 2625-2632.

Taylor, G. and Rands, B., 1992. Trees and forests in the management of rural areas in the West African Sahel. Desertification Control Bulletin 21: 49-51.

Tougiani, A., Guero, C. and Rinaudo, T., 2009. Community mobilization for improved livelihoods through tree crop management in Niger. GeoJournal 74: 377-389.

Wentling, M., 2008. Niger – annual food security report and future prospects. US Agency for International Development, Niamey, Niger.

World Resources Institute (WRI), 2008. Turning back the desert: how farmers have transformed Niger's landscapes and livelihoods. Roots of resilience: growing the wealth of the poor. World Resources Institute, Washington, DC, USA.

World Resources Institute (WRI), 2017. Restoration seminar – toward achieving greater success in restoring millions of hectares by 2020: an opportunity for knowledge transfer and idea sharing. World Resources Institute, Washington, DC, USA.

Chapter 2.
Economics of land degradation in Niger

Ephraim Nkonya*, Yating Ru and Edward Kato
International Food Policy Research Institute (IFPRI), 1201 Eye Street NW, Washington, DC 20005,
USA; e.nkonya@cgiar.org

Abstract

Land degradation poses daunting challenges to Niger and the country has designed several policies and strategies for combatting it. Building on work past studies, this study uses new satellite data which have higher resolution and run for longer time – thus capturing the long-term land management dynamics. This study also uses an improved cost of land degradation model which nets out benefits from land improvement as well analysing the impacts of land degradation on food and nutrition security. Results show that in the past 25 years, Niger has rehabilitated over 10 million ha of bare land – or 2.6% of lands south of the desert – home to more than 90% of population. The annual total economic value of degradation was 2015 US$3.535 billion or 19% of the 2015 purchasing power parity gross domestic product. Rehabilitation of degraded land will have large impacts on household food and nutrition security. Yet, adoption rates of key land management practices are very low. The results suggest the need to Niger to find other incentives for increasing adoption of improved land management – such as payment for ecosystem services and improvement of road infrastructure, education and extension services.

Keywords: land degradation, total economic value, dietary diversity, food security, Niger, land restoration

2.1 Introduction

Drylands account for about 41% of the global surface land area (CGIAR, 2014) and are home to 2.5 billion people – or a third of the world population (*ibid.*). About 90% of people living in the drylands are in developing countries (CGIAR, 2014). Compounding the water shortage challenges that populations face, severe land degradation has occurred in the drylands (Barbier and Hochard, 2016; Gerber *et al.*, 2014). The Sahelian region – which spans western to eastern Africa – is home to people facing daunting challenges of land degradation and poverty due to the fragile biophysical environment as well as weak governance (Raleigh and Dowd, 2013). Land degradation, climate change and conflicts are leading to migration out of the Sahelian region as well as other social changes (D'Odorico *et al.*, 2013). For example, a total of 360,000 – or 5% of 1990 Nigerien population – left their country between 1990-2015 (UNDP, 2016) due to climatic degradation and other reasons (IOM, 2010; Kloos and Renaud, 2016).

Niger – a country in which about 49% of the population lives below the national poverty line (UNDP, 2016) – has experienced dramatic changes in the past two decades (Moussa *et al.*, 2016). The country presents an interesting case study for understanding how rural communities are affected by land degradation and how government action influences household investments in land improvements. Niger has risen to these daunting challenges and made significant progress both in human welfare and improvement of governance. We explore the extent and severity of land degradation and the impact of rehabilitation on food and nutrition security. We use caloric intake and household dietary diversity score as indicators of nutrition security. We follow the Millennium Ecosystem Assessment (2005) definition of land degradation – long-term loss of ecosystem services and thus use the total economic value (TEV) approach to compute the cost of land degradation. This chapter builds on Moussa *et al.* (2016) by using the most recent land degradation data recently released by the European Space Agency (ESA). The ESA data have higher resolution (300 m) and cover a longer time span (1992-2015) compared to the Moderate Resolution Imaging Spectroradiometer (MODIS) data used by Moussa *et al.* (2016) – which have a lower resolution (1 km) and cover a shorter period (2001-2010). Additionally, this study nets out the value of rehabilitated lands in the analysis – an aspect which was not considered by Moussa *et al.* (2016). In contrast to Moussa *et al.* (2016), this chapter also analyses the impacts of rehabilitation of degraded lands on food and nutrition security. The rest of the chapter is organised as follows. The next section discusses the Nigerien natural resource policies and their impacts on human development. This is followed by discussion of the methodological approaches and data used. Results of the study are then discussed and the chapter ends with conclusions and policy implications.

2.2 Niger's natural resource policies and their impacts on human development

Policies significantly affect land users' decision making even in poor countries with weak market development. Before colonialism, Nigerien customary institutions vested land ownership to anyone who cleared unoccupied forested land (Gnoumou and Bloch, 2003).[1] The French colonial government passed a law 'Aubreville Decree' in 1935, which nationalised forests and all trees in other biomes (Montagne and Amadou, 2012). Additionally, the French colonial government enacted a law which stipulated that any land that is not cleared or used for at least 10 years becomes state property (Boffa, 1999). Niger gained independence in 1960 and only slightly changed the 'Aubreville Decree' since it listed almost all economically viable trees as protected species and thus public property (Boffa, 2015). All formal and informal statues and regulations before and after independence served as disincentive for planting or protecting trees. Additionally, the weak enforcement turned all forested area as open access public goods.

The prolonged drought in the 1980s-1990s led to a loss of over 50% of livestock (RoN, 2006) and the impact of the loss was protracted given that livestock accounts for 35% of agricultural

---

[1] The customary law was nicknamed the law of the ax – to highlight the land clearing criteria used for vesting ownership.

gross domestic product (GDP) and 12% of total GDP (FAOSTAT, 2016). To address this and other effects of drought and land degradation, the Nigerien government drastically changed its laws and institutions – subsequently improving significantly its government effectiveness – quality of public and civil services, degree of its independence from political pressures, the quality of policy formulation, implementation and government's credibility and commitment to such policies (Kaufman *et al.*, 2010). From 1996-2012, Nigerien government effectiveness (GE) index increased by about 43% – a level that is high in comparison to GE decline in SSA and the Western Africa sub-region (Figure 2.1).

The country enacted a Rural Code in 1993, which recognised private land rights acquired through the customary tenure system or written contracts (RoN, 2000). Additionally, the Forest Law of 2004 gave tree tenure to land owners (Stickler, 2012) – undoing the French Aubreville Decree and post-independence statutes that vested ownership of all important trees to the state.

Niger is one of four SSA countries which have formulated sustainable land use management policies (FAO, 2016). The policies include community participation integrated land-use systems; strategies that lead to direct improvement of local community welfare and land use mapping that ensures local development (*ibid.*). This has led to a significant increase in afforestation progress in Niger – much higher than the average sub-region and regional averages (Figure 2.2). In fact, the planted forest area as share of total forest area grew much faster in Niger than is the case in Western Africa and SSA (see also Chapter 1 in this volume). This illustrates that policies – which gave tree ownership to land holders who planted or protected trees in their farms – had a favourable impact.

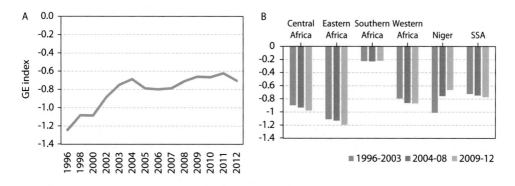

Government effectiveness (GE) Index: -2.5 (weak) to 2.5 (strong)

Figure 2.1. (A) Trend of government effectiveness (GE index), and (B) SSA, subregions and Niger GE index trends comparison, 1996-2012 (Moussa *et al.*, 2016).

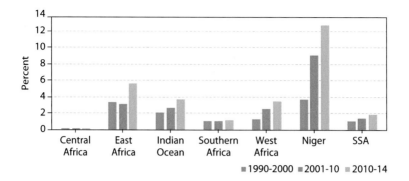

Figure 2.2. Planted forest area as share of total forest area, SSA and Niger (FAOSTAT raw data, online).

The section below discusses the approach and data used in this study. The results will reflect how the policies discussed above have affected land use/cover over the past 25 years.

2.3 Analytical approach

Our analytical approach focuses on an estimation of the cost of land degradation and impacts of rehabilitation of degraded lands on food and nutrition security.

2.3.1 Cost of land degradation

Our focus will only be on land degradation due to land use/cover change (LUCC), the leading cause of land degradation (Moussa *et al.*, 2016). Other forms of land degradation – namely degradation on static biome (cropland and livestock), i.e. land which did not experience LUCC – are adequately analysed by Moussa *et al.* (2016) and the present study does not add any new insight. Following the MEA (2005), definition, land degradation due to LUCC occurs when a low value biome replaces a high value biome. A common example in Niger is the replacement of forest by cropland. LUCC occurring in one year may be biased due to drought or other conditions. To address such potential bias, we take a three-year average LUCC in each of the 131 communes in Niger. We cannot take a three-year average at the pixel level (30 m) because of the dynamic nature of biomes. For example, pixel *i* could be a forest in 1992 but will change to grassland in 1993 and thus that pixel is no longer a forest in the baseline period and this change complicates computation of the baseline average. Analysis at the commune level helps to average out LUCC by taking the three-year average area of forest in the entire commune. To capture the trend of LUCC, we use baseline, midline and endline periods. The baseline (b), midline (m) and endline (e) periods are, respectively, b=1992, 1993 and 1994; m=2003, 2004 and 2005 and e=2013, 2014 and 2015. For example, in each commune, the forest area in the baseline period changed to another lower value biome and the LUCC between baseline and endline is given by:

$$\Delta a_{ii} = \overline{Y}_{bi} - \overline{Y}_{ei} \tag{2.1}$$

where $\overline{y_{bi}}$ is a three-year average area of forest (biome i) in baseline period b in commune I; $\overline{y_{eii}}$ is the three-year average area of high value biome i in endline period in commune i. The first difference, $\Delta a_{ii} = \overline{y_{bii}} - \overline{y_{eii}}$ is takeby sequentially pairing years such that the baseline and endline periods are about 20 years apart – i.e. $Y_{1992} - Y_{2013}$; $Y_{1993} - Y_{2013}$ and $Y_{1994} - Y_{2015}$. The average of the three-year difference is computed. The same approach is used to compute the midline land degradation. The cost of land degradation due to LUCC is given by:

$$C_{LUCC} = \sum_{i}^{\kappa} [(\Delta a_{ii} * p_1 - \Delta a_{ii} \, p_2) - \Delta a_{jir} * p_1] \qquad (2.2)$$

where C_{LUCC} = cost of land degradation due to LUCC; Δa_{ii} = change in land area of high value biome i being replaced by low-value biome j in commune i; p_1 and p_2 are total economic value (TEV) prices of high value biome 1 and low-value biome 2, respectively. By construction, $p_1 > p_2$; a_{jir} = net land area of high-value biome i restored from low value biome in a group of pixels j in commune i. The group of pixels j are mutually exclusive from those which experienced degradation – i.e. a low-value biome replaced a high-value biome. This approach ensures that the restoration efforts that Niger has done in the past 25 years are netted out of the cost of land degradation. However, TEV of a restored biome is lower than the corresponding value in its pristine state. Biodiversity builds over hundreds of years and it is not possible in a short time to fully restore a biome to its pristine TEV (CBD, 2010). For example, Catterall *et al.* (2004) observed that species bird richness in restored forests was only 8 compared to 17 in primary forests. Due to lack of data, we simply assume that the rehabilitated biomes have the same value as in their pristine state. This model is an improvement with respect to Moussa *et al.* (2016) which did not net out the TEV of rehabilitated biomes. To determine trend and pattern of land degradation, we planned to compute the midline land degradation by treating 2001, 2002 and 2003 as the midline period. Unfortunately, there is an error in the CCI ESA data as it seems there is no LUCC during this period as the biomes remained relatively stable. So, we abandoned the analysis of the midline LUCC.

2.3.2 Impacts of rehabilitation of degraded lands on food and nutrition security

In estimating the impacts of rehabilitation of degraded lands on caloric intake, we are faced with two major statistical challenges. First, the endogeneity of the sustainable land and water management (SLWM) practices used to rehabilitated degraded lands and other potentially endogenous covariates. Second, potential heteroscedasticity of unknown form, which could lead to inconsistent and/or biased estimates. We address the endogeneity problem by using an instrumental variables two-stage least square approach (IV-2SLS), which address the endogeneity bias. We will also estimate an ordinary least squares model. We address the second problem by using generalised method of moments (GMM), which combines the first moment (mean) and second moment (variance) and estimates an asymptotically efficient estimator (Cragg, 1983). The GMM is modelled as follows:

$$Y = \beta_i x_i + \mu \qquad (2.3)$$

Where Y is the per capita caloric intake; x_i is a vector of covariates that affect caloric intake – including SLWM; β_i is a vector of coefficients of the corresponding x_i and μ = population mean. We use the standard normality assumption, $E(\mu) = 0$ and $E(\mu, x_i) = 0$, i.e. we assume that covariates are exogenous and well-distributed with a mean of zero. However, we must consider the second moment – the variance to improve the estimation. The variance is given by: $E[f_h(x) u] = Var(\mu|x_i) = \sigma^2$ From this, a weighting matrix K × M of covariance-variance is formed, where K is the number of the covariates in the × vector. The weighting matrix is used to get efficient GMM estimates. To address the endogeneity bias, we also use instrumental variables (IV) thus making our estimation an IV-GMM model. The instrumental variables used include soil nutrient retention capacity – measured as low, moderate and high, elevation, and precipitation. The instrumental variables used strongly predicted the endogenous explanatory variables.[2] To determine robustness of our estimates, we use three models: OLS, IV-2SLS and IV-GMM. The empirical model will be estimated using past studies on caloric intake:

$$Y = \beta_1 x_i + \beta_2 z_i + \varepsilon \tag{2.4}$$

where z_i is a vector of endogenous variables – including SLWM practices; ε is a sample error term. Other variables are as defined above. The vector of x_i includes: household human resource endowment (level of education, household headship, family labour, etc.); physical capital (productive assets, land area, livestock owned, etc.); and rural services (access to roads, extension services, markets, etc.). Table 2.1 summarises the covariates used and compares the adopters and non-adopters of the land rehabilitation management practices included in the analysis.

2.3.3 The household dietary diversity score

The household dietary diversity score (HDDS) is an indicator of nutrition quality and is derived from groups – each of which is assigned weights to reflect its nutrient densities in terms of energy, protein and micronutrients (Figure 2.3).

---

[2] First stage estimation results are available from the authors upon request.

Table 2.1. Socio-economic characteristics of adopters and non-adopters of sustainable land and water management.[1]

	Tree planting & protection			Manure			Stony walls			Irrigation			Inorganic fertiliser		
	Adopters	Non-adopters	P-value	Adopters	Non-adopters	P-value	Adopters	Non-adopters	P-value	Adopters	Non-adopters	P-value	Adopters	Non-adopters	P-value
Number of observations	253	2,066	-	1,017	1,302	-	120	2,199	-	146	2,173	-	266	2,053	-
Household capital endowment															
Physical & financial capital endowment															
Value of durable assets, XOF[2]	46,174	52,232	0.303	55,777	48,290	0.000***	75,455	50,265	0.006***	71,717	50,245	0.000***	71,350	49,035	0.000***
Percent of households in land terciles															
Low	5.5	28.8	0.000***	9.2	3.9	0.000***	5.8	27.5	0.000***	17.8	26.9	0.015**	16.9	27.6	0.000***
Medium	33.5	24.3	0.000***	26.7	24.1	0.080*	35.0	24.7	0.006***	67.1	22.5	0.000***	44.7	22.7	0.000***
High	60.8	46.8	0.000***	64.0	36.1	0.000***	59.1	47.7	0.007***	15.1	50.6	0.000***	38.3	49.6	0.000***
Number of rooms in dwelling	2.9	2.4	0.000***	2.9	2.3	0.000***	2.8	2.5	0.054*	2.8	2.5	0.032*	3.1	2.4	0.000***
Value of productive assets, XOF[1]	30,536	25,780	0.048**	30,554	22,975	0.000***	21,369	26,568	0.433	13,594	27,153	0.000***	24,257	26,564	0.493
% households with livestock ownership	76.3	73.7	0.379	74.0	73.9	0.966	54.2	75.1	0.000***	67.8	74.4	0.078*	74.4	73.9	0.862
Percent of households in expenditure terciles															
Low	52.2	46.4	0.043**	53.2	42.3	0.000***	34.1	47.8	0.003***	20.5	48.9	0.000***	36.1	48.5	0.000***
Medium	32.8	36.7	0.219	32.8	39.0	0.002***	43.3	35.9	0.050**	46.6	35.6	0.007***	44.3	35.3	0.003***
High	15.0	16.8	0.473	13.9	18.6	0.003***	22.5	16.3	0.037**	32.9	15.5	0.000***	19.5	16.2	0.170
Human capital endowment															
Household size	6.8	6.2	0.001***	7.0	5.7	0.000***	6.1	6.3	0.585	6.3	6.3	0.769	7.2	6.2	0.000***
% of female headed households	10.3	17.6	0.003***	10.4	21.8	0.000***	13.3	17.0	0.394	5.5	17.6	0.000***	10.9	17.6	0.001***
Age household head	45.7	47.3	0.057*	47.0	47.1	0.919	46.9	47.1	0.916	47.8	47.0	0.560	46.5	47.2	0.486
Number of adults	4.9	4.4	0.005***	5.1	4.1	0.000***	4.5	4.5	0.850	4.7	4.5	0.470	5.2	4.5	0.000***
Primary economic activity of household head															
Agriculture	85.3	75.6	0.001***	80.8	73.5	0.000***	70.8	77.0	0.058*	74.6	76.8	0.543	74.8	76.9	0.435
Employed	4.3	5.1	0.613	5.8	4.4	0.059*	5.0	5.0	0.991	6.2	4.9	0.505	5.3	4.9	0.835
Non-farm	6.7	10.4	0.031**	7.8	11.8	0.001***	12.5	9.9	0.359	10.3	10.0	0.925	12.4	9.7	0.174

Table 2.1. Continued.

	Tree planting & protection			Manure			Stony walls			Irrigation			Inorganic fertiliser		
	Adopters	Non-adopters	P-value	Adopters	Non-adopters	P-value	Adopters	Non-adopters	P-value	Adopters	Non-adopters	P-value	Adopters	Non-adopters	P-value
Education of household head															
No formal education	84.1	84.5	0.878	84.1	84.9	0.598	82.5	84.6	0.530	84.9	84.5	0.886	81.9	84.8	0.219
Primary education	9.8	7.6	0.213	9.5	6.6	0.009***	8.3	7.9	0.853	6.1	8.0	0.424	9.3	7.7	0.332
Post primary	4.3	3.3	0.432	3.4	3.5	0.905	2.5	3.5	0.543	2.7	3.5	0.608	4.5	3.4	0.336
Adapted to temperature changes	42.6	45.1	0.464	46.0	43.9	0.031**	37.5	45.2	0.096	34.9	45.5	0.012**	37.5	45.7	0.011**
Adapted to rainfall changes	42.3	50.1	0.018**	48.3	50.0	0.438	48.3	49.3	0.829	28.0	50.7	0.000***	35.7	51.0	0.000***
Access to rural services															
Received extension services	11.4	11.2	0.930	12.7	10.2	0.031**	10.0	11.4	0.644	11.6	11.3	0.891	13.2	11.1	0.308
Received input credit	4.7	3.7	0.452	4.2	3.6	0.022**	2.5	3.9	0.421	5.4	3.8	0.301	4.5	3.8	0.571
Distance to all-weather road, km	19.3	19.0	0.238	12.5	24.0	0.000***	15.6	19.2	0.050**	37.3	17.8	0.000***	20.2	18.8	0.373
Distance to city, km	62.2	80.8	0.000***	64.4	89.9	0.000***	62.9	79.6	0.001***	73.9	79.1	0.248	55.5	81.8	0.000***
Distance to agricultural market, km	69.4	75.9	0.044**	64.3	83.7	0.000***	65.6	75.7	0.013***	118.4	72.3	0.000***	87.3	73.6	0.000***
Distance to international border, km	144	146	0.761	121	165	0.000***	116	147	0.000***	275	137	0.000***	171	142	0.000***
Distance to drinking water source, km	597	421	0.003***	467	664	0.000***	588	386	0.017**	580	540	0.608	604	375	0.000***

[1] Significance: * P<0.1 (trend); ** P<0.05; *** P<0.01.
[2] XOF is West African currency – Communauté Financière Africaine (CFA) Francs.

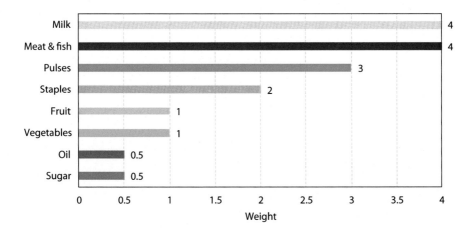

Figure 2.3. Weights of food groups (Stadlmayr *et al.*, 2010). Staples include maize porridge, rice, sorghum, millet, bread and other cereals; root and tuber crops and plantains.

A Poisson model is used since HDDS is a count variable with values ranging from 1 to 4 (Figure 2.3), i.e. HDDS = y = 1,2,3,4 with a probability of:

$$P(Y = y) = \frac{e^{-\mu}\mu^{y}}{y!} \tag{2.5}$$

Where y = mean of Y, which is equal to its variance, i.e. E(Y) = Var(Y) = μ. This means the homoscedasticity assumption does not hold because any effect that affects the first moment will equally affect the second moment (Hackbusch, 2010). The same variables used for the caloric intake (Table 2.1) will be used in the HDDS model.

2.4 Data

To analyse the cost of land degradation, we use the new climate change initiative (CCI) land cover data recently released by the European Space Agency (ESA). The data are classified and have a 30 m resolution and cover 24 years, 1992-2015. The CCI data have 22 typologies but we reduced them to only six groups by grouping those closely related and dropping those which do not exist in Niger or only to a limited extent. A recent study by Lesiv *et al.* (2017) ground-truthed CCI data covering SSA and observed an accuracy of 68% – which is comparable with MODIS accuracy of 75% (Friedl *et al.*, 2010). Excluding the desert in the north, which account for two thirds of Nigerien land area, grasslands account for the largest share of total land area (Table 2.2).

The ESA-CCI and MODIS biome classification differ significantly. Additionally, FAO biome classification also differs from CCI and MODIS. Below, we summarise the differences and the reason behind such differences. First, Table 2.3 shows that ESA-CCI has more forest area than FAO and MODIS after being reconciled with FAO's definition for forest. FAO's definition for

Table 2.2. Major biomes in Niger and their extent in 1992 and 2016.

Biome	IGBP[1] definition	Extent (million ha) & percent				MODIS, 2009
		1992-95		2012-15		
		Area	% of total	Area	% of total	
Forests	Woody vegetation with height >2 m and covering at least 60% of land area. Forest trees divided into four categories: (1) Deciduous broadleaf – broad-leaf trees that shed leaves in annual cycles; (2) Deciduous needleleaf – as deciduous broadleaf but with narrow leaves; (3) Evergreen broadleaf forests – broadleaf trees that remain green foliage throughout the year; (4) Needleleaf evergreen – like evergreen broadleaf but with narrow leaves.	1.330	0.11	1.181	0.10	0.05
Shrublands	Vegetation with mainly shrubs or short trees (shrubs) of less than 2 m. Canopy of shrublands is fairly open and allows grasses and other short plants grow between the shrubs.	26.363	2.22	26.287	2.21	10.1
Woodlands	Biome with tree cover of 5-10%, with trees reaching a height of 5 m at maturity.	61.204	5.14	65.691	5.52	0.11
Grasslands	Lands with herbaceous types of cover. Tree and shrub cover is less than 10%.	211.007	17.73	215.919	18.14	47
Cropland	Lands covered with temporary crops followed by harvest and a bare soil period (e.g. single and multiple cropping systems). Perennial woody crops are classified as forest or shrubland.	77.715	6.53	78.530	6.60	2.4
Bare land[2]		810.010	68.06	799.968	67.21	40
Wetlands	An area in which: (1) the water table is at or near the soil surface for a significant part of the growing season; and (2) soils are covered by active vegetation (during the period of water saturation.	1.847	0.16	2.043	0.17	-
Water	Water permanently covers land.	0.628	0.05	0.412	0.03	-
Urban	Built up area with large concentration of people.	0.089	0.01	0.159	0.01	0.10
Total		1,190.2	100	1,190.2	100	100

[1] IGBP = International Geosphere-Biosphere Progr Spectro radiometer.
[2] Area of bare land rehabilitated is 10.042 million ha or 2.6% of area non-desert land area in Niger.

forest area is 'land spanning more than 0.5 hectares with trees higher than 5 meters and a canopy cover of more than 10%, or trees able to reach these thresholds *in situ*'. The reason that ESA-CCI has more forest area is that when we reconciled the forest class of ESA-CCI, we also brought in the pixels with mixed mosaics, which are likely to have tree canopy over 10% but also contain other types of land, such as cropland. MODIS has significantly less forest area because it has classified a large number of pixels with mixed mosaics into shrublands rather than forest. Second, ESA-CCI has less cropland area than FAO and MODIS using FAO's definition for forest. FAO's definition for cropland area is 'the land under temporary agricultural crops, temporary meadows for mowing or pasture, land under market and kitchen gardens, land temporarily fallow, land cultivated with long-term crops which do not have to be replanted for several years, land under trees and shrubs producing flowers, and nurseries.' ESA-CCI does not distinguish temporary meadows from permanent meadows and does not include temporary meadows in the cropland area, therefore resulting in a smaller number for cropland (Table 2.3).

After the three datasets were aggregated and reclassified in accordance with the same thematic classification schema, discrepancies persisted. The discrepancies are due to the data being produced using different sources and methods. FAO land use data are primarily collected through the annual Land Use and Irrigation Questionnaire and complemented with statistics from official yearbooks and ministerial data portals (FAOSTAT, 2016). On the other hand, CCI land cover data and MODIS land cover data are derived from satellite remote sensing images.

Table 2.3. Differences in land use/cover type extent reported by FAO, ESA-CCI and MODIS in Niger.

| | Area of biome (1000 ha) and corresponding percent of total land area | | | | | |
	Forest	% of total	Cropland	% of total	Grasslands	% of total
FAO[1]						
Baseline: 1992-1995	1,729	1.37	13,250	10.46	22,000	17.37
Midline: 2004-2007	1,260	0.99	14,388	11.36	27,665	21.84
Endline: 2012-2015	1,167	0.92	16,000	12.63	28,782	22.72
ESA-CCI						
Baseline: 1992-1995	2,178	1.83	7,771	6.53	21,284	17.88
Midline: 2004-2007	2,160	1.81	7,867	6.61	21,580	18.13
Endline: 2012-2015	2,153	1.81	7,853	6.60	21,793	18.31
MODIS[2]						
Baseline: 1992-1995	-		-		-	
Midline: 2004-2007	24.03	0.01	14,414	12.11	14,568	12.24
Endline: 2012-2015	-		-		-	

[1] FAO refers grasslands as permanent meadows and pastures.
[2] The span of MODIS is from 2001 to 2013, so we only have midline data for MODIS.

But they use satellite images from different sensors and proceed with different algorithms for cloud detection, distortion correction and land classification. Even their difference in spatial resolution could cause the discrepancies, as spatial resolution correlates to accuracy in heterogenous landscape (Herold *et al.*, 2008). For permanent meadows and pastures, FAO and ESA-CCI have similar statistics under FAO's definition. FAO defines permanent meadows and pastures as 'the land used permanently (>5 years) for herbaceous forage crops, either cultivated or naturally growing'. MODIS has less area in this category because it has classified more pixels with mixed mosaics into other types of land rather than permanent meadows and pastures.

The disagreement area mostly lies in the transition zones with mixed vegetation types, where different datasets may classify the area to different classes going by various thresholds (Bai *et al.*, 2014). Nevertheless, the comparison of CCI with FAO and MODIS land cover datasets suggests that to a large extent CCI land cover data is supported by the FAO statistics but has considerable discrepancies compared to MODIS land cover – another major land cover dataset derived from satellite images. For reasons discussed earlier – high resolution and long duration – we use ESA land cover data to determine the extent and severity of land degradation.

2.5 Cost of land degradation due to land use/cover change

The extent of grasslands and woodlands increased the most while the bare land decreased by about 10 million ha – which is about 2.6% of the non-desert land area. This is consistent with other studies which have shown greater regreening of the Sahel in Southern Niger than in Northern Nigeria (Hermann *et al.*, 2005). This illustrates Nigerien achievement in its efforts to combat desertification (Table 2.4).

The total economic value (TEV) of land degradation due to land use/cover change (LUCC) is US$3.535 billion or 19% of Nigerien 2015 purchasing power parity (PPP) GDP of 19.03 billion (IMF, 2017). The on-site cost of land degradation is 2015 US$1.621 or 8.52% of the 2015 PPP GDP. Land degradation due to change of woodlands and grasslands to lower value biomes account for 96% of total cost of land degradation (Figure 2.4). The total cost of land degradation is greater than uncovered by Moussa *et al.* (2016) who estimated the cost to be only US$ 0.75 billion.[3] The difference is due to the much greater area degraded under the CCI ESA data than is the case for MODIS data. The cost of land degradation estimated in this study is even greater given that Moussa *et al.* (2016) did not net out rehabilitated biomes. Land degradation due to cropland changing into bare land contributes only 0.06% to the total cost of land degradation due to LUCC, illustrating an insignificant role of cropland LUCC to land degradation. The largest cost of land degradation on cropland is due to use of land degrading management practices (Moussa *et al.*, 2016).

---

[3] This is a constant US dollar value with baseline year of 2007.

Table 2.4. Land use/cover change, Niger, 1992-2015.

Biome	Area, baseline 1992-1995 Area, 000 ha	LUCC area (×1000 ha)	
		(2004-2007) - (1992-1995) Midline ha	(2012-2015) - (1992-1995) Endline
Forest	1,330	-150	-149
Woodlands	61,204	-1,336	4,487
Shrublands	26,363	-46	-76
Grasslands	211,007	2,778	4,912
Cropland	77,715	957	815
Wetlands	1,847	196	196
Water	628	-220	-216
Bare	810,010	-2,204	-10,042
Urban	89	23	70
Total[1]	1,190.191	-2	-3

[1] Total change is not a zero because of three points (baseline, midline and endline) are averages.

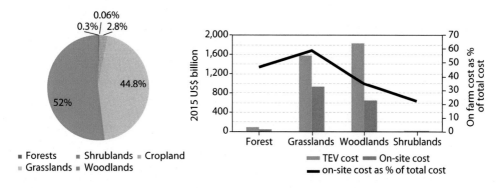

Figure 2.4. Contribution of biomes to annual total economic value (TEV) (US$ 3.535 billion) and on-site costs (US$ 1.621 billion) of land degradation, 1992-2015.

Cost of land degradation increases from north to south (Figure 2.5). There was basically no change of land use/cover in the north-eastern part of the country while the central hyper-arid region experienced rehabilitation. Land rehabilitation largely occurred in the hyper-arid communes. A large number of semi-arid and sub-humid communes also did not experience LUCC – underlining the impressive protection of land.

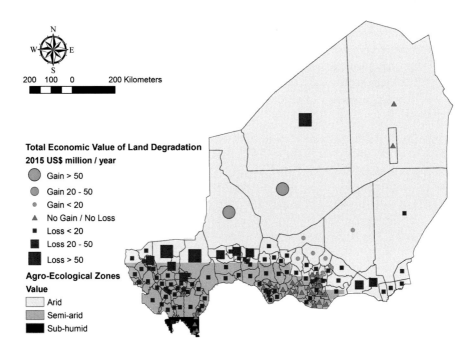

Figure 2.5. Intensity and extent of cost of land degradation across agroecological zones and communes.

The on-site cost of land degradation as percent of total cost of land degradation (TEV) is 46% – underscoring the incentive challenge in adoption of SLWM since land operators cannot internalise 54% of their benefits. The largest and smallest share of on-site cost of land degradation are those of grasslands and shrublands respectively (Figure 2.4). This is one of the reasons for the low adoption of SLWM (Figure 2.6).

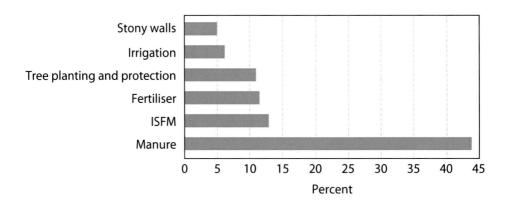

Figure 2.6. Adoption rate of sustainable land and water management.

2.6 Role of land improvement in food and nutrition security

Households who have adopted stony walls, tree planting and protection and manure generate a significantly higher yield (Table 2.5) and consequently higher HDDS and caloric intake than non-adopters (Table 2.6). Adopting stony wall and tree planting and protection increases caloric intake by 36 and 23% respectively (Table 2.6). Similarly, adoption of manure increases caloric intake by 27%. HDDS also increases significantly when farmers adopt organic soil fertility management practices. The percent change of HDDS varies from 13% for a stony wall to 5% for manure adopters. But even a small change in HDDS has a large impact on food nutritional quality. This illustrates that SLWM practices can simultaneously increase soil fertility and food and nutrition security.

Inorganic fertiliser has no significant impact on HDDS and a negative impact on HDDS and a weak positive impact on caloric intake while integrated soil fertility management (ISFM) has a negative impact on caloric intake. The results could be due to the small quantities of fertiliser used. Niger applied an average of 0.3 kg NPK/ha in 2006-10 and 0.8 kg NPK/ha in 2011-

Table 2.5. Impact of adoption of integrated soil fertility management (ISFM) on crop yield, Niger.

Crop	Yield (kg/ha)		Percent change
	With ISFM	Without ISFM	
Millet	461	350	32
Sorghum	153	110	39
Cowpea	231	176	31

Table 2.6. Household dietary diversity score (HDDS) and 7-day per capita caloric intake with and without land management practice.

Land management	HDDS				7-day per capita caloric intake (Kcal)			
	With	Without	% change	Equality test[1]	With	Without	% change	Equality test[1]
Stony wall	6.8	6.0	13	0.008***	3,561	2,627	36	0.000***
Tree planting & protection	6.6	5.9	12	0.007***	3,202	2,613	23	0.000***
Fertiliser	6.04	6.01	0	0.872	2,732	2,649	3	0.786
Manure	6.2	5.9	5	0.026**	3,105	2,450	27	0.000***
ISFM[2]	5.7	6.1	-7	0.034**	2,841	2,636	8	0.0848*

[1] Significance: * $P<0.1$ (trend); ** $P<0.05$; *** $P<0.01$.
[2] ISFM = integrated soil fertility management.

14, the lowest quantities of nitrogen, phosphorus and potassium (NPK) in SSA (Figure 2.7). Consequently, even ISFM does not seem to have an appreciable impact on food and nutrition security. However, it is worth noting the dramatic increase in quantity of NPK applied in Niger. The change is much greater than in other countries – illustrating the impressive progress Niger has made in the past decade (Moussa *et al.*, 2016).

Regression results on the association of rehabilitation of degraded lands with caloric intake and HDDS support the descriptive results discussed above. Stony wall, tree planting and protection, organic inputs (manure) are significantly positively correlated with caloric intake and the results are robust across all three models (Table 2.7). Similarly, inorganic fertiliser does not have a significant association with caloric intake. Surprisingly, irrigation is negatively related with caloric intake. It is possible that farmers practice supplemental irrigation and do so when they experience drought, which reduces caloric intake since drought is always associated with hunger. As expected, household human capital endowment has a significant correlation with caloric intake. Consistent with other studies (e.g. Akhter *et al.*, 2009), larger families have lower caloric intake. Consistent with Adelman *et al.* (2008), the level of education is associated with higher caloric intake. Household capital endowment generally relates to higher caloric intake as expected. The only exception is the number of rooms – an aspect which could be due to larger families building low-value small houses – and thus not reflecting value of housing observed in urban areas. As expected, land quality is associated with increased caloric intake as it is likely to increase agricultural productivity. Access to rural services has a weak relation with caloric intake. Only proximity to an agricultural market relates positively to caloric intake. The weak extension services in Niger could be the reason behind its lack of impact on caloric intake. Distance to

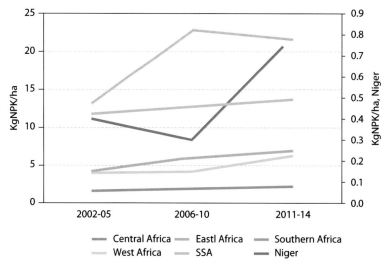

Figure 2.7. Fertiliser applied in Niger and SSA sub-regions (Calculated from FAOSTAT raw data, available at: http://www.fao.org/faostat/en/#data/RF).

Table 2.7. Impact of land improvement on caloric intake in rural Niger.[1,2]

	OLS	IV-2SLS	IV-GMM
Land and water management practices			
Tree planting and protection	0.157***	0.927**	0.164***
	(0.047)	(0.465)	(0.043)
Stony wall	0.261***	0.956***	0.239***
	(0.065)	(0.251)	(0.058)
Inorganic fertilisers	-0.003	-0.360	0.003
	(0.043)	(0.294)	(0.042)
Organic fertilisers	0.102***	0.596**	0.0959***
	(0.032)	(0.277)	(0.031)
Irrigation	-0.354***	-0.711**	-0.352***
	(0.071)	(0.346)	(0.068)
Adapted to temperature changes	0.058	0.039	0.055
	(0.045)	(0.055)	(0.049)
Adapted to rainfall changes	-0.032	-0.020	-0.018
	(0.045)	(0.060)	(0.049)
Household characteristics			
Ln (value of durable assets)	0.004	0.004	0.005
	(0.005)	(0.006)	(0.005)
Ln (household size)	-0.252***	-0.260***	-0.251***
	(0.067)	(0.080)	(0.074)
Female household head	0.019	0.047	0.036
	(0.041)	(0.052)	(0.043)
Ln (age of household head)	-0.063	-0.049	-0.052
	(0.049)	(0.066)	(0.051)
Number of adults	-0.009	-0.007	-0.008
	(0.016)	(0.019)	(0.016)
Household head level of education (cf post-primary)			
No formal education	-0.203***	-0.209***	-0.207***
	(0.057)	(0.066)	(0.062)
Primary	-0.262***	-0.315***	-0.281***
	(0.074)	(0.087)	(0.079)
Capital endowment			
Expenditure tercile (cf low)			
Medium	0.161***	0.176***	0.150***
	(0.034)	(0.041)	(0.033)
High	0.250***	0.272***	0.254***
	(0.048)	(0.058)	(0.049)

Table 2.7. Continued.

	OLS	IV-2SLS	IV-GMM
Ln (value of productive assets, XOF)	0.034***	0.027***	0.035***
	(0.005)	(0.006)	(0.005)
Livestock ownership	0.138***	0.183***	0.137***
	(0.035)	(0.046)	(0.035)
Number of rooms in dwelling	-0.049***	-0.069***	-0.049***
	(0.011)	(0.013)	(0.012)
Land quality terciles (cf low)			
Medium	0.139***	-0.009	0.146***
	(0.045)	(0.079)	(0.047)
High	0.100**	-0.165**	0.125***
	(0.040)	(0.076)	(0.040)
Primary activity of household head (cf agriculture)			
Employed	0.0509	0.0633	0.0214
	(0.067)	(0.079)	(0.063)
Non-farm	-0.0161	6.16E-05	-0.00398
	(0.049)	(0.059)	(0.048)
Unemployed	0.0315	0.0681	0.000432
	(0.079)	(0.093)	(0.088)
Access to rural services			
Extension access	0.0357	0.0453	0.0361
	(0.045)	(0.053)	(0.045)
Credit input credit	0.0476	0.0991	0.0632
	(0.073)	(0.085)	(0.058)
Ln (distance to all-weather road, km)	0.013	0.0102	0.0171
	(0.014)	(0.019)	(0.014)
Ln (distance to city, km)	0.00383	-0.0361	-0.00919
	(0.027)	(0.040)	(0.027)
Ln (distance to agricultural market, km)	-0.0677**	-0.0171	-0.0793***
	(0.027)	(0.035)	(0.025)
Ln (distance international border, km)	0.0752***	0.117***	0.0531**
	(0.022)	(0.029)	(0.023)
Distance to drinking water source	-1.06e-05	4.07e-07	-5.21e-06
	(0.000)	(0.000)	(0.000)
Constant	8.304***	8.000***	8.428***
	(0.243)	(0.305)	(0.259)

Table 2.7. Continued.

	OLS	IV-2SLS	IV-GMM
Observations	2,282	2,282	2,282
R^2	0.198	0.087	0.195
F-test (joint significance of all covariates)	0.000***	0.000***	0.000***
Endogeneity tests:			
Wu-Hausman F test (*P*-value)		0.000***	0.000***
Durbin-Wu-Hausman chi-square test (*P*-value)		0.000***	0.000***

[1] Values are given as coefficients, with corresponding standard errors in brackets. Significance: * $P<0.1$ (trend); ** $P<0.05$; *** $P<0.01$.
[2] OLS = ordinary least square; IV = instrumental variable; 2SLS = two-stage least square; GMM = generalised methods of moments.

international border increases caloric suggesting that there is significant cross-border trade that increases income and in turn enhances caloric intake. The countries bordering Niger where most surveyed farmers were located are Benin, Burkina Faso, Chad, Cote d'Ivoire, Mali and Nigeria.

Consistent with the descriptive statistics results, tree planting and protection, stony wall and organic inputs are associated with higher HDDS and the results are robust across all five models (Table 2.8). Likewise, adaptation to climate change (temperature) relates positively to HDDS. However, irrigation is negatively correlated to HDDS, an aspect which is unexpected since irrigators can grow vegetables and other foods which may not be grown under rainfed conditions. Age of household head increases HDDS – suggesting that households with older heads are likely better endowed to afford a higher dietary diversity. Surprisingly, level of education does not have a significant correlation with HDDS. This is contrary to well-established strong relationship between education and better nutrition (Adato and Bassett, 2009; Jukes *et al.*, 2007). As expected, access to agricultural extension services, proximity to all weather roads, city, and market are positively correlated with HDDS. The results underscore the importance of rural services in achieving nutrition security. Likewise, value of assets and livestock are positively associated with HDDS – supporting the well-established positive role of livestock in enhancing household nutrition security.

Table 2.8. Drivers of household dietary diversity score, Niger.[1,2]

	OLS	IV-2SLS	IV-GMM	Poisson	IV-Poisson
Land and water management practices					
Tree planting and protection	1.122**	6.44	0.929**	0.098***	13.77
	(0.461)	(6.269)	(0.426)	(0.021)	(323,896.000)
Stony wall	2.538***	14.24***	2.894***	0.239***	12.56
	(0.639)	(3.572)	(0.588)	(0.027)	(122,391.000)
Inorganic fertilisers	-1.078**	-17.04***	-1.761***	-0.111***	-1.041***
	(0.423)	(3.988)	(0.416)	(0.020)	(0.393)
Organic fertilisers	1.002***	15.09***	0.846***	0.097***	1.547**
	(0.315)	(3.833)	(0.311)	(0.015)	(0.664)
Irrigation	-0.558	9.171*	-0.333	-0.069**	0.0908
	(0.695)	(4.735)	(0.694)	(0.033)	(0.428)
Adapted to temperature changes	0.883**	0.447	1.060**	0.085***	0.179*
	(0.443)	(0.759)	(0.461)	(0.021)	(0.108)
Adapted to rainfall changes	0.0602	-0.172	0.0411	0.007	-0.0183
	(0.446)	(0.829)	(0.454)	(0.021)	(0.118)
Household characteristics					
Ln (value of durable assets)	0.0391	0.007	0.0572	0.004	0.00339
	(0.048)	(0.086)	(0.048)	(0.002)	(0.009)
Ln (household size)	0.94	0.872	1.149*	0.092***	0.104
	(0.652)	(1.082)	(0.638)	(0.031)	(0.126)
Female household head	0.336	1.481**	0.375	0.033*	0.0135
	(0.407)	(0.720)	(0.402)	(0.019)	(0.075)
Ln (age of household head)	1.142**	0.286	1.127**	0.114***	0.0235
	(0.482)	(0.908)	(0.479)	(0.023)	(0.120)
Number of adults	-0.259*	-0.153	-0.297*	-0.025***	-0.0339
	(0.155)	(0.255)	(0.153)	(0.007)	(0.036)
Household head level of education (cf post-primary)					
No formal education	0.231	0.0695	0.167	0.020	0.166
	(0.564)	(0.917)	(0.531)	(0.027)	(0.137)
Primary	1.03	0.396	0.951	0.097***	0.123
	(0.732)	(1.199)	(0.695)	(0.034)	(0.176)
Capital endowment					
Expenditure tercile (cf low)					
Medium	0.395	0.52	0.545*	0.035**	0.0533
	(0.338)	(0.571)	(0.328)	(0.016)	(0.072)
High	0.635	0.354	0.714	0.055**	0.153
	(0.468)	(0.803)	(0.467)	(0.022)	(0.110)

Table 2.8. Continued.

	OLS	IV-2SLS	IV-GMM	Poisson	IV-Poisson
Ln (value of productive assets, XOF)	0.236***	0.260***	0.248***	0.026***	0.0305***
	(0.046)	(0.081)	(0.046)	(0.002)	(0.010)
Livestock ownership	1.196***	2.316***	1.548***	0.128***	0.177**
	(0.342)	(0.627)	(0.347)	(0.017)	(0.078)
Number of rooms in dwelling	0.174*	-0.195	0.218**	0.016***	-0.0323
	(0.103)	(0.182)	(0.094)	(0.005)	(0.024)
Land quality terciles (cf low)					
Medium	-0.203	-4.541***	0.0817	-0.0172	-0.440***
	(0.443)	(1.092)	(0.438)	(0.021)	(0.136)
High	-0.35	-5.841***	-0.0988	-0.03	-0.594***
	(0.392)	(1.053)	(0.387)	(0.018)	(0.146)
Primary activity of household head (cf agriculture)					
Employed	0.656	0.407	0.881	0.0670**	0.144
	(0.660)	(1.084)	(0.615)	(0.030)	(0.127)
Non-farm	0.736	1.317	0.693	0.066***	0.185*
	(0.483)	(0.811)	(0.481)	(0.022)	(0.099)
Unemployed	-0.67	-0.204	-0.838	-0.0652*	-0.0164
	(0.768)	(1.264)	(0.822)	(0.037)	(0.140)
Access to rural services					
Extension access	0.983**	1.032	1.313***	0.090***	0.078
	(0.447)	(0.728)	(0.425)	(0.020)	(0.090)
Credit input credit	0.851	1.773	1.051	0.0785**	0.202
	(0.721)	(1.174)	(0.727)	(0.032)	(0.148)
Ln (distance to all-weather road, km)	0.192	0.108	0.279**	0.020***	0.0162
	(0.136)	(0.258)	(0.134)	(0.006)	(0.027)
Ln (distance to city, km)	-0.70***	-1.989***	-1.036***	-0.077***	-0.221***
	(0.262)	(0.544)	(0.259)	(0.012)	(0.068)
Ln (distance to agric. market, km)	-0.98***	0.283	-1.042***	-0.091***	0.025
	(0.265)	(0.479)	(0.238)	(0.012)	(0.054)
Ln(dist. to international border, km)	1.598***	1.840***	2.077***	0.171***	0.177***
	(0.217)	(0.391)	(0.240)	(0.011)	(0.060)
Distance to drinking water source	0.0002	0.0003	0.0003*	2.34e-05***	5.34e-05*
	(0.000)	(0.000)	(0.000)	(0.000)	(0.000)
Constant	-0.718	0.613	-2.336	1.154***	1.462**
	(2.387)	(4.223)	(2.416)	(0.114)	(0.719)

Table 2.8. Continued.

	OLS	IV-2SLS	IV-GMM	Poisson	IV-Poisson
Observations	2,304	2,304	2,304	2,304	2,304
F-test (significance of all covariates)	0.000***	0.000***	0.000***	0.000***	0.000***
Endogeneity tests:					
Wu-Hausman F test (*P*-value)		0.000***	0.000***		
Durbin-Wu-Hausman chi-square-test		0.000***	0.000***		
(*P*-value)					

[1] Values are given as coefficients, with corresponding standard errors in brackets. Significance: * $P<0.1$ (trend); ** $P<0.05$; *** $P<0.01$.
[2] OLS = ordinary least square; IV = instrumental variable; 2SLS = two-stage least square; GMM = generalised methods of moments.

2.7 Conclusions and policy recommendations

In the past 25 years, Nigerien efforts to combat desertification have resulted into rehabilitation of over 10 million ha of bare land – or 2.6% of non-desert land area. Planted forest as a share of total forest area in Niger was over 12% of the total forest area in 2011-2014, the highest share in West Africa. The country has also achieved an impressive progress in increasing soil fertility through a higher rate of application of nitrogen, phosphorus and potassium (NPK). From 2002-2005 to 2009-2012, the average rate of NPK application rate increased by 59% compared to only 7% for the corresponding statistics for Western Africa countries. These efforts have contributed to the country's efforts to achieve sustainable natural resource management and food and nutrition security. Accordingly, the infant mortality rate and other key indicators of wellbeing have improved significantly in Niger (Moussa *et al.*, 2016).

Despite the impressive achievement in combating desertification and land degradation in general, Niger still has a long way to go before it achieves zero net land degradation in 2030 – a target that the country has set in accordance with the United Nations Sustainable Development Goal 15 (SDG15). Niger experienced high costs of land degradation in the past 24 years (1992 to 2015). The annual total economic value (TEV) of degradation was 2015 US$3.535 billion or 19% of the 2015 PPP GDP. The on-site cost of land degradation is about US$1.621 or about 9% of the 2015 PPP GDP. Land degradation in the grasslands and woodlands accounts for more than 95% of total cost of land degradation due to LUCC. This poses a big concern given that grasslands and woodlands play key role in livestock feeding systems and that livestock sector play a key role in household nutrition and is a leading sector in the Nigerien economy.

It is important for Niger to protect land from degradation and invest in rehabilitation of degraded lands – given that the majority of the poor in Niger heavily depend on land for their livelihoods.

As shown by Moussa *et al.* (2016), for every US$ invested in rehabilitation of degraded lands, the land operator gets back US$5. Our study also shows large benefits on adoption of land management practices on food and nutrition security. Adopting stony wall, organic inputs and tree planting and protection increase caloric intake by 36, 27 and 23%, respectively. Likewise, HDDS increases by 13% for stony wall adoption to 5% for manure adoption.

Despite the high returns and favourable impacts on food and nutrition security, adoption rates of key land management practices are still very low. Among the major reasons for such low adoption is that only 46% of the investment in rehabilitation of degraded lands accrues on-site and 54% of the benefits are off-farm. This suggests the need for the Nigerien government to find cost-effective methods for providing incentives for tree planting and protection and other land management practices which have large off-farm benefits. Niger is among African countries which do not provide fertiliser subsidies and it is not prudent for the country to introduce them given their challenges seen in other countries. However, it is possible to develop a payment for ecosystem services in which the government – in collaboration with international carbon and biodiversity programs – could establish an effective mechanism for rewarding farmers. This will complement the successful efforts the country has made in the past 25 years to increase tree planting and protection through policy and institutional reforms.

Proximity to roads and higher education enhance adoption of sustainable land and water management (SLWM) (Moussa *et al.*, 2016) and as this study showed, the two factors also enhance household food and nutrition. Additionally, access to extension services play a key role in enhancing adoption, especially for knowledge intensive SLWM practices. These rural services need to be enhanced significantly as part of the country's efforts to reduce poverty and improvement of other human welfare aspects.

In summary, Niger has illustrated that sustainable development is achievable even among poorest countries. However, its efforts need to be increased in partnership with international community which is the largest beneficiary of the rehabilitation of degraded lands.

References

Adato, M. and Bassett, L., 2009. Social protection to support vulnerable children and families: the potential of cash transfers to protect education, health and nutrition. AIDS Care 21 Suppl. 1: 60-75.

Adelman, S.W., Gilligan, D.O. and Lehrer, K., 2008. How effective are food for education programs? A critical assessment of the evidence from developing countries. Food Policy Reviews 9. International Food Policy Research Institute, Washington, DC, USA. Available at: http://tinyurl.com/yag36p7w.

Albert, J. R. G, A. L. TabuAkhter, U.A., Vargas Hill R., Smith L.C. and Frankenberger, T., 2009. The poorest and hungry: characteristics and causes. In: Von Braun, R., Hill V. and Pandya-Lorch, R. (eds.) The poorest and hungry. Assessments, analyses, and actions. IFPRI 2020 Publication, Washington, DC, USA.

Bai, Y., Feng, M., Jiang, H., Wang, J., Zhu, Y. and Liu, Y., 2014. Assessing consistency of five global land cover data sets in China. Remote Sensing 6: 8739-8759.

Barbier, B. and Hochard, J.P., 2016. Does land degradation increase poverty in developing countries? PloS One 11: e015973.

Boffa, J.M., 1999. Agroforestry parklands in sub-Saharan Africa. FAO Conservation Guide 34. FAO, Rome, Italy. Available at: https://tinyurl.com/y94gzcsc.

Boffa, J.M., 2015. Opportunities and challenges in the improvement of the shea (*Vitellaria paradoxa*) resource and its management. Occasional Paper, 24. World Agroforestry Centre, Nairobi, Kenya. Available at: http://tinyurl.com/ycl7bvmr.

Catterall, C.P., Kanowski, J., Wardell-Johnson, G.W., Proctor, H., Reis, R., Harrison, D. and Tucker, N.I., 2004. Quantifying the biodiversity values of reforestation: perspectives, design issues and outcomes in Australian rainforest landscapes. In: Lunney, D. (ed.) Conservation of Australia's forest fauna. Royal Zoological Society of New South Wales, Mosman, Australia, pp. 359-393.

Consultative Group on International Agricultural Research (CGIAR), 2014. Research program on dryland systems. Annual report 2014: pathways to lasting impact for rural dryland communities in the developing world. CGIAR, Amman, Jordan.

Cragg, J.G., 1983. More efficient estimation in the presence of heteroskedasticity of unknown form. Econometrica 51: 751-763.

D'Odorico, P., Bhattachan, A., Davis, K.F., Ravi, S. and Runyan, C.W., 2013. Global desertification: drivers and feedbacks. Advances in Water Resources 51: 326-344.

Food and Agriculture Organisation (FAO), 2016. State of the world's forests. Available at: http://www.fao.org/3/a-i5588e.pdf.

Food and Agriculture Organisation Statistics (FAOSTAT), 2016. FAOSTAT land use metadata. Available at: http://www.fao.org/faostat/en/#data/RL/metadata.

Friedl, M., Sulla-Menashe, D., Tan, B., Schneider, A., Ramankutty, N., Sibley, A. and Huang, X., 2010. MODIS global land cover: algorithm refinements and characterization of new datasets. Remote Sensing of Environment 114: 168-182.

Gerber, N., Nkonya, E. and Von Braun, J., 2014. Land degradation, poverty and marginality. In: Von Braun J. and Gatzweiler, F.W. (eds.) Marginality: addressing the nexus of poverty, exclusion and ecology. Springer, Heidelberg, Germany, pp. 181-203.

Gnoumou, Y. and Bloch, P., 2003. Niger country brief: property rights and land markets. Land Tenure Center, University of Wisconsin, Madison, WI, USA.

Hackbusch, W., 2010. Elliptic differential equations. The Poisson equation. Mairdumont Gmbh & Co. KG, Ostfildern, Germany, pp. 27-37.

Hermann, S.M., Anyamba, A. and Tucker, C.J., 2005. Recent trends in vegetation dynamics in the African Sahel and their relationship to climate. Global Environmental Change 15: 394-404.

Herold, M., Mayaux, P., Woodcock, C., Baccini, A. and Schmullius, C., 2008. Some challenges in global land cover mapping: an assessment of agreement and accuracy in existing 1 km datasets. Remote Sensing of Environment 112: 2538-2556.

International Organization for Migration (IOM), 2010. Niger – migration profile highlights the need for improved migration statistics. Available at: https://tinyurl.com/ycqmsr79.

Jukes, M.C., Drake, L.J. and Bundy, D.A., 2007. School health, nutrition and education for all: levelling the playing field. CABI, Wallingford, UK.

Kaufmann, D., Kraay, A. and Mastruzzi, M., 2010. The worldwide governance indicators: methodology and analytical issues. World Bank Policy Research Working Paper No. 5430. World Bank, Washington, DC, USA.

Kloos, J. and Renaud, F.G., 2016. Overview of ecosystem-based approaches to drought risk reduction targeting small-scale farmers in sub-Saharan Africa. In: Renaud, F., Sudmeier-Rieux, K., Estrella, M. and Nehren, U. (eds.) Ecosystem-based disaster risk reduction and adaptation in practice. Springer International Publishing, New York, NY, USA, pp. 199-226.

Lesiv, M., Fritz, S., McCallum, I., Tsendbazar, N., Herold, M., Pekel, J.-F., Buchhorn, M., Smets, B. and Van de Kerchove, R., 2017. Evaluation of ESA CCI prototype land cover map at 20 m. International Institute for Applied Systems Analysis (IIASA) Working Paper No. WP-17-021. IIASA, Laxenburg, Austria.

Millennium Ecosystem Assessment (MEA), (2005). Dryland systems. In: Hassan, R., Scholes, R. and Ash, N. (eds.) Ecosystem and well-being: current state and trends. Island Press, Washington, DC, USA, pp. 623-662.

Montagne, P. and Amadou, O., 2012. Rural districts and community forest management and the fight against poverty in Niger. Field Actions Science Reports 6. Available at: https://journals.openedition.org/factsreports/1473.

Moussa, B., Nkonya, E., Meyer, S., Kato, E., Johnson, T. and Hawkins, J., 2016. Economics of land degradation and improvement in Niger. In: Nkonya, E., Mirzabaev, A. and Von Braun, J. (eds.) Economics of land degradation and improvement – a global assessment for sustainable development. Springer, New York, NY, USA, pp. 499-540.

Raleigh, C. and Dowd, C., 2013. Governance and conflict in the Sahel's 'Ungoverned Space'. Stability: International Journal of Security and Development 2: 1-17.

Republic of Niger (RoN), 2000. Programme d'action national de lutte contre la désertification et la gestion des ressources naturelles (PAN-LCD/GRN). Le cabinet du Premier ministre, le Conseil national de l'environnement pour un développement durable et le programme national pour un environnement durable, Niamey, Niger.

Republic of Niger (RoN), 2006. National adaptation programme of action. Available at: https://tinyurl.com/y8qcc7w2.

Secretariat of the Convention on Biological Diversity(CBD), 2010. Global biodiversity outlook 3. CBD, Montréal, Canada, 94 pp.

Stadlmayr, B., Charrondiere, U.R., Addy, P., Samb, B., Enujiugha, V.N., Bayili, R.G., Fagbohoun, E.G. Smith, I.F., Thiam, I. and Burlingame, B., 2010. Composition of selected foods from West Africa. Food and Agriculture Organisation, Rome, Italy.

Stickler, M., 2012. Rights to trees and livelihoods in Niger. Focus on land in Africa. Placing land rights at the heart of development. Available at: www.focusonland.com/download/51c49667b7626.

United Nations Development Programme (UNDP), 2016. Trends in international migrant stock: the 2015 revision database. UN Department of Economic and Social Affairs, New York, NY, USA. Available at: https://tinyurl.com/y83m4cpp.

Chapter 3.
Empowerment, climate change adaptation and agricultural production: evidence from Niger[1]

Fleur Wouterse

IFPRI c/o ISS, Kortenaerkade 12, 2518 AX, The Hague, the Netherlands; f.wouterse@cgiar.org

Abstract

We use new household level data from Niger and regression analysis to study the role of drought perception and human capital – including empowerment – in climate change adaptation through the digging of zaï pits and effects of these pits on agricultural productivity. We find that selection of households into adoption of zaï pits is influenced by the perception that the frequency of droughts has increased. More educated, experienced, and empowered households are also more likely to have put in place zaï pits. Accounting for endogeneity of adoption, zaï pits are found to significantly increase cereal yields. Our counterfactual analysis reveals that even though all households would benefit from adoption of zai pits, the effect would be significantly larger for households that did not adopt if they had adopted. For the latter group, empowerment in particular is associated with significantly higher yields.

Keywords: climate change adaptation, empowerment, regression analysis, West Africa

3.1 Introduction

Climate change poses potentially large risks for farmers in the developing world affecting yields, growing seasons, water availability and increasing weather uncertainties (Nelson *et al.*, 2009). Smallholders in drought-prone Niger are well-acquainted with how a changing climate affects their crop production and have long adjusted their management practices to address negative impacts of climate. One adaptative strategy that is pursued in the face of climatic stressors is the digging of zaï pits, which are small holes (diameter 20-40 cm and depth 10-20 cm) filled with compost and planted with seeds. Zaï pits contribute to both agronomic and economic productivity and resilience and adaptive capacity of households and are considered key for climate smart agriculture planning for farm-level interventions in the country. Given that climate change will likely exacerbate climate variability and extreme events, an understanding of drivers and obstacles to zaï pit adoption and returns to agricultural production is critical to facilitate and enhance adaptation to climate change and for developing well targeted policies.

Considerable research exists on adaptation strategies (see Burnham and Ma, 2016 for an overview) but empirical evidence is lacking as to the role that climate change perception plays

---

[1] Originally published as Wouterse, F., 2017. Empowerment, climate change adaptation and agricultural production: evidence from Niger. Climatic Change 145: 367-382. Permission to republish (Creative Common Licenses).

in adaptation and on the importance of a broader concept of human capital in the decision to adapt. Although it has been suggested that farmer perceptions regarding long-term climatic changes affect adaptation (Maddison, 2007), this has not yet been formally established. Formal education has been identified as a driver of adaptation but because climate change adaptation is endogenous to society and influenced by values, there is a need to consider the agency – or the ability to make strategic life choices – of adaptation decision making (Adger *et al.*, 2009). Empowerment, which is the expansion of agency, is likely to play an important role in climate change adaptation decisions but to our knowledge the contribution of empowerment to adaptation has not yet been empirically established. Establishment of a formal link between perception and adaptation and empirical evidence as to the role that empowerment plays in adaptation and productivity constitute two important gaps in the literature.

In this chapter, we aim to contribute to the literature by investigating the use of zaï pits as an adaptative strategy in Niger. Using new household level data from the Tahoua region, we model adaptation decision-making and returns to adaptation at the farm household level. In particular, we empirically establish a link between climate change perception and adaptation. We also assess the importance of empowerment in adaptation decision making and in productivity outcomes. Our results reveal that households that perceived increased drought were more likely to have employed zaï pits. Inadequacy in empowerment emerges as an important constraint to zaï pit adoption. Results from our production function estimation, show that adaptation to climate change through the digging of zaï pits is associated with higher yields. The impact of adaptation on food productivity would be particularly large for farm households that did not adapt in the counterfactual case that they adapted. Empowerment is found to contribute positively to yields in the more vulnerable non-adopting households. In terms of policy implications, this study demonstrates that climate change adaptation can be autonomous and that interventions aimed at empowering households, particularly those that are most vulnerable, would be effective in promoting adaptation and productivity.

3.2 Climate vulnerability and adaptation decision-making

Located at the heart of West Africa, Niger is a landlocked country with three quarters of its territory covered by the Sahara Desert. Niger's climate is mostly arid with a rainfall gradient ranging from 100 to 700 mm of annual rainfall and it is one of the least developed countries in the world, ranking 186th per the Human Development Index (UNDP, 2013). The clear majority of its population (82%) lives in rural areas and the country is strongly dependent on agriculture, which contributed about 36.4% to GDP in 2015 (World Bank, 2016). The agricultural sector is dominated by smallholders and generally rainfed. Yields rely on a single rainy season that runs from May to September. Although productivity has shown a positive trend, agriculture has been strongly affected in recent decades by several crises due – partly or entirely – to extreme weather events, such as the droughts of 1973, 1984-1985 and more recently 2005 and 2009 (World Bank, 2013). There is thus considerable discussion on how to make agriculture, the main sector in which the poor are involved, and especially smallholder agriculture, more resilient to extreme events as well as adapted to shifts in potential climate conditions (Howden *et al.*, 2007). Climate-smart agriculture (CSA) – farming systems that increase agricultural productivity, improve the adaptive capacity of farmers and mitigate climate change where possible – has been put forward as a solution to the food and climate challenges Africa faces (Lamanna *et al.*, 2015).

3.2.1 Adaptation strategies for soil and water conservation in rural Niger

Adaptation to climate change can be defined as an adjustment in ecological, social or economic systems in response to observed or expected changes in climatic stimuli and their effects and impacts to alleviate adverse impacts of change or take advantage of new opportunities (Adger *et al.*, 2005). Adaptation is an ongoing and dynamic process whereby societies continually respond to changing socioeconomic, technological and resource regimes. Adaptation can occur at various levels and can be autonomous or planned where the former are initiatives by private actors rather than by governments usually triggered by welfare changes induced by actual or anticipated climate change (IPCC, 2014).

During a period of severe drought in the Sahel in the early 1980s, farmers in Burkina Faso began 'innovating out of despair' by experimenting with planting pits, a technique practiced for many years by farmers elsewhere in the Sahel (Reij *et al.*, 2009). The innovation was, first, to increase the diameter (20-40 cm) and depth of the pits (10-20 cm) and second to concentrate nutrients and moisture in the pits. After digging these so-called zaï pits on severely degraded farmland that was otherwise impermeable to water, organic matter was added and – after the first rainfall – the matter would be covered with a thin layer of soil and millet and/or sorghum seeds placed in the middle of the pit. The zaï pits dramatically improved soil fertility by capturing soil and organic matter attracting termites, resulting in enhanced soil nutrients, increased water retention, and increased cost-effectiveness of manure and fertiliser application. The practice of zaï pits spread to neighbouring Niger after a study visit of farmers from the Tahoua region of Niger to Burkina Faso in 1989. The technique has spread at a surprising rate in rural Niger, adding an additional 2-3 ha per year to some holdings (IFAD, 2010). Zaï pits are autonomous rather than planned adaptations as the government of Niger and nongovernmental organisations promoted the more expensive contour stone bunds and half-moons as preferred forms of in-field soil and water conservation endorsed by researchers. Stone bunds, established along the contours of the land and where stones or rocks are available, slow water runoff to improve water-catchment capacity. Half-moon micro catchments are small, semicircular earth bunds. These are quite common on the desert margins of the Sahel. The half-moons catch water flowing down a slope. Half-moons are particularly helpful to rehabilitate degraded land.

Zaï pits have been associated with important improvements in yields because they simultaneously address issues of land degradation, soil fertility, and soil moisture. In Burkina Faso, in fields that had been yielding virtually no grain, farmers recorded yields of 300 kg/ha (in years with low rainfall) to 1,200 kg/ha (in years of good rainfall) upon digging zaï pits (Kaboré and Reij, 2004). By improving soil water holding capacity, zaï pits also help households buffer against drought-induced food shocks thereby improving resilience. Because zaï pits contribute to two of the pillars of climate smart agriculture – agronomic and economic productivity and resilience and adaptive capacity of households – they are thought to be key for climate smart agriculture planning for farm-level interventions in the country (Lamanna *et al.*, 2015). It is thus important to understand the driving forces behind climate change adaptation in the form of the adoption of zaï pits.

3.2.2 Adaptation decision-making

The discourse around limits to adaptation is traditionally constructed around three immutable thresholds – ecological and physical, economic and technological. For example, given that adaptation requires investments, studies tend to first and foremost consider its economic feasibility using cost-benefit analysis where benefits are on-site land productivity gains. Recent research has posited that socio-cognitive factors may be as important as or more important than economic ones in motivating individuals to take adaptive actions (Grothman and Patt, 2005). Relevant characteristics are thought to include beliefs, preferences, perceptions of self-efficacy and controllability. These together with, amongst others, perceptions of risk, knowledge and experience determine what is perceived to be a limit to adaptation and what is not (Adger *et al.*, 2009).

Here we focus on perception of risk and on human capital defined as the aggregation of the innate abilities and the knowledge and skills that individuals acquire and develop throughout their lifetime (Laroche *et al.*, 1999) to explain climate change adaption decision-making in the form of the implementation of zaï pits. Perception of hazard risk has long been recognised as a critical determinant of human response to environmental shocks. In Grothmann and Patt's (2005) Model of Private Proactive Adaptation to Climate Change (MPPACC), for example, perception is a key variable illustrated as influencing or being influenced by all the model's determinants of adaptive behaviour. Although the definition of human capital as given above is sufficiently broad, in practice, knowledge has often become synonymous with formal education and skills with experience. Notwithstanding the relevance of formal education and experience in adaptation decision-making, Adger *et al.* (2009) have postulated that the agency of adaptation decision making may also be important. Agency refers to the ability to define one's goals and act upon them. Agency also encompasses the meaning, motivation and purpose that individuals bring to their activity, their sense of agency or the 'power within'. The Women's Empowerment in Agriculture Index (WEAI) – originally developed for USAID's Feed the Future program – is based on the agency dimension of empowerment, which is far less studied than resources such as income or achievements (Alkire *et al.*, 2013).

The WEAI is a survey based index, which builds up a multidimensional empowerment profile for the primary male and female decision maker in a household that reflects their overlapping achievements in five domains and aggregates these. The WEAI is a weighted average of two sub-indexes: (1) the five domains of empowerment (5DE); and (2) gender parity (the gender parity index, GPI). The former captures the roles and extent of engagement in the agricultural sector in five domains: (1) decisions about agricultural production; (2) access to and decision-making power about productive resources; (3) control of use of income; (4) leadership in the community; and (5) time allocation. Table 3.1 describes the ten indicators that are used in the five domains.

Each indicator takes the value of 1 when the individual is considered as adequate and zero otherwise. The GPI is a relative inequality measure that reflects the inequality in 5DE profiles between the primary adult male and female in each household. Wouterse (2017) has used the 5DE to show for rural Niger that more empowered households are more productive while Seymour *et al.* (2016) use the 5DE scores of women measured to explain adoption of improved varieties by rural households in Ethiopia, Kenya and Tanzania. They find that the empowerment of women is positively correlated with increased participation in decisions about the adoption of improved varieties. With limits to adaptation contingent on values (Adger *et al.*, 2009), an analysis of household level decision-making, which incorporates perception and empowerment is indispensable to a better understanding of adaptation and informing policy.

3.3 Data

Data to estimate our model of adaptation decision-making were collected by the author during April-May 2015 for 500 randomly sampled households (and 769 adult individuals in these households) in 35 villages situated in three communes (Doguéraoua, Malbaza and Tsernaoua) in the Maggia valley of the Birni N'Konni department in the Tahoua region.[2] Birni N'Konni is

---

[2] 12 households were excluded from the analysis due to missing data.

Table 3.1. The domains, indicators, and weights in the Women's empowerment in agriculture index (Alkire *et al.*, 2013).

Domain	Indicator	Definition of indicator	Weight
Production	input in productive decisions	sole or joint decision-making over food, cash crop farming, livestock and fisheries	1/10
	autonomy in production	autonomy in agricultural production	1/10
Resources	ownership of assets	sole or joint ownership of major household assets	1/15
	purchase, sale or transfer of assets	whether respondent participates in decision to buy, sell or transfer his/her owned assets	1/15
	access to and decisions on credit	access to and participation in decision-making concerning credit	1/15
Income	control over use of income	sole or joint control over income and expenditures	1/5
Leadership	group member	whether respondent is an active member in a group	1/10
	speaking in public	whether the respondent is comfortable speaking in public	1/10
Time	workload	allocation of time to productive and domestic tasks	1/10
	leisure	satisfaction with the time available for leisure activities	1/10

situated in the southern part of Niger and belongs to the Sahelo-Sudanese environment, which allows for rainfed agriculture. Household level data were collected using a standard agricultural household survey while individual level empowerment data were collected using the standard WEAI survey (Alkire *et al.*, 2013). The WEAI survey tool collects data from the primary male and female decision-maker in a household on the five domains (production, resources, income, leadership and time) that are envisaged to make up empowerment. To calculate household-level empowerment we take the average of the sum of the weighted adequacy scores for the primary male and female decision-maker. Weighted scores of each indicator for men and women in our sample and their contribution to empowerment are given in Figure 3.1.

Figure 3.1 shows that women are much more disempowered compared to men. We can also see that leadership – composed of speaking in public and group membership – strongly contributes to disempowerment for both men and women in our sample.

Farm and household descriptives by zaï adoption status are given in Table 3.2. Farming systems are extensive agropastoral millet and sorghum based. In our sample, about a fifth of households had dug zaï pits on their cereal plots. Less common soil and water conservation measures are stone bunds and half-moons. The table shows that yield or the quantity of cereals harvested in kilograms per hectare during the 2014 agricultural season is significantly higher for households that had put in place zaï pits. Table 3.2 also shows that households that had employed zaï pits are significantly better endowed in terms of cultivated land and dispose of more valuable farming equipment. As to variable inputs, households that employ zaï pits use more days of household labour in production but there is no significant difference in terms of the quantity of fertiliser applied between households that employ zaï pits and those that do not. In general, synthetic fertiliser use is low in the study area with less than half of households applying fertiliser and

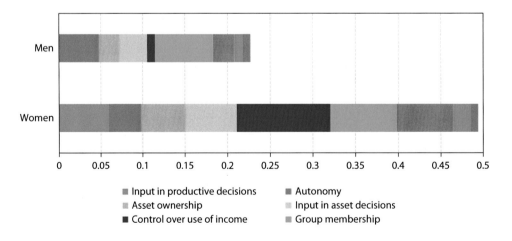

Figure 3.1. Contributors to inadequacy in empowerment.

Table 3.2. Farm and household descriptives (World Bank, 2016).

	Adopter[1]	Non-adopter[1]	t-test
Household level			
Cereal yield (kg/ha)	441.28 (313.52)	352.71 (270.81)	-2.80
Cultivated acreage (ha)	6.16 (6.85)	4.01 (3.43)	-1.77
Household labour (days/ha)	36.25 (34.14)	30.23 (30.23)	-1.72
Fertiliser (kg/ha)	3.64 (7.92)	3.77 (9.29)	0.13
Seed (kg/ha)	11.71 (14.72)	10.14 (10.26)	-1.23
Manure (kg/ha)	442.69 (567.15)	410.15 (684.32)	-0.43
Number of cattle	0.76 (1.22)	0.70 (1.43)	-0.76
Lagged value of equipment (FCFA)[2]	44,488 (68,726)	26,588 (38,859)	-3.41
Sex of the household head (1 = male)	0.87 (0.34)	0.73 (0.44)	-2.78
Literacy of household head (1 = yes)	0.44 (0.50)	0.30 (0.46)	-2.53
Schooling of most educated adult (years)	2.46 (2.97)	1.93 (3.17)	-1.49
Koranic schooling of adult	0.59 (0.49)	0.27 (0.45)	-6.22
Experience of adults (years)	28.11 (12.00)	26.03 (10.74)	-1.67
Empowerment	0.66 (0.17)	0.65 (0.17)	-0.56
Perceives increased drought	0.81 (0.40)	0.67 (0.47)	-2.56
Village level			
High participation in migration	0.70 (0.46)	0.53 (0.50)	-3.04
Distance to minibus stop	7.61 (9.61)	5.09 (8.21)	-2.15
Number of observations	101	387	

[1] Standard deviation in parentheses.
[2] FCFA 225 = US$ 1 (purchasing power parity for 2015).

application rates well below recommended dosages. Table 3.2 also shows that households that employ zaï pits are significantly more likely to have perceived an increased frequency of droughts during the five years preceding the survey. In terms of human capital, households that had adapted to climate change by digging zaï pits were more likely to be headed by a male, have heads who are literate and contain more experienced adults, where experience is measured as the average age of adults minus years of formal education received minus five. Households that adopted are also more likely to contain an adult member who attended Koranic school as a child but empowerment levels of households that had and had not employed zaï pits do not significantly differ.

3.4 Methods

The zaï adoption decision as a function of drought perception and human capital and its implications in terms of an outcome of interest can be modelled in the setting of a two-stage framework (see also Abdulai and Huffman, 2014; Di Falco *et al.*, 2011). In the first stage, we use a selection model for zaï adoption where a representative risk averse farm household chooses to implement the pits if it generates net benefits. We can therefore represent the net benefits derived from zaï adoption by a latent variable D_j^*, which is not observed but can be expressed as a function of the observed characteristics and attributes, denoted as Z in a latent variable model as follows:

$$D_j^* = \gamma\, Z_j + \varepsilon_j \quad \text{with } D_j = \begin{cases} 1, \text{ if } D_j^* > 0 \\ 0, \text{ otherwise} \end{cases} \tag{3.1}$$

In Equation 3.1 D_j is a binary variable that equals 1 for households that implement zaï pits and zero otherwise, γ denotes a vector of parameters to be estimated. Household j will choose to adopt ($D_j = 1$) by employing zaï pits only if the perceived net benefits are positive $D_j^* > 0$. The error term ε_j with mean zero and variance σ_ε^2 captures measurement errors and factors unobserved to the researcher but known to the farmer. Variables in Z include factors that influence the decision to adopt such as farm level and household characteristics including perception of increased drought. Although the perceived net benefits of implementation are unknown to the researcher, the characteristics of the farm household and the attributes of the technology are observed during the survey period.

In the second stage, we model the effect of adoption on productivity via a representation of the production technology. Following Di Falco *et al.* (2011) we use a quadratic specification of a single output production function. As cereals – millet and sorghum – constitute the bulk of agricultural production and are cultivated by all households in our sample and zaï pits are employed on plots under cereals, we use the total yield of cereals as our outcome variable. The simplest approach to examine the impact of adoption of zaï pits on farm households would be to include a binary variable which takes the value of 1 if the household employed zaï pits and then use ordinary least squares to estimate the production function. However, because the decision to employ zaï pits may be based on individual self-selection, this approach would yield biased results. This is so because there may be unobserved heterogeneity which drives the decision to adopt and affects output. Farmers that adopt may have systemically different characteristics from farmers that did not and may have decided to adopt based on expected benefits. Given that we dispose of cross section data only and thus have no information on the counterfactual situation and the fact that we have an actual interest in examining the determinants of household level climate change adaption, we follow Di Falco *et al.* (2011) and Abdulai and Huffman (2014) and employ the endogenous switching regression model developed by Lee (1982).

The endogenous switching regression approach as a generalisation of Heckman's selection correction approach, accounts for selection on unobservables by treating selectivity as an omitted variable problem (Heckman, 1979). In the switching regression approach, households are classified per their status as adopters and nonadopters to capture the differential responses of the two groups. Regimes are defined as follows:

Regime 0 (not adopt): $Y_{Nj} = X_{Nj}\beta_N + u_{Nj}$ if $D_j = 0$ (3.2a)

Regime 1 (adopt): $Y_{Aj} = X_{Aj}\beta_A + u_{Aj}$ if $D_j = 1$ (3.2b)

In Equation 3.2a and 3.2b, Y_j is quantity produced per hectare in regimes 0 and 1 and X_{Nj} and X_{Aj} are vectors of weakly exogenous inputs (seed, labour and fertiliser) and farm and household characteristics; β_N and β_A are vectors of parameters and u_{Nj} and u_{Aj} are independently and identically distributed errors. The error terms in Equations 3.1 and 3.2a-b are assumed to have a trivariate normal distribution with mean vector zero and the following covariance matrix:

$$\text{cov}(\varepsilon, u_A, u_N) = \Sigma = \begin{bmatrix} \sigma_\varepsilon^2 & \sigma_{\varepsilon A} & \sigma_{\varepsilon N} \\ \sigma_{A\varepsilon} & \sigma_A^2 & \cdot \\ \sigma_{N\varepsilon} & \cdot & \sigma_N^2 \end{bmatrix}$$

Where $\text{var}(u_A) = \sigma_A^2$, $\text{var}(u_N) = \sigma_N^2$, $\text{var}(\varepsilon) = \sigma_\varepsilon^2$, $\text{cov}(u_A, \varepsilon) = \sigma_{A\varepsilon}$ and $\text{cov}(u_N, \varepsilon) = \sigma_{N\varepsilon}$. The covariance between u_A and u_N is not defined because Y_{Nj} and Y_{Aj} are not observed simultaneously. An important implication of the error structure is that because the error term of the selection equation is correlated with the error terms of the productivity functions, the expected values of u_{Nj} and u_{Aj} conditional on sample selection are non-zero:

$$E(u_{Aj}|D = 1) = \sigma_{A\varepsilon}\rho_A \frac{\varphi(Z_j\gamma)}{\Phi(Z_j\gamma)}$$

and $E(u_{Nj}|D = 0) = -\sigma_{N\varepsilon}\rho_N \dfrac{\varphi(Z_j\gamma)}{1 - \Phi(Z_j\gamma)}$

Where φ and Φ are the probability density and cumulative distribution function of the standard normal distribution respectively and ρ_A is the correlation coefficient between u_{Aj} and ε_j and ρ_N is the correlation coefficient between u_{Nj} and ε_j. The ratio of φ and Φ evaluated at $Z_j\gamma$ is referred to as the inverse Mills ratio and accounts for self-selection into one of the two regimes. If the estimated covariances $\hat{\sigma}_{A\varepsilon}$ and $\hat{\sigma}_{N\varepsilon}$ are statistically significant, then the decision to employ zaï pits and yields are correlated, we would thus reject the absence of sample selectivity bias and use an endogenous switching regression model. The conditional expectation of yields with respect to households that adopted is then given by:

$$E(Y_{Aj}|D = 1) = X_{Aj}\beta_A + \sigma_{A\varepsilon}\rho_A \frac{\varphi(Z_j\gamma)}{\Phi(Z_j\gamma)}$$ (3.3a)

The expected output had the household chosen not to adopt zaï pits is given as:

$$E(Y_{Nj}|D = 0) = X_{Nj}\beta_N - \sigma_{N\varepsilon}\rho_N \frac{\varphi(Z_j\gamma)}{1 - \Phi(Z_j\gamma)}$$ (3.3b)

Expected yields in the hypothetical counterfactual case that the nonadopted farm household adopted are given by:

$$E(Y_{Aj}|D = 0) = X_{Aj}\beta_A - \sigma_{A\epsilon}\rho_A \frac{\varphi(Z_j\gamma)}{1 - \Phi(Z_j\gamma)} \qquad (3.3c)$$

while expected yields in the hypothetical case that the adopted farm household did not adopt are given by:

$$E(Y_{Nj}|D = 1) = X_{Nj}\beta_N + \sigma_{N\epsilon}\rho_N \frac{\varphi(Z_j\gamma)}{\Phi(Z_j\gamma)} \qquad (3.3d)$$

The change in the outcome due to adoption can then be specified as the difference between adoption and nonadoption. Thus, the expected outcomes from Equations 3.3a and 3.3d are used to obtain unbiased estimates of the effects of adoption. These estimates represent the average treatment effect on the treated (TT) (Lokshin and Sajaia, 2004):

$$TT = E[Y_{Aj}|D = 1] - E[Y_{Nj}|D = 1] = X_{Aj}(\beta_A - \beta_N) + (\sigma_{A\epsilon}\rho_A - \sigma_{N\epsilon}\rho_N) \frac{\varphi(Z_j\gamma)}{\Phi(Z_j\gamma)} \qquad (3.4)$$

Similarly, we can calculate the effect of treatment on the untreated (TU) for the farm households that did not adopt zaï pits as:

$$UT = E[Y_{Aj}|D = 0] - E[Y_{Nj}|D = 0] = X_{Nj}(\beta_A - \beta_N) + (\sigma_{A\epsilon}\rho_A - \sigma_{N\epsilon}\rho_N) \frac{\varphi(Z_j\gamma)}{1 - \Phi(Z_j\gamma)} \qquad (3.5)$$

We can also use the expected outcomes to calculate heterogeneity effects. For example, farm households that adopted may have produced more compared to farm households that did not adopt irrespective of the fact that they decided to adopt but because of unobservable characteristics (Di Falco *et al.*, 2011).

$$BH_A = E[Y_{Aj}|D = 1] - E[Y_{Aj}|D = 0] = \beta_A(X_{Aj} - X_{Nj}) + \sigma_{A\epsilon}\rho_A \left(\frac{\varphi(Z_j\gamma)}{\Phi(Z_j\gamma)} - \frac{\varphi(Z_j\gamma)}{1 - \Phi(Z_j\gamma)} \right) \qquad (3.6)$$

Similarly, for the group of households that decided not to adopt, 'the effect base heterogeneity' is formulated as:

$$BH_N = E[Y_{Nj}|D = 1] - E[Y_{Nj}|D = 0] = \beta_N(X_{Aj} - X_{Nj}) + \sigma_{N\epsilon}\rho_N \left(\frac{\varphi(Z_j\gamma)}{\Phi(Z_j\gamma)} - \frac{\varphi(Z_j\gamma)}{1 - \Phi(Z_j\gamma)} \right) \qquad (3.7)$$

We use full-information maximum likelihood to simultaneously fit the binary and continuous part of our model to yield consistent standard errors (Lokshin and Sajaia, 2004).

3.4.1 Econometric issues

Although the variables in the vectors X in Equation 3.2 and Z in Equation 3.1 may overlap, it is important to note that accurate identification requires that at least one variable in Z does not appear in X. For the model to be identified we use as exclusion restrictions not only those automatically generated by the nonlinearity of the selection model of adoption but also other variables that directly affect the selection variable but not the outcome variable. Our selection instruments are a binary variable that takes the value of 1 if the household perceives increased frequency of drought over the five years preceding the survey and two village-level variables that capture dedication to agriculture and lagged availability of financial resources. The former measures the distance from the center of the village to the nearest mini bus stop while the latter is a binary variable that takes the value of 1 when more than 50% of households participated in the exode – or seasonal migration – 10 years ago. We establish the admissibility of these instruments by performing a simple falsification test: if a variable is a valid selection instrument, it will affect the adoption decision but it will not affect the quantity produced among farm households that did not adopt. The results from the falsification test (not reported) reveal that drought-sensitivity, remoteness and past labour availability can be considered jointly statistically significant drivers of the decision to adapt to climate change.[3]

An issue that needs to be addressed in estimating both the adoption and outcome specification is the potential endogeneity problem that may arise with the empowerment variable. Empowerment is likely to be endogenous to the production process due to simultaneous effects. Though it may be intuitively appealing to believe that more empowered individuals are more productive, the direction of causality between empowerment and productivity is difficult to establish. Increased empowerment could lead to increased productivity but it is equally possible that increased productivity leads to higher incomes, thereby improving an individual's status of empowerment. Both formal schooling of the highest educated adult and Koranic schooling of adults could also be endogenous with adaptation and agricultural output due to simultaneous effects but this source of bias is likely to be much smaller as educational attainment of an adult has most likely taken place in the past. To account for this potential source of bias, we employ the Rivers and Vuong approach (1988), since one of our dependent variables is dichotomous. The estimation is carried out by first specifying the potential endogenous variable as a function of all other explanatory variables given in the adoption equation, in addition to a set of instruments in the first stage regressions. That is, the specification used is:

$$T_i = \gamma\, Z_{ij} + \psi\, V_{ij} + \zeta_{ij} \tag{3.8}$$

Where T_i is a vector of the potential endogenous variables (empowerment), Z_{ij} is as described previously, and V_{ij} is a vector of instruments that is correlated with the given endogenous variable but uncorrelated with the error terms in Equation 3.1 and is therefore excluded in estimating this equation. Rather than using the predicted values from the first-stage equation as in a habitual two-stage estimation approach, the approach involves specifying the adoption equation in Equation 3.3 as:

---

[3] A potential endogeneity problem may arise with the drought-sensitivity variable due to omitted variable bias. E.g. more conscientious households that are more drought-sensitive and more likely to have dug zaï pits. However, we do not dispose of suitable instruments to control for this potential bias and we will refrain from any causal inference as to the relation between drought-sensitivity and adaptation.

$$D_{ij}^* = \beta Z_{ij} + \varphi T_i + R_{ij} + \upsilon_{ij} \tag{3.9}$$

where R_{ij} is a vector of the residual terms from the first-stage regressions of the endogenous variables. The probit estimates of the potential endogenous variables in Z are then consistent (Wooldridge, 2002). To ensure identification in the estimation of the adoption specification, some of the variables included in the first stage estimation (Equation 3.8) are excluded from the selection Equation 3.9. Instruments are a variable that describes the difference between the primary male and female in the capacity to be interviewed alone as assessed by the household. A second instrument is a binary variable that takes the value of 1 if the household had indicated to have had access to generic information transmitted via the radio. These variables are expected to be suitable instruments because they are correlated with empowerment but do not independently explain the decision to employ zaï pits or farm output.

Levels of variable inputs (seed, labour and fertiliser) could also be simultaneously determined with current output because a disturbance in the production equation for example a late start of the rainy season could affect output but also levels of input. This source of bias could render single equation estimates inconsistent. Instrumental variables – often prices of the various inputs – could be used to address this source of bias. However, as we did not record price information and other instruments are not available, it would be challenging to address this potential source of bias. Instead we postulate that variable inputs are determined for the current period by household maximization with respect to anticipated output. Because any shifts in the production relation affect actual but not anticipated output, when these shifts occur the level of input is unaffected (Hoch, 1958).

3.5 Estimation results

The results of the estimation of the latent variable model specified in Equation 3.9 are given in the third right hand side column of Table 3.3 and suggest that our three selection variables: increased drought-perception, distance to the minibus stop and high participation in seasonal migration at the village level explain the implementation of zaï pits. If the household perceives that the drought frequency has increased over the five years preceding the survey, it is more likely to have put in place zaï pits. This is important as it confirms that perceptions of climatic impacts are a driver of adaptation. The larger is the distance to the minibus stop from the center of the village, the lower the probability of engagement in activities outside own-farm agriculture and the greater is therefore the dedication to agriculture increasing the probability that a household has dug zaï pits. Similarly, the higher was the village-level participation in seasonal migration 10 years before the survey took place, the larger the influx of resources in the village through remittances and the more likely it is that households invested in zaï pits.

Our human capital variables – formal and koranic school education, experience and empowerment – are also positively associated with adaptation (see also Maddison, 2007). The variable representing the level of formal education of the highest educated adult household member is positive and significantly different from zero, suggesting that more-educated farmers are more likely to construct zaï pits on their land, a finding that is consistent with the notion that education is important in helping farmers in their decisions on adopting new innovations and technologies (Abdulai and Huffman, 2014; Huffman, 2001). The more empowered is the household, the more likely it is to have adapted to climate change by putting in place zaï pits. This means that in addition to the commonly used dimensions of human capital – skills and experience – an expansion in the ability to make strategic life choices will also affect adaptation behaviour. In terms of assets, the value of productive equipment is also positive and significant pointing to the importance of resources in determining the capacity to adapt.

We now turn to the productive implications of adoption. The simplest approach to investigate the effect of adoption on production consists of estimating a production function that includes a binary variable, which takes the value of 1 if the farm household implemented zaï pits and 0 otherwise. Estimation results in the first right and second right-hand side columns of Table 3.3 show that there are significant and positive returns to zaï pits. Yields also respond positively and significantly to the seeding rate and to labour but to the latter at a decreasing rate. Both literacy of the household head and average empowerment are positively and significantly correlated with cereal yields. This approach, however, assumes that adoption of zaï pits is exogenously determined while it is potentially an endogenous variable. The estimates presented in the last two columns of Table 3.3 account for the endogenous switching in the cereal production function. Both the estimated coefficients of the correlation terms ρ_j are not significantly different from zero (Table 3.3, bottom row) indicating that the hypothesis of absence of sample selectivity bias may not be rejected. However, there are some differences in the production function of farm households that adapted to climate change by employing zaï pits and those that did not. Households that did not adopt, experience decreasing returns to the seeding rate. It also needs to be noted that returns to empowerment are positive and significant only for households that did not adopt. These differences in the coefficients of the production function between farm households that adopted and those that did not illustrate the presence of heterogeneity in the sample.

Table 3.4 presents the expected quantity produced per hectare under actual and counterfactual conditions. Cells (a) and (b) represent the expected quantity produced observed in the sample. The expected yield of farm households that adopted is about 385 kg per hectare while it is about 325 kg per hectare for the group of farm households that did not adopt zaï pits. This simple comparison, however, can be misleading and drive the researcher to conclude that on average farm households that adopted produced about 60 kg per hectare (or 18%) more than households that did not. The last column of Table 3.4 presents the treatment effects of zaï pit adoption on cereal productivity. In the counterfactual case (c), farm households who adopted would have produced almost 47 kg per hectare less (about 14%) less if they had not adopted. In the counterfactual case (d) that farm households that did not adopt adopted, they would have produced about 110 kg (or about 34%) more. These results imply that adaptation to climate change by putting in place zaï pits significantly increases cereal productivity for households in the

Table 3.3. Endogenous switching regression results for adoption and impact of adoption on cereal yields (kg/ha).[1]

	OLS	IV[2]	Adoption	Zaï=0	Zaï=1
Zaï (1=yes)	47.33 (21.14)b**	43.99 (22.30)*			
Household labour (days/ha)	4.77 (0.77)**	4.69 (0.78)**		4.34 (0.90)**	6.86 (1.95)**
Household labour squared (/100)	-2.44 (0.42)**	-2.35 (0.42)**		-2.15 (0.53)**	-3.30 (0.84)**
Fertiliser (kg/ha)	3.84 (2.93)	4.19 (2.90)		4.59 (3.54)	1.39 (4.85)
Fertiliser squared (/100)	-0.33 (6.72)	-0.77 (6.43)		-2.02 (7.99)	12.60 (12.26)
Seed (kg/ha)	5.86 (1.90)**	5.62 (1.85)**		8.17 (2.24)**	-0.36 (3.51)
Seed squared (/100)	-3.12 (2.58)	-2.95 (2.33)		-6.92 (3.33)**	2.56 (3.32)
Manure (kg/ha)	0.02 (0.03)	0.03 (0.03)		-0.01 (0.03)	0.13 (0.08)*
Manure squared (/100)	-0.00 (0.00)	-0.00 (0.00)		0.00 (0.00)	-0.00 (0.00)
Value of equipment (FCFA[3]/10.000)	-2.08 (2.17)	-3.75 (2.48)	0.04 (0.02)**	-3.55 (3.55)	-0.76 (3.70)
Cattle holdings (number)	5.69 (7.82)	3.98 (8.59)	-0.05 (0.06)	10.94 (9.58)	-4.27 (14.36)
Sex of the household head (1=male)	32.28 (23.93)	43.27 (26.97)*	0.23 (0.19)	12.08 (27.30)	103.96 (54.53)*
Literacy of household head (1=yes)	46.31 (23.04)**	46.28 (25.42)*	-0.14 (0.18)	27.30 (27.69)	15.80 (35.21)
Schooling of most educated adult (years)	-3.23 (3.00)	-3.10 (3.11)	0.04 (0.02)*	-0.25 (3.27)	-0.55 (7.32)
Koranic schooling of adult	-56.58 (21.66)**	-40.61 (26.13)	0.88 (0.17)**	-57.80 (53.24)	-87.11 (70.28)
Experience of adults (years)	0.08 (0.88)	0.50 (0.87)	0.01 (0.01)*	0.75 (1.24)	1.71 (1.94)
Empowerment[4]	180.46 (50.27)**	394.95 (230.84)*	0.79 (0.45)*	197.65 (70.69)**	-20.96 (109.46)
Perceives increased drought			0.35 (0.18)*		
High participation in migration (lagged)			0.58 (0.15)**		
Distance to minibus stop			0.04 (0.01)**		
σ_i				183.82 (1.95)**	154.39 (19.55)**
ρ_i				0.05 (0.77)	-0.30 (0.60)
R-squared	0.29	0.26			

[1] OLS = ordinary least squares; IV = instrumental variables; Robust standard errors are given in parentheses. ** significant at the 5% level, * significant at the 10% level.
[2] Community fixed effects not reported.
[3] FCFA 225 = US$1 (purchasing power parity for 2015) (World Bank, 2016).
[4] Predicted from first stage regression (see Appendix Table 3.A1 for estimation results).

Table 3.4. Impact of zaï pits on cereal yields.[1]

Impact	Decision stage		Treatment effects
	To adopt	Not to adopt	
Farm households that adopted	(a) 385.11 (14.42)	(c) 338.44 (10.19)	46.67 (11.01)***
Farm households that did not adopt	(d) 435.14 (8.29)	(b) 325.26 (5.73)	109.88 (6.07)***
Heterogeneity effects	-50.03 (6.08)***	13.18 (2.72)***	-63.21 (6.70)***

[1] Standard errors in parentheses. *** Significance at the 1% level.

Tahoua region of Niger. However, the transitional heterogeneity effect is negative and significant, that is, the effect is significantly smaller for the farm households that did adopt relative to those that did not. The last row of Table 3.4, which adjusts for the potential heterogeneity in the sample, shows that farm households who adopted would have produced significantly more than farm households that did not adopt in the counterfactual case (c).

To reiterate, four important findings emerge from our analysis. First, the perception of climatic change is a driver of adaptation. This means that agricultural adaptation in the face of climate change can be expected to occur autonomously to some extent and that the role for government could centre on lowering barriers to adaptation (see also Maddison, 2007). Second, empowerment positively affects adaptation behaviour. This means that an expansion in the ability to make strategic life choices will contribute to adaptation to climate change. Because the leadership domain – comprising of group membership and ease of speaking in public in front of a mixed audience – is an important contributor to inadequacy in empowerment, relatively soft interventions such as encouraging households to become a member of an existing group or organising leadership training could contribute to climate change adaptation and productivity. Third, adaptation to climate change by putting in place zaï pits significantly increases cereal productivity and thereby household incomes and welfare. These findings are consistent with the view that adoption of new agricultural technologies can improve farm productivity and household incomes (Abdulai and Huffman, 2014). Fourth, farm households belonging to the group of adapters have some characteristics (e.g. unobserved skills) that would make them more food secure even without the implementation of the adaptation strategies. This finding highlights, in line with findings of Di Falco *et al.* (2011) for rural Ethiopia, that there are some important sources of heterogeneity that make adopters 'better producers' compared to those that did not irrespective of the issue of climate change. Therefore, adoption of zaï pits seem to be particularly important for the most vulnerable farm households, those who are less able to produce food, by helping them to close the productivity gap with less vulnerable farm households (Di Falco *et al.*, 2011).

3.6 Conclusions

The objectives of this study were to analyse the driving forces behind the decision of farm households in the Tahoua region of Niger to adapt to climate change by implementing zaï pits and to investigate the productive implications of this decision. We have contributed to the existing literature by empirically establishing a relationship between drought perception and adaptation and by assessing the role that empowerment plays in adaptation and productivity. We have used recent household and individual level WEAI data to estimate a simultaneous equation model with endogenous switching to account for household self-selection into adoption. We find that households that perceived increased drought were more likely to have employed zaï pits but that important human capital-related obstacles to adaptation exist. We find, for example, that inadequacy in empowerment hampers zaï pit adoption. Our results reveal that productivity is higher in households that had implemented zaï pits. Heterogeneity effects imply that yield gains would be particularly large for non-adopting households if they were to adopt.

Our findings have considerable implications for policy measures aimed at enhancing and facilitating climate change adaption in rural Niger and elsewhere. First, they suggest that the perception of an increase in drought frequency can prompt households into adaptative action. Climate change adaptation can thus take place autonomously and rather than planning climate change adaptation strategies, programs and interventions could more usefully focus on alleviating barriers to adaptation. Second, our findings speak to the importance of empowerment as a development goal, both for its intrinsic value, and as demonstrated here for its instrumental value in promoting adaptation and its productivity effects, particularly for vulnerable households. It is therefore important for policy makers aiming to enhance agricultural productivity of those households to consider empowerment-augmenting programs and interventions. For households in rural Niger, softer interventions such as leadership training or encouraging membership of groups such as producer groups or rotating savings schemes, are expected to be particularly effective.

References

Abdulai, A. and Huffman, W., 2014. The adoption and impact of soil and water conservation technology: an endogenous switching regression application. Land Economics 90: 26-43.

Adger, W.N., Arnell, N.W. and Tompkins, E.L., 2005. Successful adaptation to climate change across scales. Global Environmental Change 15: 77-86.

Adger, W.N., Dessai, S., Goulden, M., Hulme, M., Lorenzoni, I., Nelson, D.R., Naess, L.O., Wolf, J. and Wreford, A., 2009. Are there social limits to adaptation to climate change? Climatic Change 93: 335-354.

Alkire, S., Meinzen-Dick, R., Peterman, A., Quisumbing, A.R., Seymour, G. and Vaz, A., 2013. The women's empowerment in agriculture index. World Development 52: 71-91.

Burnham, M. and Ma, Z., 2016. Linking smallholder farmer climate change adaptation decisions to development. Climate and Development 8: 289-311.

Di Falco, S., Veronesi, M. and Yesuf, M., 2011. Does adaptation to climate change provide food security? A micro-perspective from Ethiopia. American Journal of Agricultural Economics 93: 825-842.

Grothmann, T. and Patt, A., 2005. Adaptive capacity and human cognition: the process of individual adaptation to climate change. Global Environmental Change 15: 199-213.

Heckman, J., 1979. Sample selection bias as a specification error. Econometrica 47: 153-161.

Hoch, I., 1958. Simultaneous equation bias in the context of the Cobb-Douglas production function. Econometrica 26(4): 566-578.

Howden, S.M., Soussana, J.F., Tubiello, F.N., Chhetri, N., Dunlop, M. and Meinke, H., 2007. Adapting agriculture to climate change. Proceedings of the National Academy of Sciences of the USA 104: 19691-19696.

Huffman, W.E., 2001. Human capital: education and agriculture. In: Gardner, B.L. and Rausser, G.C. (eds.) Handbook of agricultural economics IB. Elsevier Science, Amsterdam, the Netherlands.

Intergovernmental Panel on Climate Change (IPCC), 2014. Climate change 2014 – impacts, adaptation and vulnerability: regional aspects. Cambridge University Press, Cambridge, UK.

International Fund for Agricultural Development (IFAD), 2010. Niger: managing rainfall with tassa. IFAD, Rome, Italy.

Kaboré, D. and Reij, C., 2004. The emergence and spreading of an improved traditional soil and water conservation practice in Burkina Faso. Vol. 114. International Food Policy Research Institute, Washington, DC, USA.

Lamanna, C., Ramirez-Villegas, J., Van Wijk, M., Corner-Dolloff, C., Girvetz, E. and Rosenstock, T.S., 2015. Evidence- and risk-based planning for food security under climate change. Results of a modeling approach for climate-smart agriculture programming. CCAFS, Wageningen, the Netherlands.

Laroche, M., Mérette, M. and Ruggeri, G.C., 1999. On the concept and dimensions of human capital in a knowledge-based economy context. Canadian Public Policy/Analyse de Politiques 25(1): 87-100.

Lee, L.-F., 1982. Some approaches to the correction of selectivity bias. Review of Economic Studies 49: 355-372.

Lokshin, M. and Sajaia, Z., 2004. Maximum likelihood estimation of endogenous switching regression models. Stata Journal 4: 282-289.

Maddison, D.J., 2007. The perception of and adaptation to climate change in Africa. World Bank Policy Research Working Paper No. 4308. World Bank, Washington, DC, USA.

Nelson, G.C., Rosegrant, M.W., Koo, J., Robertson, R., Sulser, T., Zhu, T. and Ringler, C., 2009. Climate change: impact on agriculture and costs of adaptation. International Food Policy Research Institute, Washington, DC, USA.

Reij, C., Tappan, G. and Smale, M., 2009. Agroenvironmental transformation in the Sahel. Another kind of 'Green Revolution. International Food Policy Research Institute, Washington, DC, USA.

Rivers, D. and Vuong, Q.H., 1988. Limited information estimators and exogeneity tests for simultaneous probit models. Journal of Econometrics 39: 347-366.

Seymour, G., Doss, C.R., Marenya, P., Meinzen-Dick, R. and Passarelli, S., 2016. Women's empowerment and the adoption of improved maize varieties: evidence from Ethiopia, Kenya, and Tanzania. Selected Paper prepared for presentation at the 2016 Agricultural & Applied Economics Association Annual Meeting. July 31-August 2, 2016. Boston, MA, USA.

United Nations Development Programme (UNDP), 2013. Human Development Report 2013: the rise of the south: human progress in a diverse world. UNDP, New York, NY, USA.

Wooldridge, J.M., 2002. Introductory econometrics: a modem approach. Thomson South-Western, Mason, OH, USA.

World Bank, 2013. Agricultural sector risk. Assessment in Niger: moving from crisis response to long-term risk management. Report no. 74322-NE. World Bank, Washington, DC, USA.

World Bank, 2016. Agriculture, value added (% of GDP). Available at: https://tinyurl.com/y8y4969u.

Wouterse, F.S., 2017. The returns to empowerment in diversified rural household: evidence from Niger. Vol. 1611. International Food Policy Research Institute, Washington, DC, USA.

Appendix 3.

Table 3.A1. First stage regression for empowerment.

	Empowerment
Household labour (days/ha)	0.001 (0.001)
Household labour squared (/100)	-0.001 (0.001)
Fertiliser (kg/ha)	-0.003 (0.002)
Fertiliser squared (/100)	0.005 (0.003)
Seed (kg/ha)	0.000 (0.001)
Seed squared (/100)	-0.000 (0.002)
Manure (kg/ha)	-0.000 (0.000)
Manure squared (/100)	0.000 (0.000)
Value of equipment (FCFA/10.000)	0.005 (0.002)**
Cattle holdings	0.015 (0.006)**
Sex of the household head (1=male)	-0.045 (0.019)**
Literacy of household head (1=yes)	-0.055 (0.019)**
Schooling of most educated adult (years)	0.005 (0.002)**
Koranic schooling of adult	-0.037 (0.019)**
Difference in capacity to be interviewed alone between primary male and female	-0.096 (0.025)**
Access to generic information via the radio	0.069 (0.017)**
R-squared	0.21
Adjusted R-squared	0.18
Kleibergen-Paap Wald rk F statistic	13.90
Stock-Yogo critical values	
10% maximal IV relative bias	19.93
15% maximal IV relative bias	11.59
20% maximal IV relative bias	8.75
Hansen J-statistic (P-value)	0.50 (0.48)
Durbin (score) X^2 (1) (P-value)	1.03 (0.31)
Number of observations	488

Chapter 4.
Does small irrigation boost smallholder agricultural production – evidence from a small irrigation programme in Niger

Pascal Tillie[1]*, Kamel Louhichi[1,2] and Sergio Gomez-Y-Paloma[1]
[1]European Commission, Joint Research Centre (JRC), Directorate D – Institute for Sustainable Resources, Edificio Expo. C/ Inca Garcilaso 3, 41092 Seville, Spain; [2]INRA-UMR Economie Publique, 78850 Thiverval Grignon, France; pascal.tillie@ec.europa.eu

Abstract

In Niger, an important objective of the agricultural policy aims at promoting the development of small irrigation infrastructures in order to diversify agricultural production, extend the cropping season, raise land productivity and secure farmers' revenue. Small irrigation infrastructures are regarded as a possible alternative to large irrigation infrastructure since they are cheaper to implement and maintain and easier to manage. This paper explores the impacts of a program of small irrigation development in Niger on land allocation, agricultural production and income generation using a farm-level model and data from a nationally representative sample of farm households. A static positive programming model was applied to every individual farm household included in sample to capture the full heterogeneity of impacts across farm households. The results show the large potential impact of irrigation on agriculture production and income generation, especially during the dry season and in regions of Niger with high-potential irrigable land. Farm income would increase by around 7% at country level if small irrigation was made available to all farmers. Small irrigation infrastructure would also contribute to reducing income inequality.

Keywords: small irrigation, policy impacts, farm modelling, positive mathematical programming, Niger

4.1 Introduction

Niger is one of the least developed countries in the world, according to the classification of the United Nation Development Program (UNDP). According to the population projection of the United Nation, its population was around 20.7 million people in 2016, and is one of fastest growing in the world. More than 80% of this population still lives in rural areas, and 75% live with less than 2 US dollar per day. The last Human Development Report of 2016 (UNDP, 2016) ranked Niger second-to-last country in the world (187th) in terms of Human Development Index. However, the extreme poverty rate has decreased in the last decades, from 63% in 1990 to 48% in 2011. The GDP per capita has also increased by almost 75% between 2000 and 2014, to reach approximately 427 USD per annum.

The demographic trend is another important feature of the Nigerien economy. According to United Nation figures, the annual growth rate of the population averaged 4% over the 2011-2015 period, which makes the country rank third in the world for population growth. This impressive population growth has important consequences on land pressure in rural areas. The burgeoning population both increases the pressure on the existing agricultural areas and further extends the boundaries of the agricultural frontier beyond the less favourable land. Between 1980 and 2012, the ratio of arable land to agricultural worker shrank from 11.8 to 1.1 ha worker (INS, 2012). Overall, this implies a reduction of rotation time for cropping. Considering that most of Niger's soils are *arenosol* (particularly prone to erosion and loss of nutrients), this increased pressure on land contributes to a rapid acceleration of land degradation, exacerbating conflicts between different land users, such as farmers and pastoralists.

Despite the constraints faced by the agricultural sector in Niger, its development is essential to meet the growing demand of the rural and urban population, and achieve both economic growth and poverty alleviation. The current agricultural policy, embedded in the *initiative 3N: les Nigériens nourrissent les Nigériens* (Nigeriens feed Nigeriens), focuses on land recuperation, development of irrigation and provision of extension services to farmers. It is aimed at facing land degradation problem and raising land productivity through a higher use of inputs, such as fertilisers. The development of irrigation infrastructures should also increase yields and secure farmers' revenue by allowing a diversification of cropping systems. Contrary to practices of the past, an important focus is placed on the development of small irrigation infrastructures, where water management is regarded as more efficient than in larger infrastructures.

The objective of this chapter is to assess the potential impacts of the development of small irrigation infrastructure currently promoted in Niger on irrigated land allocation, agricultural production and agricultural income, using a farm level model based on data collected in 2011 from a representative sample of 2,300 farm households.

4.2 Development of agriculture in Niger

4.2.1 Agriculture and constraints for farmers

Agricultural production in Niger is accomplished under very hostile conditions, due to the arid climate regime of the country characterised by low, uncertain rainfall, a short rainy season and high temperatures. Despite these adverse conditions, agriculture is the most important sector of the economy in Niger, from both a social and economic point of view. More than three-quarters of the population is active in agriculture (INS, 2012), while the sector contributed to about 45% of the GDP in 2010. The agricultural sector has actually grown faster than the other sectors of the economy over the last ten years. It is also the second sector contributing to export revenues after mining, primarily through the export of live animals and agricultural products such as onions or sesame to its neighbouring countries (Ministère de l'Agriculture, 2014).

Most of Niger's agricultural production relies on small-scale family farms, generally less than 2 hectares in size. Typical rain-fed agricultural systems are based on staple crops such as millet and sorghum, most of the time in mixed cropping systems with legume crops such as peanuts or *niébé* (the local name of one of the cultivars of cowpea, or *Vigna unguiculata*). When they have access to irrigated land, farmers generally add some vegetable crops, such as onions, sweet pepper, lettuce, or eggplants to their production of staple cereals. Overall, irrigated crops contribute to 30% of the value added of the agricultural production and up to 90% of the exports. Vegetable production represents the only source of cash for many agricultural households, in the absence of other alternatives.

Aside from the obvious agro-climatic factors that constrain agriculture production in Niger, there are other barriers that could be more easily lifted. Access to most productive factors (agricultural inputs and equipment) or to extension services is still limited for most farmers. Market access is also hindered by an underdeveloped road network and poor market facilities. Access to credit remains virtually inexistent for farmers. In addition, the country is also on the front line regarding the potential negative impacts of climate change. It could suffer significant drops in cereal yields if agricultural systems are not adapted to the changing climatic conditions. Due to the high importance of cereals in the diet of most agriculture households, the consequences for the food security and the nutrition of the population could be dramatic.

4.2.2 Potential of irrigation for Nigerien farmers

Most of cultivated land in Niger belongs to the Sahelo-Sudanian climatic zone, which receives between 300 to 600 mm of rain every year, from June to September. This amount of water, although small, could be better exploited for agricultural production with the use of proper techniques or infrastructure in order to avoid water run-off or infiltration and retain as much as possible of water. In addition, the water resources from the main watersheds of Niger, the Niger River and Lake Chad, are also not fully exploited. Altogether, the total irrigated potential of Niger was estimated to 270,000 hectares, of which only one third is currently imperfectly exploited (Ministère de l'Agriculture, 2015a).

Therefore, the challenge for agriculture in Niger will be to better manage the water supply and soil fertility. The yields of cereal and vegetable products could be increased and their variability reduced thanks to the use of improved varieties, the adoption of anti-erosion techniques, the increased use of animal traction for farming operations, or the introduction of agro-ecological innovations. Better exploitation of rain water, together with a better management of irrigation systems to improve water efficiency also represents an important development lever for agriculture in Niger. The improvement and stabilisation of crop yields would allow farming households to meet their subsistence needs and to generate some surpluses for sale. This would in turn strengthen their resilience to climatic change.

In 2012, to support the development of its agriculture sector, Niger adopted a common framework for all rural and agriculture policies, called the 'Initiative 3N', that stands for '*Les Nigériens Nourrissent les Nigériens*' (Nigeriens feed Nigeriens). The main goal of this initiative, and of its further *plan d'accélération* adopted in 2014, is to foster the domestic production of food products, in order to build up the supply side and the resilience of the country to food crises and natural disasters (HCi3N, 2012). Agricultural development is also supposed to be in line with the principles of sustainable development. The Initiative 3N agricultural policy intends to solve market failures with the deployment of a network of community-based one-shop stop facilities – so-called *maison du paysan* (farmers' house) – where farmers could gain access to microcredit, inputs, extension services and a workshop for agricultural tools.

Moreover, the Initiative 3N places a strong emphasis on the development of small irrigation, for several reasons. First of all, cereal yields in Niger have been decreasing over the last decades, as a result of soil degradation, shortening or disappearance of fallow periods, and increased pest pressure. Irrigated crops such as vegetables are therefore regarded as new opportunities for traditional cereal farmers, especially in the context of dynamic urbanisation observed in the country. Second, irrigation allows to stabilise yield in the face of erratic rainfall and to virtually expand the cropped area by using the land during both the dry and the rainy seasons or by cultivating land that cannot be used during the dry season (for instance in the riverbed of temporary watercourses, where humidity remains at low depth during the dry season). Finally, small irrigation is also regarded as a viable alternative to the large hydraulic installations that have been the priority until the end of the 1990s, and whose profitability and management turned out to be complex (Ministère de l'Agriculture, 2015b).

These elements have contributed to a change in the rural development strategy of Niger, which now emphasises the development of small irrigated perimeters managed locally at village scale. This new priority has led the Ministry of Agriculture to elaborate a specific strategy for the development of small irrigation, in the framework of the Initiative 3N, namely the *Stratégie de la Petite Irrigation au Niger* (SPIN) (Ministère de l'Agriculture, 2015b). The objective of the SPIN is to increase the use of irrigated land in order to boost agricultural productivity, achieve food and nutrition security, and increase the resilience of rural households faced with climatic hazards in Niger. In concrete terms, the government will support small irrigation projects proposed by local authorities, villages or groups of farmers, in exchange for a payment or physical (work) participation by beneficiaries. Small irrigation infrastructures have the benefit of flexibility and are easily adapted to many different local situations and water sources (surface water, groundwater, rainfalls). The most common forms of small irrigation infrastructure that the SPIN intends to develop are: wells and shallow forage (less than 15 m deep) with pumps, agricultural ponds, small hillside catchment reservoirs, river weirs, and small pumping stations for permanent watercourses. The SPIN started to operate and to grant funds for small irrigation projects in 2016. This strategy is intended to last for the next ten years.

4.3 Methodology: farm level modelling for policy impact assessment

4.3.1 Overview of the farm level model FSSIM-Dev

How to measure food security has been a point of debate in recent years due to the multidimensionality of food security (food availability, food access, utilisation and stability) and the time span to be considered. Different approaches, either qualitative or quantitative, have been developed to assess and/or proxy the impact of policy and technology on food security at micro and macro levels. For instance, food availability has been estimated through econometric techniques (Feleke *et al.*, 2005; Larochelle *et al.* 2015; Oluyole *et al.*, 2009) or measures through specific surveys based on indicators such as dietary energy supply per capita or household expenditure.

Farm and farm household models have also been used for the assessment of policy and market impacts on food security and poverty alleviation, especially in developing economies. Farm household models are well suited for taking into account the peculiarities of rural economies in low income countries where production, consumption and labour allocation decisions are non-separable due to market imperfections (De Janvry *et al.*, 1991; Singh *et al.*, 1986). Such models are able to take into account the effects of transaction costs on market participation decisions. In sum, farm household models represent a useful tool to capture key features of the agricultural sector in developing countries and to assess the systemic effects of policies on farming systems. They can provide information on resource uses, agricultural production, changes in crop rotation, food consumption, participation to input and factor markets, agriculture and household income, poverty level, etc. All data can be generated at household and aggregated levels, which can also give the distribution of any impact across all farms, and not only average effects. Louhichi and Gomez-y-Paloma (2014) have recently reviewed studies based on farm household models in developing countries, stressing the advantages and drawbacks offered by the different methodology, geographical coverage and behavioural hypotheses proposed.

We use a farm household model called FSSIM-Dev (Louhichi and Gomez y Paloma, 2014) to assess *ex-ante* the impacts of the deployment of a small irrigation schemes on smallholder farmer livelihood and on food security in Niger. FSSIM-Dev is a micro-simulation tool that is well adapted to assess the policy impacts on food security and rural poverty alleviation in the specific context of low-income developing countries. As in any farm household model, the tool solves simultaneously the household's production and consumption decisions. However, contrary to most other household models, FSSIM-Dev is a positive programming model and this makes it able to properly reproduce the observed situation taking into account the existence of implicit costs not always captured in the dataset used to calibrate the model.

FSSIM-Dev model reproduces the dual character of farm households in developing countries. In particular, food surplus/deficit is created as a difference between food and cash crop production and household food demand. Both food production and food demand are affected by prices.

Household prices are endogenous in order to account for the existence of transaction costs that influence farmer's decisions regarding market participation. Production prices are a function of international markets and trade, infrastructure and market efficiency. In sum, FSSIM-Dev is a comparative static and non-linear optimisation model which relies on both the general household's utility framework and the farm's production technical constraints, in a non-separable regime. Consequently, it maximises farm household income subject to resource constraints (includes land and labour), cash, market clearing conditions, linear expenditure system (LES), price bands and complementary slackness conditions.

The general mathematical formulation of the model is the following:

Max $U = \Sigma_h w_h R_h$

Subject to:
- resource constraints;
- LES;
- price bands & complementary slackness conditions;
- market clearing conditions;
- cash constraint.

where U is the value of the objective function, h denotes a farm household and w its weight within the village, region or country and R is the farm household expected income. For more details on the mathematical structure of the model and its functioning, see Louhichi and Gomez-y-Paloma (2014).

Farm household income (R) is defined as the income earned from all economic activities of family members of the same household. It is made up of three components: farm income, income from marketed factors of production (off-farm agricultural wages, rent of land and equipment) and non-farm income. Farm income is defined as the income earned by households from selling or consuming their own agricultural products. Non-farm incomes are defined exogenously and can originate from different sources, such as non-agricultural wages, self-employed activities (petty trading, craftsmanship, etc.), pensions, transfers (including remittances) and donations.

Farm income is computed as the sum of agricultural gross margin minus a non-linear (quadratic) activity-specific function. Gross margin is the total revenue from agricultural activities, including sales and self-consumption, minus the accounting variable costs of production activities. The accounting costs include costs of seeds, fertilisers, crop protection, and other specific costs. The quadratic activity-specific function is a behavioural function introduced to calibrate the farm model to an observed base year situation, as is usually done in Positive Mathematical Programming (PMP) models. The PMP methodology (Howitt, 1995), recently refined by Mérel and Bucaram (2010), intends to replicate households' production and consumption decisions in a precise way, allowing to capture the effects of factors that are not explicitly included in the model such as price expectation, risk-averse behaviour, labour requirement, capital constraints and other unobserved costs (Heckelei, 2002). The principal outputs generated by FSSIM-Dev for a specific policy scenario are forecasts on resource use, agricultural production, food consumption, market factors exchange, farm household income and poverty level at farm household and aggregated levels.

For the present study, the consumption module of FSSIM-Dev was switched-off due to missing data on income elasticities. The supply module was implemented for the cropping season 2010/2011, corresponding to the period covered by the Niger LSMS-ISA survey. The model calibration was performed at the individual farm household level using the Highest Posterior Density (HPD) estimator with prior information on supply elasticities (Louhichi *et al.*, 2015). Model parameters were calibrated so that the model exactly replicates an observed land allocation among irrigated and non-irrigated crops, as well as an exogenous set of supply elasticities. The calibration to the exogenous supply elasticities is performed in a non-myopic way. In other words, we take into account the effects of changing dual values on the simulation response (Heckelei, 2002, Mérel and Bucaram, 2010).

The parameters of the behavioural function are estimated only for observed activities in each farm household, meaning that the well-known self-selection problem is not explicitly handled in this estimation. The self-selection problem is the misrepresentation of economic behaviour with regard to production activities that are not observed during the base year (i.e. activities whose initial observed supply level is zero during the base-year). In other words, while farmers do observe any crop that is cultivated in their village or region and make their own assessment for their individual gross margin and costs of production and implicit costs, those are not directly available from the dataset of observed activities. To cope with this problem, we adopted the following ad-hoc modelling decisions in the simulation phase: in each region, the gross margin of the non-observed activities for a given farm is equal to the farm-type average gross margin, the activity's quadratic function parameter is equal to the activity's average quadratic function parameter within the farm type, and the linear term's quadratic function is derived from the difference between the gross margin and the dual values of constraints. By doing so, the model is able to select optimal production activities from all possible activities present in the region.

4.3.2 Data used for the calibration

The research described in this chapter and the simulation exercise are based on the exploitation of the dataset of farm households originated by the 2011 Living Standard Measurement Survey – Integrated Survey of Agriculture (LSMS-ISA). This very comprehensive survey was conducted by the National Institute of Niger with the technical support of the World Bank. Data were collected in two waves, in order to cover both the off season (from December 2010 to May 2011) and the rain-fed (June 2011 to November 2011) cropping cycles. The full sample includes about 3,970 households, all involved in agriculture (including livestock) activities. The survey sample was designed following a random two-stage process and was stratified by four agro-ecological areas, namely urban, agricultural, agro-pastoral and pastoral. The final sample is representative both at country and regional level, for urban and rural areas. Three different questionnaires were used, at different levels of data collection: at community level, at household level, and the last one specific to agricultural activities.

The Niger 2011 LSMS-ISA survey featured many different modules, and gathered information on many different aspects of household livelihoods. Those modules used for the purpose of this study cover three topics:

1. Household activities, consumption and livelihood. Data were collected in order to trace all food and non-food expenses of households surveyed. A seven-day recall methodology was used to collect data on food consumption. All non-farm activities, as well as any source of income, are reported, for any member of the household.
2. Agricultural activities. Data on agricultural activities include a comprehensive description of all fields of the farm, land tenure, type of soil and available infrastructure (anti-erosion, irrigation, etc.). Production cost (labour and input) are collected at plot level. The quantity of family labour, labour exchange and hired labour used for each crop and for different farming operations is also available. Crop output is collected for each plot and each crop on the plot. Plot size was measured by GPS, at least in most of the cases.
3. Livestock activities. Data on livestock activities include a comprehensive description of all type of herds of animals owned by the farmers, the output (sales) and production costs.

The 2011 LSMS-ISA dataset was prepared for the purpose of this research. Variables such as crop yield, quantity of input used and prices were treated for outliers (using either Tukey's method based on Interquartile Range and trimmed mean) and missing values. However, the main limitation of this dataset is that, at the time of the data collection, the entire country suffered a severe drought that dramatically affected the rain-fed cropping season. Therefore, the yields calculated from the survey data are very low, especially for cereals, such as millet and sorghum. As they do not correspond to farmer's expectations at time of planting, we have replaced those data by the expected yields, calculated notably using the estimation of losses by farmers.

For this research, we focused on those households with cropping activities. This results in the exclusion of those households that are involved in livestock production only, but mixed farms are included. The final size of our analytical sample is therefore 2,322 households. The key features of the sample used for this research are presented in Table 4.1.

4.4 Baseline and simulation of the effects of the SPIN

The baseline scenario is interpreted as a projection in time including the most probable future development in terms of technological, structural and market changes. It is used as a reference point for the comparison of the effects of the simulation scenario. In our case study, the baseline scenario is assumed to be similar to the base-year, which means that all model parameters are assumed to remain unchanged including output prices, yields, variables costs, implicit costs (i.e.

Table 4.1. Sample characteristics of farm households.

Regions	Agadez	Diffa	Dosso	Maradi	Tahoua	Tillaberi	Zinder	Niamey	Niger
Number of farm households	108	227	389	389	378	374	384	73	2,322
Total area covered (ha)	116	856	1167	803	863	2,035	994	214	7,048
Average farm size (ha)	1.1	3.8	3.0	2.1	2.3	5.4	2.6	2.9	3.0
Standard deviation	0.9	3.3	2.5	2.5	2.5	5.1	3.4	12.0	4.0
Number of farms with irrigation	89	53	37	7	54	41	20	46	347
Average irrigated land (ha)	0.9	2.1	0.6	0.2	1.0	1.7	2.3	3.2	1.5
Land use in rainy season (% by region)									
Millet	18.7	57.0	46.9	38.3	43.8	57.1	39.6	64.2	47.2
Sorghum	13.9	15.0	7.3	22.0	23.3	10.0	20.9		15.5
Paddy rice	16.4							6.0	0.6
Cowpea	4.4	10.1	28.3	33.1	26.4	21.6	30.7	22.9	25.6
Peanut		4.3	6.5		4.7				3.6
Onion	34.9								0.6
Land use in off-season (% by region)									
Paddy rice		15.7	28.6			48.6		19.3	16.9
Sweet potato			27.3			19.8			5.1
Sweet pepper		74.8					7.8		22.3
Chili				10.9		6.2	6.0		2.9
Cabbage				23.8	8.8		6.5	16.2	5.1
Tomato				10.1	6.3		8.3	20.1	6.5
Jaxatu							52.2		8.1
Onion	45.2				7.9	77.4	7.5		16.5
Pumpkin						7.9	5.2		2.4

PMP terms), farm resource endowments and farm weighting factors (no structural change). As in the base-year, the local labour markets are not modelled in the version of the model used for this simulation, which means that while farmers can hire some labour to work on their farm, there is no constraints requiring this exchange to be balanced and labour cost (wage) is not depending on the equilibria between offer and demand.

The policy scenario that is simulated for this study attempts to estimate the potential impacts of the implementation of the 'strategy for small irrigation development in Niger' (SPIN in French) (Ministère de l'Agriculture, 2015b). In concrete terms, we simulated increased access to irrigated land for farmers in Niger and assess the potential impacts in terms of land use change, agricultural production and income change. This scenario will therefore enlighten the potential effects of the implementation of the SPIN for farm households in Niger. The objective of the SPIN is to increment the land area suitable for small irrigation by 152%, from the 107,000 hectares as currently to 270,000 hectares over the next ten years (Table 4.2). The SPIN will finance projects of small irrigation development at the request of farmers, groups of farmers or local authorities. The SPIN considers two types of requests: the 'social' one and the 'normal' one. The first type targets specifically the most vulnerable farmers, either on economic or on climatic grounds. For those farmers, the project will be implemented at no cost, while for the other it will be partially subsidised and partially financed by credit. For this simulation exercise, we focused on the first type of request, because it is very much in line with the objective of strengthening food security and alleviate poverty in Niger.

Therefore, we assumed that the cost of the investment (the implementation of the irrigation infrastructure) for those farmers benefiting from a small irrigation project will be zero, since the overwhelming majority of farmers in Niger could be considered marginal. However, all other costs linked to the farm operations on the 'new' irrigated land, if any, including the costs specific to the irrigation systems, have to be supported by the farmers. In the simulated scenario, we have set for each region and farm a potential irrigated area that would correspond to the increase of irrigated land that is forecast by the SPIN, based on the potential irrigable land for each region of Niger. Therefore, all farms could potentially obtain access to irrigated land, at no cost, and they will decide whether to use it based on the gross margin for irrigated crops in the region, their own factor endowment and cost structure. In this scenario, the adoption of irrigation is therefore only based on economic considerations, in a broad sense (there is no 'technical infeasibility' of irrigation in a strict sense although this should be reflected by high and prohibitive implicit costs).

Based on these assumptions, the expected results of the simulation scenario would be: (1) an increase in irrigated land at national and regional level; (2) a switch in the overall pattern of

Table 4.2. Small irrigation in Niger, current situation and estimated potential (Ministère de l'Agriculture et de l'Elevage du Niger, 2012, 2015b).

Watershed	Region	Potential irrigable land (ha)	Irrigated land with modern water management (ha)	Other irrigated land (ha)
Niger River	Tillabéri, Dosso, Niamey	144,000	9,233	93,150
Dallols-Adder-Doutchi-Maggia	Tahoua	69,000	3,592	
Goulbis-Tarka	Maradi, Tahoua	17,000	570	
Korama-Damagaram-Mounio	Zinder	10,000		
Manga	Diffa	20,000	295	
Aïr-Azaouagh	Agadez	10,000		
Total Niger		270,000	13,850	93,150

cultivated crops in favour of irrigated ones (for instance, vegetable production); (3) an increase of household income.

4.5 Results and discussion

We present here the impacts of the simulation scenario on a set of indicators generated from FSSIM-Dev at farm level, subsequently aggregated at region or country level. These indicators are: land allocation among irrigated and rain-fed crops, crop area and agricultural income. The results are generally expressed in relative change compared to the baseline.

4.5.1 Irrigated area by region

We simulated the possibility for every farm to gain access to irrigated land, with an upper bound corresponding to the potential irrigated area for each region, as indicated in the SPIN strategy documents. The question is, will farmers use this possibility, and if they do, to what extent?

Figure 4.1 provides a summary of the results of the simulated policy scenario. As expected, the irrigated area in Niger would dramatically increase. During the dry season, the irrigated area would increase by 208%, while during the rainy season it would be multiplied by 6. However, this increase has different explanations depending on the season considered. During the rainy season, farmers substitute rain-fed crops with irrigated crops which are much more profitable. Therefore, the total cultivated area remains the same in most of the country, but the share of irrigated crops in total land expands from 1% to almost 6%. In contrast, the extension of irrigated land during the dry season is achieved by enlarging the total cultivated area, from 2.4% of the total agricultural land to 7.3%.

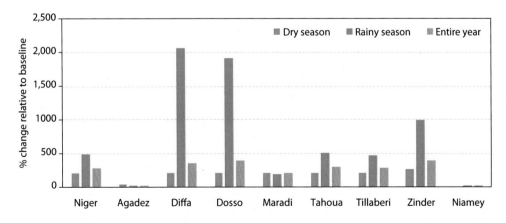

Figure 4.1. Use of irrigated land area under the simulation scenario (relative change compared to the baseline – population weighted).

Overall, improved access to small irrigation would lead to an increase of the total cropped area in Niger by about 5%. The trend described above for the entire country also applies to every region in Niger, but in different proportions. The largest increase of total cultivated area would occur in Diffa (+22%) while there would be a contraction of 4.1% in the Niamey region (the only region to actually show a decrease). The largest increase of irrigated area during the dry season is observed in the Zinder, Dosso and Tahoua regions, with a relative change to the baseline of 260, 219 and 213%, respectively. In these regions, the production of off-season vegetables is already quite important. The increase of irrigated land in relative terms is much higher during the rainy season, but this is also explained by the small irrigated area during this season in the baseline. In absolute terms, the Tillabéri region would remain the first region for irrigated area (for both seasons), followed by Tahoua and Zinder.

At the level of the individual farm, the results of the simulated policy scenario show that approximately 83% of the farmers in Niger would engage in irrigation if they were given the possibility to do so. Also, the mean increase of irrigated area would be of 0.56 hectare for the entire country, while only 16.7% of the farmers would actually increase their irrigated area by more than 1 hectare. Figure 4.2 displays the distribution of this increase irrigated area for the whole sample of farmers.

4.5.2 Crop land use

A closer look at the relative change of area cultivated by crop gives additional insights into the choices made by farmers when they are given access to irrigated land. In fact, the most important changes in land use occur during the dry season, which makes sense since gaining access to irrigation makes it possible to develop cropping activities that previously were impossible during

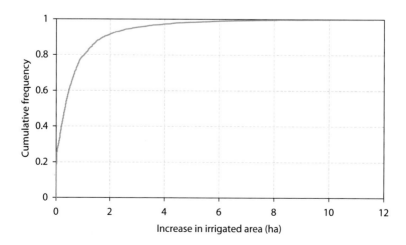

Figure 4.2. Cumulative distribution of the absolute change of irrigated area.

the dry season. However, as the total area cultivated during the off-season is still far from the area cultivated during the rainy, the impact of this change on the land use over the full year is rather limited (Figure 4.3). Millet, cowpea and sorghum remain the three most important crops in terms of cultivated area, although the cumulated proportion of the total cultivated area declines slightly from 87.8 to 82.1%. On the contrary, paddy rice area is growing significantly, and its share of the total cultivated area increases from less than 1 to about 3.5%. Cassava and peanuts follow the same pattern but to a lesser extent.

At the regional level, the changes tend to be more marked. For instance, the production of staple crops (millet, sorghum and cowpea) would shrink at a higher level in Diffa and Niamey region, while there would be no change in Maradi. Rice production expansion is occurring mainly in Diffa, Dosso and Tillabéri.

Focusing on the changes occurring during the off-season for land use reveals other patterns of changes (Figure 4.4). It shows that the extended access of irrigation would make paddy rice the first crop during this season instead of onion. Although onion cultivation would increase by 168% during the dry season, its share of the total cultivated area would decline from 25.7 to 22.4%. On the contrary, paddy rice would represent more than one third of the total area cultivated during the dry season. Other crops that would lose importance are sweet pepper, sweet potatoes, pumpkin, cabbage, sugar cane, or carrots. On the other hand, eggplant, cassava, tomato and lettuce would represent a larger share of the total cultivated area during the dry season. The largest increase of cultivated area in relative terms (compared to the baseline) would be observed for cassava, paddy rice and okra, in this order.

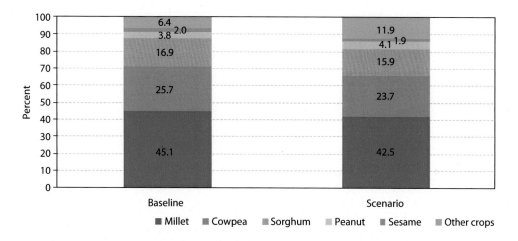

Figure 4.3. Crop land use in Niger over one entire year.

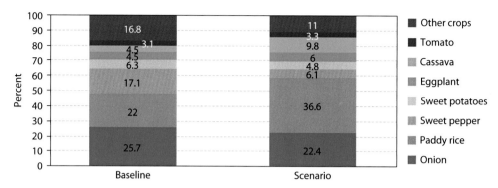

Figure 4.4. Crop land use in Niger over the dry season.

4.5.3 Agricultural income

The economic impacts of the increased access to irrigation are assessed in two ways: at country and regional aggregate level and in terms of income change by income decile. As expected, access to small irrigation would increase agricultural income by around 7% at country level. The largest increase is observed in Diffa, while there is virtually no effect in Maradi and Niamey. As shown in Figure 4.5, most of the changes in agricultural income are driven by the reallocation of land during the dry season, that is to say the extension of irrigated area. However, the regions where agricultural income has the greatest increase are not necessary those where the irrigated land expands the most. This is because the kind of agricultural production that is available to farmers also matters. Some crops are more profitable than others. In this respect, paddy rice plays an important role in the large income increase in Diffa.

Figure 4.6 shows how the benefits of the enlarged access to small irrigation would be distributed among the different categories of income. The big picture is that this policy would have a clear

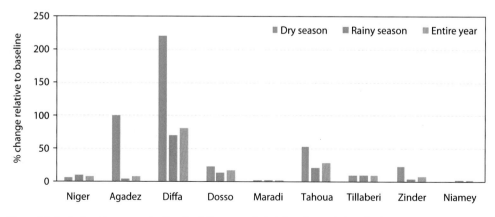

Figure 4.5. Agricultural income under the simulation scenario (relative change to baseline).

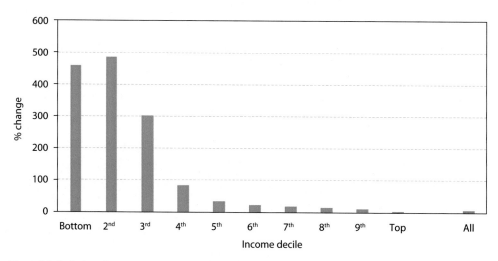

Figure 4.6. Agriculture income change by income decile (relative change to baseline).

effect in terms of closing the inequality gap among farm households in Niger. Indeed, the largest income increase would be obtained by the poorest households. This is explained by the very low agricultural income that households with poor endowments in land and capital are earning in the baseline. Those households typically derived their agricultural income from traditional cropping systems of millet, sorghum, and possibly, cowpea, with low yields and low income. If these households are given the possibility to practice off-season, irrigated agriculture, they would therefore benefit from the high-value added of vegetable crops or other more diversified staple crops.

4.6 Conclusion

This chapter has sought to assess *ex-ante* the impacts of the small irrigation scheme (SPIN) on the livelihoods and food security of smallholder farmers in Niger. This is performed using a micro-simulation model named FSSIM-Dev (Farm System Simulator for Developing Countries). FSSIM-Dev is a static positive programming model that is applied to every individual farm household of a sample of 2,300 farm households drawn from the 2011 LSMS-ISA survey. This allows to capture the full heterogeneity across farm households and to obtain results of the simulation at the level of the individual farm.

From a policy perspective, the main finding of applying this model is the large effect of small irrigation on crop allocation, production and farm income. The total cropped area would increase by 5% in Niger, representing a positive impact for the availability of food and food security. The cultivated areas of paddy rice and cassava, two staple crops with an important role in the diet of farm households, would see dramatic increases. Agricultural income at the national level would increase by around 7%. At the regional levels the impact would be even more pronounced (reaching more than 15% in three regions). At individual level, about 20% of farm households would receive an increase higher than 100% (accounting for household weighting factors). Finally, an important contribution of irrigation to food security, that is not considered here, is the stabilisation of crop yields. Irrigation smooths the potential dramatic impacts of drought and rainfall variability on yields.

These findings have to be considered, however, with some caution on account of the model's assumptions. First of all, output prices are assumed to be exogenously given. This implies that the market feedback (output price changes) is not taken incorporated into the model. However, this effect tends to be important in developing countries in general, and in Niger in particular, where high transaction costs tend to isolate the various local markets from each other, hampering price transmission. This issue is even more acute for vegetable crops that are less easy to transport than cereals. Therefore, our model probably overestimates the overall effects of the simulated scenario.

Another important limitation to our approach is that there are other constraints to the extension of irrigated production that are not treated here, such as the soil type or possible inefficiencies in the management of small irrigation equipment at community level. The challenge of commercialising vegetables is another issue. In reality, vegetable production tends to develop near city centres where some demand exists.

Despite these limitations, the simulation results presented here can be useful to policy makers that are currently developing small irrigation support programs in Sub-Saharan African countries. Further development of the FSSIM-Dev model will take into account the above-mentioned limitations.

References

De Janvry, A., Fafchamps, M. and Sadoulet, E., 1991. Peasant household behaviour with missing markets: some paradoxes explained. Economic Journal 101: 1400-1417.

Feleke, S.T., Kilmer, R.L. and Gladwin, C.H., 2005. Determinants of food security in Southern Ethiopia at the household level. Agricultural Economics 33: 351-363.

HCi3N, 2012. Cadre Stratégique de l'Initiative 3N. Haut Commissariat à l'Initiative 3N, Niamey, Niger.

Heckelei, T., 2002. Calibration and estimation of programming models for agricultural supply analysis. Habilitation Thesis. Agricultural Faculty, University of Bonn, Bonn, Germany.

Howitt, R.E., 1995. Positive mathematical programming. American Journal of Agricultural Economics 77: 329-342.

INS, 2012. Recensement général de la population et de l'habitat. Institut National de la Statistique du Niger, Niamey, Niger.

Larochelle, C., Alwang, J., Norton, G.W., Katungi, E. and Labarta, R.A., 2015. Impacts of improved bean varieties on poverty and food security in Uganda and Rwanda. In: Walker, T.S. and Alwang, J. (eds.) Crop improvement, adoption and impact of improved varieties in food crops in Sub-Saharan Africa. CABI Publishing, Wallingford, UK, pp. 314-337.

Louhichi, K. and Gomez-y-Paloma, S., 2014. A farm household model for agri-food policy analysis in developing countries: application to smallholder farmers in Sierra Leone. Food Policy 45: 1-13.

Louhichi, K., Ciaian, P., Espinosa-Goded, M., Colen, L., Perni, A. and Gómez-y-Paloma, S., 2015. Farm-level economic impacts of EU-CAP greening measures. In: Agricultural and Applied Economics Association and Western Agricultural Economics Association Annual Meeting. San Francisco, USA. Available at: http://tinyurl.com/y9n6ts4x.

Mérel, P. and Bucaram, S., 2010. Exact calibration of programming models of agricultural supply against exogenous supply elasticities. European Review of Agricultural Economics 37: 395-418.

Ministère de l'Agriculture, 2012. Résultats définitifs de la campagne horticole 2012. Direction des Statistiques – Ministère de l'Agriculture, Niamey, Niger.

Ministère de l'Agriculture, 2014. Résultats définitifs de la campagne agricole d'hivernage 2014 et perspectives alimentaires 2014-2015. Direction des Statistiques – Ministère de l'Agriculture. Niamey, Niger.

Ministère de l'Agriculture, 2015a. Evaluation du potentiel en terre irrigable du Niger. Direction Générale du Génie Rural – Ministère de l'Agriculture, Niamey, Niger.

Ministère de l'Agriculture, 2015b. Stratégie de la petite irrigation au Niger. DG du Génie Rural, Ministère de l'Agriculture du Niger, Niamey, Niger.

Oluyole, K.A., Oni, O.A., Omonona, B.T. and Adenegan, K.O., 2009. Food security among cocoa farming households of Ondo State, Nigeria. ARPN Journal of Agricultural and Biological Science 4: 7-13.

Singh, I., Squire, L. and Strauss, J., 1986. A survey of agricultural household models: recent findings and policy implications. World Bank Economic Review 1: 149-179.

UNDP, 2016. Human Development Report 2016: human development for everyone. United Nations Development Programme, New York, NY, USA.

Chapter 5.
Gender parity and inorganic fertilizer technology adoption in farm households: evidence from Niger

Mahamadou Roufahi Tankari

IFPRI-Dakar, Titre 3396, Lot #2, BP 24063 Dakar Almadies, Senegal; m.tankari@cgiar.org

Abstract

This study seeks to address the gap in understanding the role of gender parity in inorganic fertiliser technology adoption in Niger. The empirical strategy is firstly based on the calculation of the household parity indicator following the Women's Empowerment in Agriculture Index (WEAI) approach and, secondly, it relies on binary regressions. It appears that gender parity in the household affects negatively the adoption of inorganic fertiliser. Thus, accompanying measures are needed to correct this negative effect of gender parity on the fertiliser technology adoption. The study also highlights a number of determinants of gender parity and adoption of fertilisers in agricultural households that can serve policy design.

Keywords: gender, agricultural technologies, Niger

5.1 Introduction

Gender parity is increasingly seen as both a strategy and a prerequisite for economic and social development in poor countries. The World Bank (2011), in its 2012 World Development Report, identifies the equality between women and men as a major asset to the economy with greater parity increasing productivity, benefiting the next generation with improved living conditions and making institutions more representative.

In sub-Saharan Africa, where women comprise approximately 46% of the agricultural labour force (Quisumbing *et al.*, 2014), gender parity in agriculture may play a key role in agriculture development on which thousands of households depend for their livelihood. One of the major constraints facing this sector relates to limited inorganic fertiliser use despite the broad consensus that its increased use is necessary for sustained productivity growth (Jayne and Rashid, 2013). Wanzala and Groot (2013) argue that the stagnation of agricultural production in sub-Saharan Africa during the last fifty years was primarily the result of low fertiliser use. This indicates that the adoption of inorganic fertiliser technology is necessary to boost agricultural production in farm households.

Women's bargaining power may affect many aspects of household production, including the allocation of labour to various activities, including homework, agricultural work and wage work (Doss, 2013). It should be noted that decisions about technology adoption often involve inputs from both men and women in farm households (Lambrecht *et al.*, 2016; Love *et al.*, 2014; Marenya *et al.*, 2015). A clear understanding of how intra-household dynamics affect technology adoption is important from a policy point of view as the adoption of modern inputs is at the forefront of the government agenda reflected by the re-emergence of input subsidy programs in African countries (Ricker-Gilbert and Jayne, 2017).

Gender parity in a household exists when women are equally empowered to the men in their households. However, this may negatively or positively affect fertiliser technology adoption in farm households depending on the effects of unobserved characteristics, such as risk aversion, time preference or knowledge which are important determinants of agricultural technology adoption. For example, in Niger the country on which we are focusing Adesina *et al.* (1988) and Sanou *et al.* (2015) have shown that risk aversion matters among Nigerien farmers for fertiliser technology adoption. In addition, in a poverty context and with a lack of access to credit, time preference will importantly affect the allocation of household's resources between investment and consumption. Finally, the knowledge about returns to a technology may also influence its adoption. For example, there is evidence for Niger that living in a woman-headed household improves caloric consumption for all members compared to living in a male-headed household (Tankari, 2015) and the positive expected return of fertiliser could induce women to support adoption of this technology to increase yields and subsistence consumption.

However, the literature on technology adoption, rarely considers gender and intra-household issues although there is a growing interest in understanding if and how gender parity in terms of empowerment affects agricultural outcomes (Seymour *et al.*, 2016). Most existing studies, have not addressed this issue appropriately. In fact, these studies emphasise differences between male- or female-headed households but neglect the behaviour of women within male-headed households (e.g. Doss and Morris 2001; Ndiritua *et al.*, 2014). A lack of intra-household data often means that only the sex of the household head is included in the analysis, making it difficult to determine how gender influences technology adoption in households with more than one decision-maker (e.g. Marenya *et al.*, 2015; Uaiene *et al.*, 2009). In addition, the small number of female-headed households in developing countries often results in statistically insignificant results when examining outcomes for this group (Quisumbing *et al.* 2014). Nevertheless, it is important to point out that to circumvent these limitations the disaggregation by the sex of the plot manager, rather than by sex of the household head has been proposed in the literature (Peterman *et al.*, 2011).

The aim of this chapter is to add to the literature on gender and intra-household issues with respect to technology adoption by highlighting the impact of gender parity on the adoption of inorganic fertiliser technology in farm households by focusing on primary males and female as data on co-wives are not available. The gender parity measure within the household is derived from the 5 domains of empowerment in agriculture used in the Women Empowerment Agricultural Index (WEAI) calculation. These domains are (1) decisions about agricultural production; (2) access to and decision-making power about productive resources; (3) control of use of income; (4) leadership in the community; and (5) time allocation. The study is set in the context of Niger, a poor country where agriculture is the main income generating activity for the population. Findings will reveal whether gender parity in agriculture can affect the adoption of technologies and thus be defined as a pathway to increase inorganic fertiliser adoption. In a context where gender parity negatively affects fertiliser adoption, accompanying measures should be devised to ensure that the effect is positive. This negative effect may occur due to risk aversion or time preference under resources constraint or lack of knowledge about the importance of this technology adoption.

This chapter adds to the literature on gender access to agricultural technologies in which findings are rather mixed. For instance, in Ghana, after controlling for access to complementary inputs (land, education, labour) no significant difference in rates of adoption between male and female farmers was found (Doss and Morris, 2001) while Jagger and Pender (2006) found in Uganda that female heads of household are significantly more likely to adopt inorganic fertiliser than their male counterparts. In addition, in the context of Kenya (Freeman and Omiti, 2003) and Zimbabwe (Bourdillon *et al.*, 2002), the gender of household head has no significant effect on adoption and intensity of use of inorganic fertiliser while, in Malawi, men and women plot owners do not differ significantly with respect to fertiliser adoption (Chirwa, 2005). Furthermore, in Niger, the more empowered the household is, the more likely it is to have adapted to climate change by putting in place zaï pits (Wouterse, 2017) while in Ethiopia, Kenya, and Tanzania women's empowerment is positively correlated with greater participation by women in decisions about the adoption of improved maize varieties, the acquisition of credit for the purchase of improved maize varieties and the acquisition of extension services related to improved maize varieties (Seymour *et al.*, 2016).

The chapter continues as follows: after this introduction, the context of the study will be presented (Section 5.2). Next, the methodology will be detailed (Section 5.3) and the data source and sample description will be presented (Section 5.4). Subsequently, the descriptive and econometric findings will be presented (Section 5.5). Finally, the study ends with a conclusion (Section 5.6).

5.2 Context of the study

Niger faces major problems in the field of chronic, seasonal and acute food insecurity and malnutrition. The country is landlocked with a low income per capita and level of human development. In 2013, Niger's population, growing at a rate of 3.3%, was estimated at 17.8 million people with a Gross Domestic Product (GDP) per capita of US $ 413, less than a third of the GDP per capita of the entire sub-Saharan region (World Bank, 2015). The first corollary of this is that poverty reduction takes place at a relatively low rate. For example, the national poverty rate varied from 63% in 1993 to 59.5% in 2007 (INS-Niger, 2008), which is relatively low compared to other countries in sub-Saharan Africa such as Uganda, for which the poverty rate declined from 56% in 1992 to 24.5% in 2009 (World Bank, 2015).

Agriculture continues to be the main source of employment and plays a key role in the formation of GDP in Niger. Indeed, a sizable proportion of the workforce is involved in agriculture and the contribution of this activity to GDP is about 37.2% in 2013 (INS-Niger, 2014). However, the Sahara Desert covers about two-thirds of Niger's land area. Very little rain falls in this arid region. To the south of the desert lies the pastoral belt with slightly more rainfall but not enough to support rainfed agriculture. The agro-pastoral zone to the south of the pastoral zone receives enough rainfall to permit good harvests in non-drought years but rainfall is variable. Rainfed agriculture is most successful in a band across the southern border of the country, widest in the southwest (FEWS NET, 2011). Altogether, crop land represents around 13% of Niger's total land area. As most Sahelian countries, Niger suffers from low natural fertility of the soil to which are added the drastic reduction of fallow and cultivation of certain marginal lands. However, the application rate of inorganic fertilisers in the country is between 3.7 and 5.6 kg/ha, one of the lowest in the sub-region and far below the target of 2006 Abuja Declaration. The Niger government has recognised the importance of the use of fertilisers to increase agricultural productivity. This has led to the establishment of the Centrale d'Approvisionnement en Intrants et Matériels Agricoles (CAIMA). This Centre is the main supplier of subsidised fertilisers in Niger, however the quantity supplied is far below the national demand. CAIMA's officials reported that national fertiliser demand during the 2013 agricultural season was about 70,000 tons. CAIMA funded and supplied less than 30% of this amount or approximately 20,000 tons. The country relies on other supply channels to cover the gap but needs are often not met. Development partners, such as the Alliance for a Green Revolution in Africa (AGRA), supplied about 25,000 tons or 36% of demand. Thus, only about 65% of the estimated national demand for fertilisers in 2013 was satisfied even with the contribution of donors.

According to the Ministry of Women and Child Protection of Niger (2007), the Nigerien society is characterised by a rich cultural diversity, evidenced by the coexistence of several ethnic groups, the Hausa, the Zarma or Songhai, the Fulani, the Tuareg, the Kanuri, the Budumas, the Arabs, the Toubo and the Gourmantchés. Spread across the entire territory, these ethnic groups essentially share the same cultural values based on the habits and customs specific to each group; these are reinforced by Islam, the dominant religion in Niger (virtually the entire population is Muslim). The traditional social organisation of the Nigerien society is patriarchal in most communities. Ethnic groups in Niger, despite the diversity of their beliefs and practices, share the same differentiated perception of gender roles. In all groups, family relations between men and women are built from a fundamental inequality between the man, the household head and the woman, the mother and wife.

Also, according to the Ministry of Women and Child Protection of Niger (2007), traditionally in Niger, it is the man who embodies authority in the household, he sets the rules and the code of conduct, he ensures the control and management of family property and he takes key decisions and provides livelihoods to household members. The woman, meanwhile, tends to take on a the burden of the operation of domestic life, realises housework and takes care of children and other family members. In the performance of activities, the sexual division of labour determines the distribution of tasks between girls and boys, men and women. Joined in the context of production, reproduction and at the level of the community, this differentiation means that men take on formal and valued production work and women are engaged in maintenance and care activities which are undervalued.

5.3 Methodology

We derive our measure of intrahousehold gender parity from the indicators of the Women's Empowerment in Agriculture Index (WEAI) (Alkire *et al.*, 2013). The theoretical foundation of our econometric model that justifies the inclusion of gender parity indicator as a regressor is based on Browning and Gørtz (2012) and Browning and Chiappori (1998) collective models.

5.3.1 Gender parity indicator

We use the five dimensions of empowerment defined for the establishment of the Women's Empowerment in Agriculture Index (Alkire *et al.*, 2013). The five domains of the WEAI are (1) decisions about agricultural production; (2) access to and decision-making power about productive resources; (3) control of use of income; (4) leadership in the community; and (5) time allocation. These domains also reflect aspects of empowerment found in the literature. The first domain follows directly from the definition of empowerment as the ability to make choices; in this case, in key areas of agricultural production. The resource domain reflects control over assets that enable one to act on those decisions: a woman may decide to plant trees, but if she does not have rights to the land or credit to purchase inputs, she may not be able to do so. Thus, the resource domain combines both whether the woman can potentially make decisions over the asset – because her household possesses it – and whether, in fact, she decides how to use it. Control over income is a key domain for exercising choice, and it reflects whether a person can benefit from her or his efforts. The leadership domain captures key aspects of inclusion and participation, accountability, and local organisational capacity, key elements of empowerment. Finally, time, like income, reflects the workload of an individual and satisfaction with time available for leisure.

Following the procedure established by Alkire *et al.* (2012) from these areas and indicators a score is calculated for each individual by assigning weights as indicated in Table 5.1. The value of the score varies from 0 to 1, the greater the value of the score, the greater the inadequacy in empowerment.

Following Alkire *et al.* (2012), a 20% inadequacy threshold is chosen, meaning that an individual is not empowered if his or her inadequacy score is greater than 20%. Comparatively, an individual is identified as empowered if he or she has adequate achievements in 4 out of 5 domains. Thus, in a household it is assumed that there is gender parity when women are equally empowered as the men in their households. Accordingly, the gender parity indicator is a binary variable that takes a value of 1 for households in which there is gender parity and 0 otherwise. Furthermore,

Table 5.1 The domains, indicators, and weights in the WEAI (Alkire *et al.*, 2012).

Domain	Indicator	Weight
1. Production	a) Input in productive decisions	1/10
	b) Autonomy in production	1/10
2. Resources	a) Ownership of assets	1/15
	b) Purchase, sale or transfer of assets	1/15
	c) Access to and decisions about credit	1/15
3. Income	a) Control over use of income	1/5
4. Leadership	a) Group member	1/10
	b) Speaking in public	1/10
5. Time	a) Workload	1/10
	b) Leisure	1/10

another variable was generated, the normalised gender empowerment gap, which is the relative gap between the primary male and primary female in the household. It equals to zero if there is gender parity and the gap if not (continuous).

5.3.2 Estimation strategy

We use a binary model for inorganic fertiliser technology adoption, where a representative farm household chooses to adapt this technology if it generates net benefits. We can therefore represent the net benefits derived from inorganic fertiliser adoption by a latent variable Y_j^*, which is not observed but can be expressed as a function of the observed characteristics and attributes, denoted as X and Z, in a latent variable model as follows:

$$Y_j^* = \alpha Z_j + \beta X_j + \varepsilon_j \text{ with } Y_j = \begin{cases} 1, \text{ if } Y_j^* > 0 \\ 0, \text{ otherwise} \end{cases} \qquad (5.1)$$

In Equation 5.1, Y_j is a binary variable that equals 1 for households that adopt inorganic fertiliser and zero otherwise, α and β are the coefficient and vector of parameters to be estimated. Household j will choose to adopt ($Y_j = 1$) inorganic fertiliser only if the perceived net benefits are positive $Y_j^* > 0$, ε_j are the error terms with mean zero and variance σ_ε^2 capturing measurement errors and unobserved factors. In Equation 5.1 X_j is a vector of control variables composed of plot characteristics (tenure, the distance from home to plot, plot size, soil type and topography of the plot) and farm household characteristics (age and education level of women and men, household size and possession of animal traction unit and dwelling type). Z_j is the variable indicating parity in the household. The model is estimated using probit regression.

Another complication in the estimation of Equation 5.1 is the potential endogeneity of gender parity. However, given the focus of the binary outcome model on the decision to adopt a technology, this possibility is deemed unlikely, as it is not clear how the decision to adopt would lead to gender parity in a household or increases in the indicators comprising the WEAI (e.g. participation by women on agricultural, credit, or income decisions, group membership, speaking in public, etc.). Lastly, since the data analysed are cross-sectional, it is not possible to establish a causal connection between gender parity and inorganic fertiliser adoption. Thus, while the results presented below may be suggestive of causality, they are best interpreted only as proof of correlation between gender parity and technical inorganic fertiliser adoption.

5.4 Data source and description

5.4.1 Data Source

Data were collected during February-June 2016 by the author for households and adult individuals in these households in the departments of Gaya, Koulou and Konni in Niger for a project funded by the Millennium Challenge Corporation (MCC). These households are from 8 irrigation blocks. Konni belongs to the Tahoua region, while Gaya and Koulou are in Dosso. In the three departments (Koulou, Konni and Gaya), there are about 5,936 farm households, 10% were randomly selected to be surveyed across the irrigation blocks. Gaya has four irrigation blocks Albarkaizé, Kouanza, Sia and Gatawani. Koulou has two blocks: Koulou and Ouna; and Konnis has two blocks: Konni 1 and Konni 2. Some blocks contain very few households and the sampling was essentially a census. In other blocks, households were randomly drawn from an exhaustive list drawn up by the enumerators for each block. The total number of households surveyed in the eight blocks is 641 and 1,107 for adult individuals, with the two Konni blocks representing more than half of the total number of respondents. As we are only interested in intra-household gender parity, we only consider dual households including primary male and female. This means that the number of households retained is 338. Data was only collected for the primary male and primary female, which means that empowerment information on co-wives was not recorded.

5.4.2 Data description

Table 5.2 displays the descriptive statistics of the sample used for this analysis. The total plot number is 767, belonging to the two types of households. The proportion of plots on which inorganic fertilisers is used is 43.9% while 45.4% of plots received organic fertiliser. Households are owners of plots in 84.1% of cases. We also note that the average plots size is 1.1 ha and plots are 2.3 km from the household dwelling on average. Soils are mainly sandy (38.6%) and clay (38.6%). The proportion of loamy plots is 17.6%. Regarding the topography of the plots, we note that 55.7% of the plots are plains, 22.7% valleys and 11.9% gentle slopes.

With respect to household characteristics, it appears that only 25.1% of households have gender parity and that households are composed of 6 members on average. The average age is 36 years for women and 46.6 years for men. In addition, 35.2% of women are in a polygamous union.

Table 5.2. Sample descriptive statistics.

Variables	Observed	Mean	Standard deviation	Min	Max
Organic fertiliser (1=yes)	767	0.454	0.498	0	1
Inorganic fertiliser (1=yes)	767	0.439	0.497	0	1
Plot tenure (1=yes)	767	0.841	0.366	0	1
Plot size (in ha)	767	1.097	0.884	0	5
Distance home-plot (in km)	767	2.306	2.389	0	30
Soil type					
Loamy (1=yes)	767	0.176	0.381	0	1
Clay	767	0.386	0.487	0	1
Glacis	767	0.051	0.220	0	1
Topography					
Plain (1=yes)	767	0.557	0.497	0	1
Gentle slope	767	0.119	0.324	0	1
Steep slope	767	0.038	0.191	0	1
Valley	767	0.227	0.419	0	1
Normalised gender empowerment gap	328	0.155	0.118	0	0.571
Gender parity (1=yes)	338	0.251	0.435	0	1
Household size	338	6.442	3.262	2	20
Woman age	338	36.125	11.232	7	70
Woman age square (/100)	338	14.308	8.595	0.490	49
Woman education (1=no)	338	0.926	0.262	0	1
Man age	338	46.577	14.222	5	90
Man age square (/100)	338	23.659	13.561	0.250	81
Man education (1=no)	338	0.754	0.431	0	1
Housing type					
Compartmentalised house (1=yes)	338	0.198	0.399	0	1
Hut or traditional house	338	0.047	0.213	0	1
Number of room	338	3.459	2.394	1	20
Animal traction unit (1=no)	338	0.766	0.424	0	1

The illiteracy rate is higher among women than among men. Indeed, 92.6% of women cannot read, write and count in French, while this proportion is 75.4% among men.

In addition, the proportion of households living in compartmentalised houses is 19.8% and only 4.7% of households lived in isolated huts (traditional houses). The average number of rooms per household is 3.46. Finally, in relation to agricultural assets, more than76.6% of households do not own an animal traction unit.

5.5 Results

5.5.1 Descriptive analysis

The analysis starts with the calculation of the WEAI displayed in Table 5.3 for dual households in the Tahoua and Dosso regions. The empowered headcount shows that only 23.6% of women have an adequacy score lower than 20% against almost 41.8% of men; and 76.4% of women who are not yet empowered have, on average, inadequate achievements in 38.2% of the domains. Thus, the women's disempowerment index (M0) is 76.4% × 38.2% = 0.292 and 5DE is 1 − 0.292 = 23.6% + (76.4% × [1 − 38.2%]) = 0.708. In these two regions, 58.6% of men are not yet empowered, and the average inadequacy score among these men is 31.8%. So, the men's disempowerment index (M0) is 58.6% × 31.8% = 18.6, and the men's 5DE is 1 − 0.186 = 0.814.

The second subindex (the Gender Parity Index; GPI) measures gender parity within dual households. Table 5.3 shows that 40.9% of women are equally empowered as the men in their households. For those 59.1% of households that have not achieved gender parity, GPI shows that the empowerment gap that needs to be closed for women to reach the same level of empowerment as men is quite large, being 20.8%. Thus, the overall GPI is 0.877.

Table 5.3. Niger dual households Women Empowerment Agricultural Index (WEAI).

Indices[1]	Women	Men
Disempowered headcount (H)	0.764	0.586
Empowered headcount (1-H)	0.236	0.414
Average inadequacy score (A)	0.382	0.318
Average adequacy score (1-A)	0.618	0.682
Disempowerment index (M0=H × A)	0.292	0.186
5DE index (1-M0)	0.708	0.814
% of women without gender parity (H_{GPI})	59.1	
% of women with gender parity (1-H_{GPI})	40.9	
Average empowerment gap (I_{GPI})	20.8	
GPI (1 − H_{GPI} × I_{GPI})	0.877	
Number of observations used	744	
Total number of dual households	372	
WEAI (0.9 × 5DE + 0.1 × GPI)	0.725	

[1] GPI = Gender Parity Index; M0 = Men's disempowerments index; 5DE = five domains of empowerment.

The contribution of each indicator to disempowerment of men and women is depicted in Figure 5.1. It appears that, in general, differences in empowerment for men and women in these two regions of Niger are mainly explained by having less autonomy in production. Main contributing indicators to disempowerment are group membership, speaking in public, access to and decision about credit for women; purchase sale and transfer of assets, group membership and access to and decision-making about credit for men.

Table 5.4 shows the results of the tests of a difference in shares of parcels on which organic or inorganic fertilisers are adopted among households in which there is parity compared to those without gender parity. Regarding organic fertilisers, there seems to be no significant difference between the proportion of the parcels on which one applies organic fertiliser in the household group with gender parity and in households without gender parity. However, the difference is significant with regards to inorganic fertiliser. Indeed, the proportion of plots receiving the inorganic fertilisers among households with gender parity is significantly lower than the proportion of plot which received inorganic fertilisers among households without gender parity.

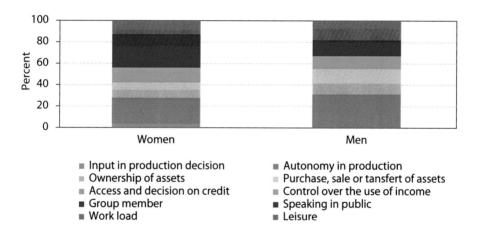

Figure 5.1. Contribution of each indicator to disempowerment by gender.

Table 5.4. Tests of proportions' difference.

	Plots of households with parity (1)	Plots of households without parity (0)	Differences (1-0)
Organic fertiliser	0.450 (0.034)	0.455 (0.021)	-0.005 (0.040)
Inorganic fertiliser	0.308 (0.032)	0.489 (0.021)	-0.181 (0.038)***
Number of observations	211	556	

5.5.2 Estimation results

Table 5.5 reports the binary outcome model results for inorganic fertiliser technology adoption estimated using probit regression. Several results are noteworthy. First, the coefficient of gender parity is negative and significant in the different equations of adoption of inorganic fertiliser at the 10% level. In other words, gender parity in the household correlates negatively with the adoption of inorganic fertiliser. This can be partly explained by the fact that with gender parity, the decision and negotiation power of a woman increases in the household and this determines the degree to which her unobserved characteristics, such as risk aversion, may affect the choice

Table 5.5. Probit regression results of inorganic fertiliser regressions (standard errors in parentheses).

Variables	Inorganic fertiliser[1]
Gender Parity (1=yes)	-0.203 (0.122)*
Woman age	-0.056 (0.027)**
Woman age square (/100)	0.061 (0.035)*
Woman education (1=no)	-0.539 (0.213)**
Man age	-0.061 (0.025)**
Man age square (/100)	0.067 (0.027)**
Man education (1=no)	0.119 (0.141)
Household size	0.078 (0.026)***
Number of rooms	-0.083 (0.031)***
Compartmentalised house (individual house)	-0.007 (0.151)
Hut or traditional house	0.276 (0.246)
Animal traction unit (1=no)	-0.249 (0.133)*
Plot tenure (1=yes)	-0.278 (0.151)*
Plot size (in ha)	-0.092 (0.060)
Distance home-plot (in km)	-0.018 (0.025)
Loamy (sandy)	-0.063 (0.156)
Clay	0.301 (0.142)**
Glacis	-0.263 (0.256)
Plain (hill)	-0.565 (0.228)**
Gentle slope	-0.382 (0.273)
Steep Slope	-0.473 (0.326)
Valley	-0.174 (0.262)
Block fixed effects	Yes
Constant	2.431 (0.683)***
Pseudo R2	0.24
Observations	761

[1] *** $P<0.01$; ** $P<0.05$; * $P<0.1$

of agricultural technologies. In fact, according to Di Falco *et al.* (2006) fertiliser is an input that can increase production but also increases the risk of production since households often do not have the mastery of the techniques needed for its proper use (Guttormsen and Roll, 2014) or climate variability (Sheremenko and Magnan, 2015). This may explain the reluctance of farmers to use fertiliser in an intensive way (Hardaker *et al.*, 2004). The negative impact of risk aversion on both the fertiliser buying decision and demand seems to be well acknowledged in the literature (Dercon and Christiaensen, 2011; Lamb, 2003; McIntosh *et al.*, 2013; Simtowe *et al.*, 2006) and even in the Niger context (Adesina *et al.*, 1988; Sanou *et al.*, 2015). In addition, most risk preference studies have demonstrated that women are more risk averse than men (Bauer and Chytilová, 2009; Croson and Gneezy, 2009; Eckel and Grossman, 2008; Gary and Gneezy; 2012; Holt and Laury, 2002; Wik *et al.*, 2004).

Another explanation is that in a context of poverty with lack of liquidity and credit, the fertiliser purchase price may be too high for farmers. For example, in Niger, 1 kg inorganic fertiliser was sold to farmers through their farmer organisations for FCFA 270 although the actual price of fertiliser was FCFA 380 indicating a subsidy of about 30%. Despite the subsidy, compared to household purchasing power in Niger this price is high. With gender parity, women could induce the household to foresee in the satisfaction of its immediate needs instead of investing in agriculture. In other words, it may be more of a priority for women to satisfy the daily food needs of the household as is evidenced by the fact that living in a woman-headed household improves the caloric consumption of all members compared to living in a male-headed household (Tankari, 2015). This is reinforced by the fact that in Niger, a woman often handles the operation of domestic life, realizes housework and takes care of children and other family members (Ministry of Women and Child Protection of Niger, 2007). Therefore, gender parity alone cannot guarantee the adoption of fertilisers in agricultural households. This result is important because it shows that gender parity which is increasingly seen as a strategy to increase agricultural productivity can have negative investments effects.

As to other determinants of fertiliser use, it should be noted that both the age of the woman and of the man explain the use of inorganic fertilisers following a convex relationship. In other words, there is a threshold below which the ages of the primary male and female relate negatively to the probability of adopting fertiliser and a reverse effect beyond the threshold. For education, it appears that limited education of women relates negatively to fertiliser adoption while for the primary male there is no relationship. This result underlines the importance of formal education of women in particular for agricultural innovation. In addition, it is important to note that the education of women seems more important than that of men in this context. Another important finding is the positive relation between household size and the inorganic fertiliser adoption decision. This can be explained by the fact that the household size can circumvent some constraints in farming such as the necessary labour for fertiliser application. Furthermore, the non-possession of animal traction unit reduces the probability of adoption this could be due to transportation cost. Finally, it appears that plot size does not to relate to the probability of inorganic fertilisers adoption.

To unpack the negative relationship between gender parity and inorganic fertiliser adoption, the hypotheses of risk aversion or time preferences under a resource constraint are tested. To better understand whether this negative result holds across technologies, we consider organic fertiliser adoption as an outcome. The rationale behind this choice is that organic fertiliser does not have the same cost as inorganic fertiliser in Niger and is generally free, thus relaxing the constraint of elevated risk. The binary outcome model was again estimated using a probit model. The results are displayed in Table 5.A1 in the appendix. Interestingly, we found that gender parity relates positively, though not significantly, to the adoption of organic fertiliser. This finding may effectively support our hypotheses of risk aversion or time preference under a resource constraint.

Finally, recall that it is assumed that there is gender parity in a household if the woman has an inadequacy score that is lower or equal to the score of her husband. Because the gender parity variable was generated based on a threshold, its effect could depend on the threshold that was chosen. We therefore estimate the different models for organic and inorganic fertilisers by using the normalised gender empowerment gap, which is the relative gap between the primary male and primary female in the household, equal to zero if there is gender parity and the gap if not (continuous). The results of the estimations are displayed in Table 5.A2 in the appendix. The findings are similar to the previous ones. The gender gap for empowerment is significant at 5% and positive in inorganic fertiliser models indicating that the increase in the gender empowerment gap is positively associated with inorganic fertiliser adoption. In other words, households with gender parity that is with a smaller empowerment gap have a smaller chance to adopt this technology. With respect to organic fertiliser, it is found that the gender empowerment gap is negative though not significant which is in line with the previous finding.

5.6 Conclusions

The objective of this chapter was to highlight the impact of gender parity on the adoption of inorganic fertiliser technology in farm households. The methodology used is based on the gender parity indicator based on the Women's Empowerment in Agriculture Index (Alkire *et al.*, 2013). Furthermore, binary regressions have been performed. Results suggest that gender parity in the household relates negatively to the adoption of inorganic fertiliser. This finding can be partly explained by the fact that with gender parity, the decision and negotiation power of a woman in the household determines the degree to which her unobserved characteristics like risk aversion or time preference may affect agricultural technologies choice more significantly under resource constraints. For the other determinants of fertiliser use, it appears that plot size and absence of animal traction unit relate negatively to the probability of using inorganic fertiliser. Another important finding is that female illiteracy relates negatively to fertiliser adoption and that female education seems more important than that of man in this context.

References

Adesina, A.A., Abbott, P.C. and Sanders, J.H., 1988. Ex-ante risk programming appraisal of new agricultural technology: experiment station fertilizer recommendations in Southern Niger. Agricultural Systems 27: 23-34.

Alkire, S., Malapit, H., Meinzen-Dick, R., Peterman, A., Quisumbing, A., Seymour, G. and Vaz, A., 2013. Instructional guide on the women's empowerment in agriculture index. IFPRI, Washington DC, USA.

Alkire, S., Meinzen-Dick, R., Peterman, A., Quisumbing, A., Seymour, G. and Vaz, A., 2012. The women's empowerment in agriculture index. IFPRI Discussion Paper 01240. IFPRI, Washington, DC, USA.

Bauer, M., and Chytilová, J., 2009. Women, children and patience: experimental evidence from Indian villages. Discussion Paper, N° 4241. IZA, Bonn, Germany.

Bourdillon, M., Hebinck, P., Hoddinott, J., Kinsey, B., Marondo, J., Mudege, N. and Owens, T., 2002. Assessing the impact of HYV maize in resettlement areas of Zimbabwe. Summary report. International Food Policy Research Institute, Washington, DC, USA.

Browning, M. and Chiappori, P.A., 1998. Efficient intra-household allocations: a general characterization and empirical tests. Econometrica 66: 1241-1278.

Browning, M. and Gørtz, M., 2012. Spending time and money within the household. Scandinavian Journal of Economics 114: 681-704.

Chirwa, E.W., 2005. Adoption of fertiliser and hybrid seeds by smallholder maize farmers in southern Malawi. Development Southern Africa 22: 1-13.

Croson, R. and Gneezy, U., 2009. Gender differences in preferences. Journal of Economic Literature 47: 448-474.

Dercon, S. and Christiaensen, L., 2011. Consumption risk, technology adoption and poverty traps: evidence from Ethiopia. Journal of Development Economics 9: 159-173.

Di Falco, S., Chavas, J.P. and Smale, M., 2007. Farmer management of production risk on degraded lands: the role of wheat variety diversity in the Tigray region, Ethiopia. Agricultural Economics 36: 147-156.

Doss, C.R., 2013. Intrahousehold bargaining and resource allocation in developing countries. Policy Research Working Paper 6337. World Bank, Development Economics, Washington, DC, USA.

Doss, C.R. and Morris, M.L., 2001. How Does gender affect the adoption of agricultural innovations? The case of improved maize technology in Ghana. Agricultural Economics 25: 27-39.

Eckel, C.C. and Grossman, P.J., 2008. Men, women and risk aversion: experimental evidence. Handbook of Experimental Economics Results 1: 1061-1073.

FEWS NET, 2011. Livelihoods zoning 'plus' activity in Niger. USAID FEWS NET, Washington, DC, USA.

Freeman, H.A. and Omiti, J.M., 2003. Fertilizer use in semi-arid areas of Kenya: analysis of smallholder farmers' adoption behavior under liberalized markets. Nutrient Cycling in Agroecosystems 66: 23-31.

Gary, C. and Gneezy, U., 2012. Strong evidence for gender differences in risk taking. Journal of Economic Behavior and Organization 83: 50-58.

Guttormsen, A.G. and Roll, K.H., 2014. Production risk in a subsistence agriculture. Journal of Agricultural Education and Extension 20: 133-145.

Hardaker, J.B., Huirne, R.B.M. and Anderson, J.R., 2004. Coping with risk in agriculture. CAB International, Wallingford, UK.

Holt, C.A. and Laury, S.K., 2002. Risk aversion and incentive effects. American Economic Review 92: 1644-1655.

INS-Niger, 2008. Tendances, Profil et Déterminants de la Pauvreté au Niger 2005-2007/08. Ministère de l'Economie et des Finances.

INS-Niger, 2014. Comptes Economiques de la Nation, Institut National de la Statistique du Niger.

Jagger, P. and Pender, J., 2006. Influences of programs and organizations on the adoption of sustainable land management technologies in Uganda. In: Pender, J. Place, F. and Ehui, S. (eds.) Strategies for sustainable land management in the East African Highlands. IFPRI, Washington, DC, USA, pp. 277-308.

Jayne, T.S. and Rashid, S., 2013. Input subsidy programmes in sub-Saharan Africa: a synthesis of recent evidence. Agricultural Economics 44: 547-562.

Lamb, R.L., 2003. Fertilizer use, risk, and off-farm labor markets in the semi-arid tropics of India. American Journal of Agricultural Economics 85: 359-371.

Lambrecht, I., Vanlauwe, B. and Maertens, M., 2016. Agricultural extension in Eastern Democratic Republic of Congo: does gender matter? European Review of Agricultural Economics 43: 841-874.

Love, A., Magnan, N. and Colson, G.J., 2014. Male and female risk preferences and maize technology adoption in Kenya. In: Agricultural and Applied Economics Association's 2014 AAEA Annual Meeting. July 27-29. DOI: https://doi.org/10.1017/CBO9781107415324.004.

Marenya, P., Kassie, M. and Tostao, E., 2015. Fertilizer use on individually and jointly managed crop plots in Mozambique. Journal of Gender, Agriculture and Food Security 1: 62-83.

McIntosh, C., Sarris, A. and Papadopoulos, F., 2013. Productivity, credit, risk, and the demand for weather index insurance in smallholder agriculture in Ethiopia. Agricultural Economics 44: 399-417.

Ministère de la Promotion de la Femme et de la Protection de l'Enfant du Niger (2007). Politique Nationale Genre. République du Niger.

Ndiritua, W., Kassieb, M. and Shiferaw, B., 2014. Are there systematic gender differences in the adoption of sustainable agricultural intensification practices? Evidence from Kenya. Food Policy; 49: 117-127.

Peterman, A., Quisumbing, A.R., Behrman, J. and Nkonya, E., 2011. Understanding the complexities surrounding gender differences in agricultural productivity in Nigeria and Uganda. Journal of Development Studies, Special Issue on Agriculture 47: 1482-1509.

Quisumbing, A., Peterman, R.A., Behrman, J.A., Croppenstedt, A., Raney, T.L. and Meinzen-Dick, R., 2014. Gender in agriculture: closing the knowledge gap. FAO/Springer, Heidelberg, Germany.

Ricker-Gilbert, J. and Jayne, T.S., 2017. Estimating the enduring effects of fertilizer subsidies on commercial fertilizer demand and maize production: panel data evidence from Malawi. Journal of Agricultural Economics 68: 70-97.

Sanou, A., Liverpool-Tasie, L.S.O. and Shupp, R., 2015. Technology adoption when risk attitudes matter: evidence from incentivized field experiments in Niger. In: 2015 AAEA and WAEA Joint Annual Meeting, July 26-28, San Francisco, CA, USA.

Seymour, G., Doss, C., Marenya, P., Meinzen-Dick, R. and Passarelli, S., 2016. Women's empowerment and the adoption of improved maize varieties: evidence from Ethiopia, Kenya, and Tanzania. In: 2016 Agricultural and Applied Economics Association Annual Meeting, July 31-August 2, Boston, MA, USA.

Sheremenko, G. and Magnan, N., 2013. Gender-specific risk preferences and fertilizer use in Kenyan farming households. In: 2015 Agricultural and Applied Economics Association and Western Agricultural Economics Association Annual Meeting, July 26-28, San Francisco, CA, USA.

Simtowe, F., Mduma, J., Phiri, A., Thomas, A. and Zeller, M., 2006. Can risk-aversion towards fertilizer explain part of the non-adoption puzzle for hybrid maize? Empirical evidence from Malawi. Journal of Applied Sciences 6: 1490-1498.

Tankari, M., 2015. Is the calorie-income elasticity low in Niger? Review of Agricultural and Environmental Studies 95: 473-491.

Uaiene, R.N., Arndt, C. and Masters, W.A., 2009. Determinants of Agricultural Technology Adoption in Mozambique. National Directorate of Studies and Policy Analysis Discussion Papers No. 67E. Ministry of Planning and Development, Republic of Mozambique.

Wanzala, M. and Groot, R., 2013. Africa – fertilizer market development in sub-Saharan Africa. In: International Fertilizer Society, on 24 May 2013, Windsor, UK.

Wik, M., Kebede, T.A., Bergland, O. and Holden, S.T., 2004. On the measurement of risk aversion from experimental data. Applied Economics 36: 2443-2451.

World Bank, 2011. World Development Report 2012. Gender equality and development. World Bank, Washington, DC, USA. Available at: http://tinyurl.com/ohlnfgd.

World Bank, 2015. World bank open data. Available at: http://data.worldbank.org.

Wouterse, F., 2017. Empowerment, climate change adaptation, and agricultural production: evidence from Niger. Climatic Change 145: 367-382.

Appendix 5.

Table 5.A1. Probit regression results of organic fertiliser regressions.

Variables	Organic fertiliser
Gender parity (1=yes)	0.083 (0.117)
Woman age	0.034 (0.024)
Woman age square (/100)	-0.043 (0.032)
Woman education (1=no)	-0.366 (0.216)*
Man age	-0.067 (0.024)***
Man age square (/100)	0.062 (0.025)**
Man education (1=no)	0.197 (0.141)
Household size	0.074 (0.022)***
Number of rooms	-0.035 (0.029)
Compartmentalised house (individual house)	-0.723 (0.151)***
Hut or traditional house	-0.616 (0.248)**
Animal traction unit (1=no)	0.112 (0.127)
Plot tenure (1=yes)	0.106 (0.155)
Plot size (in ha)	-0.026 (0.058)
Distance home-plot	-0.049 (0.021)**
Loamy (sandy)	-0.196 (0.147)
Clay	-0.707 (0.132)***
Glacis	0.135 (0.254)
Plain (hill)	-0.019 (0.238)
Gentle slope	-0.334 (0.273)
Steep slope	-0.043 (0.354)
Valley	-0.168 (0.272)
Block fixed effects	Yes
Constant	0.674 (0.632)
Pseudo R2	0.19
Observations	761

Standard errors in parentheses; *** $P<0.01$, ** $P<0.05$, * $P<0.1$.

Table 5.A2. Organic and inorganic fertiliser regressions using gender empowerment gap.

	Inorganic fertiliser	Organic fertiliser
Gender empowerment gap	1.023 (0.425)**	-0.205 (0.423)

Standard errors in parentheses; ** $P<0.05$.

Chapter 6.
Information technology and farm households in Niger

Chantal Toledo[1] and Christopher Ksoll[2]*
[1]Mathematica Policy Research, 600 Alexander Park, Princeton, NJ 08540, USA; [2]Mathematica Policy Research, 505 14th Street, Suite 800, Oakland, CA 94612, USA; cksoll@mathematica-mpr.com

Abstract

Mobile telephone use in Sub-Saharan Africa has increased dramatically in recent years, fundamentally changing how people communicate and creating an opportunity to affect agricultural outcomes for both producers and consumers. This chapter is a review of the literature on the effects of information and communication technologies (ICTs) on agricultural outcomes in Niger. The review is contextualised with references to the broader literature. Evidence reveals that ICTs can have a substantial effect on agricultural price dispersion, prices, and crop choice, but this is not always the case. Moreover, even where ICTs do have positive effects, their effects on farm gate and consumer prices vary depending on the setting, access to ICTs, rural versus urban location, farming experience, and the farmer's gender. Studies of the effects of ICTs on agricultural outcomes thus do not point to a single, most effective approach. Instead, the evidence suggests that the chosen approach will depend on the constraint to be addressed, the population experiencing the constraint, and the ability to tailor the chosen approach to address the needs of the specific population. A needs assessment should be done to inform the design and choice of the approach, and the assessment should be based on high-quality quantitative and qualitative information from surveys and discussions with local stakeholders.

Keywords: information technology, ICT, agriculture, Niger, price information, mobile phones

6.1 Introduction

Mobile telephone usage in Sub-Saharan Africa has increased greatly in recent years, fundamentally changing the way in which many communications are undertaken. In Sub-Saharan Africa in general, mobile cellular telephone subscriptions increased from 12 to 77% between 2005 and 2016, and from 23 to 46% between 2010 and 2015 in Niger alone (ITU, n.d.). The dramatic increase of mobile telephone subscriptions in Niger rivals that of developing countries as a whole in percentage change, where mobile cellular telephone subscriptions increased from 82 to 127% between 2010 and 2015. Whereas landlines initially outpaced mobile telephone networks in the United States, Canada and Europe, mobile telephone networks far exceed landlines in Africa (Aker and Mbiti, 2010).

Mobile telephones can potentially provide economic benefits to consumers and producers in many ways. For example, they (1) improve access to and use of information; (2) improve firms' productive efficiency by allowing them to better manage their supply chains through the increased communication; (3) create new jobs to satisfy the demand for mobile-related services; (4) promote responsiveness to emergencies; and (5) facilitate the delivery of financial, agricultural, health, and educational services (Aker and Mbiti, 2010). As a result, availability of mobile telephone networks has been shown to affect agricultural outcomes in Africa, such as grain price dispersion, among others (Aker, 2010). Information and communication technologies (ICTs) such as mobile telephones can also play a role in adaptation to climate change by enabling the tracking of 'big data' on people's movements. The information derived from these data can be used to examine the dynamics of human mobility in a changing climate (Ford *et al.*, 2016).

This paper reviews the evidence of links between ICTs[1] and outcomes of farm households in Niger and situates this literature within the broader literature on ICTs in developing countries.[2] Where possible, we refer to Sub-Saharan Africa, but when evidence is sparse we also refer to papers more broadly, but always within developing country settings. In the Appendix, we provide a table that summarises the setting, findings, methods and conclusions of the papers discussed in this review. Our review has a particular focus on the channels through which ICTs might affect agricultural outcomes. The ICTs of particular interest in this paper are mobile phone access and usage, as well as internet access. Intuitively, we expect ICTs to affect agricultural outcomes in various ways. For example, ICTs might reduce both the costs of obtaining and providing information and transaction costs. In addition, ICTs might promote more timely and location specific information, thereby increasing the general quality of the information. By obtaining better quality information at a lower cost, ICTs might increase farmers' ability to use the information to their advantage. ICTs can also be utilised to enhance development projects by offering new methods of communicating information. Finally, ICTs can be used to improve service delivery to farm households in terms of enabling access to better information and by facilitating service delivery.

The remainder of the paper is organised as follows. To inform the discussion, background information on agriculture and ICTs in Niger is presented in Section 6.2. Existing literature on the effects of ICTs on agricultural markets, focusing on Niger, is discussed in Section 6.3. Section 6.4 includes a discussion on the use and potential of ICTs in the Nigerian agricultural setting. Finally, Section 6.5 offers conclusions.

---

[1] ICTs refer to the integration of telecommunications (telephone lines and wireless signals), computers, software, storage, and audio visual systems that enable users to access, store, transmit, and manipulate information.
[2] This chapter is not meant to be a systematic review of the broader literature on ICTs and agriculture. We do however include papers in the review that we found by searching on Google Scholar for 'Niger ICT' and in references from papers that provide rigorous quantitative evidence. In the discussion section, when discussing new trends where there is no evidence yet, we do not restrict ourselves to quantitative evidence.

6.2 Background

6.2.1 Agriculture in the economy

Agriculture plays a fundamental role in the economy of Niger. With a per capita gross domestic product (GDP) of 363 USD and an estimated 45% of the population living on less than 1.90 USD per day, the Human Development Index for Niger is ranked second to last (Jahan *et al.*, 2016). In 2016, approximately 87% of the population was employed in agriculture and contributed to approximately 36% of GDP (CIA, n.d.). The majority of the population of Niger depends on rain to support agriculture for food and income. The main grains grown are millet, sorghum, and rice, and cash crops are cowpeas, peanuts, and sesame.

A landlocked country, Niger has a largely agrarian and subsistence-based economy that is prone to political instability, chronic food insecurity, and natural crises, particularly droughts, floods, and locust infestations (CIA, n.d.; World Bank, n.d.-a). Between 1980 and 2010, Niger experienced seven droughts (World Bank, 2013). Average temperatures in Niger have increased by 0.6 °C since 1975, amplifying the effect of droughts (Funk *et al.*, 2012). Variations in rainfall directly affect agricultural output because yields depend upon the timing and quantity of rainfall. The timing and quantity of rainfall can, in turn, affect a series of other economic, social, and political outcomes. For example, the civil war that ended in 1998 has commonly been attributed to the increasing poverty of the pastoral Tuaregs, a population that was severely affected by droughts in the 1970s and 1980s. Conflict was common and rainfall was scarce during the early 1990s; the end of the conflict in the late 1990s was marked by increasing rainfall in three out of four years between 1998 and 2001 (Miguel *et al.*, 2004).

As of 2016, Niger had one of the most rapidly increasing population rates in the world – 3.9%. With a population density of 16.3 people per square kilometre and a population of 20 million spread over a large territory, density is low compared to the neighbouring countries of Nigeria, Senegal, and Burkina Faso (with population densities of 194, 77, and 48, respectively). Low population density can generate large price variations in harvested goods if distances between sources and markets are great and transportation and communication infrastructure is not well developed. In Niger, for example, inter-market distances vary from 8 km to over 1,200 km.

6.2.2 ICTs in Niger

As GDP doubled from 2006 to 2016, Niger has also benefited from vastly expanded coverage of and access to ICTs. The number of mobile cellular telephone subscriptions has increased greatly, with mobile cellular subscriptions per 100 people doubling in five years, from 23% in 2010 to 46% in 2015. Despite increasing numbers of mobile cellular telephone subscriptions, Niger continues to face challenges in extending ICTs throughout the country. Barriers to access include low per capita incomes, relatively high prices, lack of electricity, and a large, landlocked territory. For example, the probability of having a mobile phone tower in a particular location is positively correlated with demand factors, such as population density, per capita income, and the competitiveness of the mobile phone sector within the country. Similarly, higher elevation, steeper slopes, and distance from a main road and major urban centres are negatively associated with mobile phone coverage (Buys *et al.,* 2009).

In 2015, only 2.2% of the population was able to access the internet (ITU, n.d.), even with significant decreases in prices over the last decade. For example, the price of a fixed asymmetric digital subscriber line (ADSL17) subscription in Niger has fallen by more than 50% (in local currency) between 2008 and 2011 (Domínguez-Torres and Foster, 2011). Contributing to the slow advances in internet usage, infrastructure is not well developed beyond major centres (Aker and Ksoll, 2016). For example, in 2015, there was only one landline for every 100 people (CIA, n.d.).To understand the reach of ICTs in rural areas, we provide descriptive statistics of ICT ownership and use in Niger, based on a detailed household and community survey collected by the Niger National Institute of Statistics and funded by the World Bank. In particular, we examine data collected in 2011 and 2014 as part of the Niger National Survey on Living Conditions and Agriculture (Niger National Institute of Statistics, 2011, 2014). This integrated multi-topic household survey is conducted for the purpose of evaluating poverty and living conditions in Niger. The survey is publicly available through the World Bank's micro data website (Niger National Institute of Statistics, 2011, 2014).

The sample for the year 2011 survey includes approximately 4,000 households. The sample is nationally representative, as well as representative of Niamey, other urban and rural areas. Households visited in 2011 were revisited in 2014. We present survey data on ICTs (mobile and internet) ownership and use.

In the survey and among respondents who report data, mobile access and use was quite high, given Niger's poverty levels. In 2011, 39% of individuals reported owning a mobile phone. Among those who do not own a mobile phone, an additional 24% had access to a mobile phone in the past 30 days preceding the survey. In 2014, 50% of individuals reported owning a mobile phone, and an additional 29% still had access to a mobile phone in the past 30 days. Although the majority of the population had access to a mobile phone, the vast majority did not use internet. In 2011, 5% of individuals had used internet in the previous 12 months and in 2014, approximately 6% of individuals used internet. The data show a slower (1 point, or 20%) increase in internet use between 2011 and 2014, compared to a larger increase (11 points, or 28%) in mobile ownership, suggesting that in the short and medium term, mobile phones might play a larger role than the internet on agricultural outcomes. There were large differences in mobile telephone ownership, mobile telephone use (but not ownership) in the past 30 days, and internet usage in the past 12 months between urban and rural areas. These descriptive statistics are summarised by year in Table 6.1.

Table 6.1. Summary statistics of mobile ownership, mobile use, and internet use by year (Niger National Survey on Household Living Conditions and Agriculture, 2011 and 2014).

Variable	2011	2014
Mobile telephone ownership (overall)	39%	50%
Mobile telephone ownership (urban)	66%	76%
Mobile telephone ownership (rural)	19%	32%
Mobile telephone use (but not ownership) in the past 30 days (overall)	24%	29%
Mobile telephone use (but not ownership) in the past 30 days (urban)	48%	46%
Mobile telephone use (but not ownership) in the past 30 days (rural)	16%	25%
Internet usage in the past 12 months (overall)	5%	6%
Internet usage in the past 12 months (urban)	11%	15%
Internet usage in the past 12 months (rural)	0.13%	0.52%

6.3 ICTs in agriculture – evidence in the literature

This section discusses the literature on ICTs in Niger and situates it within a broader review of the literature on ICTs on agriculture in developing countries. Where possible, we refer to Sub-Saharan Africa, but when evidence is sparse we also refer to papers from developing countries more broadly. Where available, we discuss papers from Niger first, then papers from Sub-Saharan Africa and finally papers from other developing countries. Given that the papers discussed come from different countries and contexts, the comparison of outcomes should be undertaken with caution, and they may not immediately be transferable to Niger.

One of the mechanisms through which access to ICTs can improve the functioning of agricultural markets is by reducing spatial price dispersion and changing farm gate or consumer prices. ICTs can also affect farmer welfare if gains or losses are experienced as a result of access (or lack of access) to ICTs. We begin with a review of the literature on the effect of ICTs on agricultural prices and continue to the literature on ICTs and crop choice. Then, we discuss how ICTs can be associated with farmer training, service delivery, and early warning systems.

6.3.1 ICTs and agricultural prices[3]

Market integration and spatial price dispersion in consumer and producer markets

If information is limited or access to it is costly, agents might be unable to engage in optimal arbitrage, excess price dispersion across markets can arise, and goods might not be allocated efficiently. In such a setting, ICTs might reduce price dispersion.

Tack and Aker (2014) provide a mechanism through which ICTs can lead to a reduction in price dispersion. The authors construct a theoretical model of search whereby traders search for the optimal sales price over multiple markets. The duration of mobile phone coverage is associated with an increase in search activity, and this effect is stronger for larger traders (compared to smaller traders), who also engage in arbitrage over longer distances.

In order for ICTs to have an effect on price dispersion, information costs and/or market power of traders must exist that lead to a lack of market integration. Two studies provide evidence of a lack of market integration and thus the potential for ICTs for Niger using very different approaches. Goundan and Tankari (2016) use a spatial dynamic panel data model applied to Niger's millet market and find that that the millet market is merely partly integrated, and that locally traded commodities (millet and sorghum) are linked by a cross-commodity price transmission. They also find that prices of the most imported cereals (maize and rice) do not affect the millet market, but that a change in the price of sorghum was capable to be transmitted to millet price for around 10%. No cross-region price transmission occurred for the millet market.[4] Essam (2013) analyses staple food prices and market performance in Niger using remotely sensed vegetation indices through a normalised differenced vegetation index (NDVI). The idea is that weather-related vegetation production conditions captured through NDVI are a proxy for millet yields, and thus millet availability. The author finds that inter-market price spreads and levels of market integration can be reasonably explained by deviations in vegetation index outcomes from the growing season. In particular, negative (or positive) NDVI shocks are associated with better (or worse) than expected market performance, as measured through converging inter-market price spreads. Further, as the number of markets affected by negatively abnormal vegetation production conditions in the same month of the growing season increases, inter-market price dispersion declines. However, positive NDVI shocks do not produce the mirroring pattern.

---

[3] Throughout the paper, we refer to different agricultural prices. Consumer prices are prices faced by consumers. Farm gate prices are prices received by farmers for their produce at the farm location. The costs of transporting from the farm gate to the nearest market or first point of sale and market charges (if any) for selling the produce are, by definition, not included in the farm gate prices. Producer prices are prices determined at the farm gate or first-point-of-sale transactions when farmers participate in their capacity as sellers of their own products. Wholesale prices refer to the price of agricultural products that leave the farm-gate, they may pass through one or even two wholesale markets and a chain of middlemen before reaching the retailer from whom the ultimate consumer buys the products (http://tinyurl.com/yacbk4se).

[4] This latter finding is very different from the literature and raises some questions on the appropriateness of the methodology employed.

Several empirical studies that contribute to this literature are set in Niger. Using a market and trader panel dataset and a difference-in-differences model, Aker (2010) exploits the exogenous variation of mobile phone rollout to identify its impact on agricultural market performance in Niger. Aker (2010) finds that the introduction of mobile phone service between 2001 and 2006 explains a 10 to 16% reduction in grain price dispersion and that the effect is stronger for market pairs with higher transportation costs. The effect is larger when a higher percentage of markets have mobile coverage, which is suggestive of network externalities. The paper also examines alternative explanations for the empirical results by studying spill-over effects and collusive behaviour among traders, but finds little evidence of such mechanisms. The primary measure of market performance is the absolute value of the price difference between two markets during a certain month. Mobile phones are more likely to be useful as network coverage increases, since traders are able to search over a larger number of markets. By 2004/2005, mobile phone coverage reached 31% of all market pairs, and was associated with a 2.98 CFA/kg and statistically significant reduction in price dispersion across markets, compared to a not statistically significant reduction during the initial years of mobile coverage. While Aker (2010) shows that increased access to information technology has reduced grain price dispersion for consumer markets, Aker and Fafchamps (2015) focus on the impacts of ICTs on producer price dispersion in Niger. Aker and Fafchamps estimate the impact of mobile phone coverage on producer price dispersion for three commodities in Niger and find that mobile phone coverage reduces spatial producer price dispersion by 6% for cowpeas. The effect is strongest for remote markets and during certain periods of the year. On the other hand, Aker and Fafchamps (2015) find no effect on producer price dispersion for millet and sorghum. Whereas cowpeas are a semi-perishable commodity, millet and sorghum are less perishable and are commonly stored by farmers, suggesting that effects can vary by farmers' ability to store the commodity.[5] Perishability matters because goods that are more perishable are likely to be traded more locally and are likely to exhibit more temporal and spatial variation. While a reduction in search costs might reduce price variation, it could also extend the radius in which transportation is profitable more for non-perishable goods. Thus, the theoretical predictions with respect to the impact of ICTs on price dispersion for perishable and non-perishable goods are ambiguous (Aker and Ksoll, 2016).

Outside of Niger, there is also evidence that ICTs can reduce price dispersion. For example, Andersson *et al.* (2017) studied whether regional warehouses in Ethiopia that are connected to a national commodity exchange achieve reduced transaction costs and price dispersion between regions. Through the Ethiopian Commodity Exchange (ECX), traders in local markets can receive market information via SMS, interactive voice response, internet, radio, television, newspaper, or electronic tickers placed in rural markets that display real-time prices of all commodities traded on the platform. Warehouses that are connected to the ECX were sequentially rolled out and, using retail price data and information about warehouse operation, Andersson *et al.* (2017) finds the average price spread between market pairs is reduced by 0.86-1.775 Ethiopian birr (ETB)

---

[5] Perishability of crops is potentially an important determinant of price dispersion across time, as non-perishable crops can be stored by farmers or traders and sold when prices are high, and across space, as traders can transport non-perishable crops over longer distances.

when both markets have an operating warehouse. The effect is large, given that the average price spread over the full period is 3.33 ETB. The clearest example of a reduction in price dispersion is described in Jensen (2007). Using a quasi-experimental setting provided by the gradual roll-out of mobile phones, Jensen (2007) demonstrates that the adoption of mobile phones by fishermen and wholesalers in India is associated with a large reduction in price dispersion. In particular, the mean coefficient of variation of price across markets declined from 60-70% to 15% or less.

ICTs and farm gate and consumer prices

In addition to affecting price dispersion, ICTs also have the potential to affect the level of farm gate prices and the level of consumer prices through different channels.

Evidence on whether ICTs can increase farm gate prices is mixed. In Niger, Aker and Fafchamps (2015) find no effect of ICTs on the level of producer prices (although they do find a reduction in spatial producer price dispersion by 6% for cowpeas). Similarly, Aker and Ksoll (2016) find that a mobile phone-based education intervention does not increase the farm gate price received. Niger does have a public market information system that provides information on prices for certain goods and livestock for larger markets which may explain a lack of effect (FEWS NET, 2017).[6] Outside of Niger, Fafchamps and Minten (2012) find that receiving market and weather information delivered to farmer mobile phones in India has no effect on the average price received by farmers. Similarly, Mitra *et al.* (2018) find that potato farmers in India who receive wholesale price information do not experience changes in their farm gate sales or prices. These differences may be partially explained by differences in the program being studied. Some of the programs delivered only price information, while others included price and other additional information, such as weather information (e.g. Fafchamps and Minten, 2012). However, others studies outside of Niger do find effects of ICTs on farm gate prices. Taking advantage of exogenous differences in access to radio broadcasts, Svensson and Yanagizawa (2009) find evidence suggesting that farmers in Uganda who were better informed bargained for higher farm gate prices on their surplus production. In particular, improved access to information about prices is associated with a significant increase in farm gate prices; radio access in a market information service district was associated with a 15% increase in farm gate prices. Goyal (2010) finds farm gate prices increased in India after internet kiosks and warehouses that provide wholesale price information were established. This intervention was different than mobile phone interventions in that they provided both price and quality information to soybean farmers. Similarly, Nakasone and Torero (2016) find that farmers from randomly selected villages in Peru who received access to detailed price information through a short message system (SMS) for the most relevant local crops got

---

[6] SIMA monitors more than 70 staple food markets in Niger, including 48 regular markets, 18 'sentinel markets', and 8 cross-border markets. In addition, SIM-Bétail, a livestock-specific market information system, monitors livestock sales and prices in more than 70 markets, including 7 cross-border markets. As in most countries in the region, market information monitoring systems in Niger are constrained by limited or unstable funding. In particular, they lack a clear institutional status, end of project phases, technical capacity, and updated equipment and materials for data collection and analysis (FEWS NET, 2017). ICTs might be used to interact with and facilitate the functioning of market information systems by providing cheaper information on markets located closer to the respondent.

higher sales prices, compared to households in the control group. The effect was mostly driven by increases in the prices for relatively more perishable crops. Using data on mobile phone coverage and household panel data on farmers from the Philippines, Labonne and Chase (2009) find evidence consistent with the argument that easier access to information allows farmers to strike better price deals within their existing trading relationships and to make better choices in terms of where they choose to sell their goods.

Heterogeneous effects of ICTs on farm gate and consumer prices

There is evidence that effect of ICTs on farm gate and consumer prices varies not only across setting, but that different groups are differentially affected, particularly with respect to access to ICTs, rural versus urban welfare, prior experience in farming, and farmer gender. In addition, when farm gate prices do rise this is typically at the expense of traders.

Svensson and Yanagizawa's (2009) study addresses the impact of an intervention in Uganda that distributes information on urban market prices of food crops through rural radio stations. Using a differences-in-differences approach, Svensson and Yanagizawa (2009) find the information leads to a substantial increase in average crop revenue for farmers with access to the radio broadcasts; they credit the increase to higher farm gate prices and a higher share of output sold to traders. However, in a follow-up paper, the same authors show that because the radio broadcasts were received by millions of farmers and led to an increase in production and sales, the intervention lead to a decrease in market prices (Yanagizawa-Drott and Svensson, 2012). When taking into account the general equilibrium effect on prices and the impacts on farmers without access to the broadcasts, the authors find that the intervention had no impact on average crop revenue, but important distributional consequences. In particular, consumers benefited from lower prices and farmers with access to radio benefited from higher farm revenues, while crop income decreased for farmers without access to radio.

For distributional purposes, a program that encourages the diffusion of agricultural price information through ICTs could target specific populations, for example women or young farmers. In Niger, Aker and Ksoll (2016) find that households in villages that gained access to shared mobile phones were more likely to grow okra, a marginal cash crop grown by women, showing differential effects by gender. As opposed to saturated markets or populations that have already benefited from the first expansion of mobile phones, female populations could benefit from information not otherwise obtainable. In a study in India, Fafchamps and Minten (2012) find suggestive evidence that delivering market and weather information to younger farmers led to a small increase in the likelihood of grading or sorting the output. Following model predictions, Fafchamps and Minten (2012) argue that if price information helps farmers negotiate better prices with traders, then farmers who sell at farm gate before receiving the information should collect higher prices and that the effect is expected to be the largest for poor and inexperienced farmers.[7] To the extent that young and female populations are the poorest and most inexperienced, targeting these populations could increase program benefits. Also in India, Tata and McNamara (2016) find that socio-economic factors including gender, age, educational qualification and internet access have an impact on challenges faced by extension agents using Farmbook, an ICT application that enables extension agents to help farmers plan their businesses, assess productivity, and profitability of their farming enterprise. Similarly, in Uganda, Svensson and Yanagizawa (2009) argue that improving access to information may help poorly functioning markets work better, improve (relatively uninformed) farmers' bargaining position with respect to (relatively well-informed) wholesalers or middlemen, and thus increase the incomes of the poor.

In his general review of the literature, Jensen (2010) studies the potential effects of ICTs on welfare, both in terms of potential efficiency gains and welfare transfers among agents in the supply chain. Jensen finds most empirical studies report significant gains in consumer and/or producer welfare, particularly when there was no previous source of information available. Jensen (2010) underscores that any gains observed are likely to be permanent because they represent a structural improvement in the efficiency of market functioning. However, Jensen cautions that changes in price dispersion alone do not capture the welfare effects. The analysis cannot focus just on producers or consumers in isolation because one or the other might lose while the other gains (even when there is a positive net effect). Furthermore, some of the gains might come through increases in production and/or changes in the mix of crops produced. Similarly, the analysis should not focus solely on the villages whose residents have mobile phones because one village might experience welfare gains while another one might experience welfare losses. Overall, Jensen (2010) recommends a comprehensive approach for assessing the impact of mobile phones on welfare, which includes many agents, sectors, and regions.

6.3.2 ICTs and crop choice

In addition to influencing price, ICTs can have a direct effect on farmers' crop diversity and choice. There are at least three potential mechanisms through which farmer access to mobile phones can impact their production choices. First, mobile phones can improve buyer-seller coordination, which can in turn lower post-harvest losses due to trader storage constraints, making perishable crops more profitable. Second, they can improve farmers' knowledge of the optimal plantation date which can contribute to decreased losses from perishable crops. Third, they can increase the price of perishable crops received by farmers if farmers can learn the price

---

[7] The extent to which the provision of prices to farmers would affect their incomes depends on the market power of traders, as reflected in the size of their profits and the degree to which their costs of operation depend on search costs for prices. In an earlier study, Fafchamps and Gabre-Madhin (2006) find that the largest transactions costs are search and transportation in Benin and Malawi, and that the use of modern technology is limited. In such a context with high costs of searching for prices, a reduction in costs of providing price information could have larger effects on prices. Similarly, contexts in which traders have market power profits there may be more scope for price information to influence prices. Mitra *et al.* (2017) find that potato traders in West Bengal, India, earn large margins.

of perishable crops in nearby markets. There is relatively little evidence on this effect, but the existing literature suggests this effect is possible, at least for some crops.

In Niger, ICTs have been shown to affect crop diversity. Using a randomised experiment in which individuals were provided with access to shared mobile phones and learned how to use them in the context of an adult education program, Aker and Ksoll (2016) find that households in villages with increased access to ICTs and capacity to use ICTs through the experiment planted a more diverse basket of crops, particularly marginal cash crops grown by women. Further, the effects were stronger among households that had not previously owned a mobile phone, where a woman was the primary beneficiary, and among households living in villages where a market was not present. Households were also more likely to engage in sales of crops, although the average quantities sold did not increase.

Outside of Niger, there is further evidence that ICTs can affect crop choice. Using exogenous variation in the timing of when different districts received kiosks and hubs that provide wholesale price information in the Indian state of Madhya Pradesh, Goyal (2010) finds access to soy price information through the internet kiosks increases soy crop area. In particular, the presence of kiosks in a district is associated with a 19% increase in soy crop area. Also in India and using a difference-in-differences model, Cole and Fernando (2016) study the effect of farmers' access to a cell phone-based extension service, *Avaaj Otalo*, on several outcomes, including crop choice. *Avaaj Otalo* allowed farmers to call a hotline, ask questions and receive responses from agricultural scientists and local extension workers, and listen to answers to questions posed by other farmers. In addition, *Avaaj Otalo* included a weekly push content, delivering time-sensitive information such as weather forecasts and pest planning strategies directly to farmers. The authors find that individuals with more treated peers plant more cumin, a risky crop. In Pakistan and using administrative village census data and primary household survey data, Asad (2016) studies the impact of cell phone access on crop choice, among other outcomes. The author exploits a policy that restricts cell phone coverage in Pakistan from villages located within 10 km of the Indian border. Regression discontinuity estimates of village-level data show that cell phone access causes a 23-27% increase in the probability of producing perishable crops.

6.3.3 ICTs and farmer training

In addition to providing price information, ICTs have the potential to interact with traditional training pathways, such as agricultural extension services. The traditional extension model, the 'training and visit' extension, is generally characterised by government-employed extension agents visiting farmers individually or in groups to demonstrate agricultural best practices (Birner and Anderson, 2007). Traditional extension systems face many challenges. In particular, the delivery of extension services is challenged by limited transportation infrastructure in rural areas and high costs of delivering information in person, which are common in developing countries. In addition, because agricultural extension services are usually provided through infrequent and irregular meetings, there is limited scope to provide timely information, such as how to adapt to inclement weather or unfamiliar pest infestations. Further, the information may be distributed in an uneven or strategic way. For example, monthly performance quotas might lead agents to target the easiest-to-reach farmers, or political targeting might lead service agents to focus on groups affiliated with the local government, rather than to marginalised groups for whom the incremental benefit might be higher.

In contrast, mobile phone-based extensions have the ability to reach a larger number of farmers at a lower cost, at different points in time in the agricultural cycle, and at any location with mobile service. However, while mobile phone-based extension services offer many advantages over traditional extension services, they eliminate in-person demonstrations, which might be particularly effective for demonstrating agricultural practices (Cole and Fernando, 2016).

Studies generally find positive effects of agricultural extension services provided via ICTs on agricultural outcomes. For example, Casaburi *et al.* (2014) find that sending SMS messages with agricultural advice to smallholder farmers in Kenya increased yields by 11.5%, relative to a control group with no messages, and that the effects are concentrated among farmers who had no agronomy training and little interaction with the sugar cane company staff at baseline. However, a study using a similar intervention but with a separate population did not find significant effects on cane yields (Casaburi and Kremer, 2017). In India, by randomly assigning toll-free access to an agricultural extension information service, Cole and Fernando (2016) find that treated farmers were significantly more likely to adopt agricultural practices and inputs recommended by the service (farmers adopted recommended seed varieties, fertilisers, pesticides, and irrigation practices and cotton yields increased by approximately 9% and cumin yields by 28%).

ICTs can also deliver training through other media, such as video. In a small-scale pilot study in India, Gandhi *et al.* (2009) study the effect of a research project, *Digital Green,* which disseminates targeted agricultural information to small and marginal farmers using digital video. Using a matched treatment-control design and a 13 month trial involving 16 villages (8 control villages and 8 experimental villages, balanced for parameters such as size and mix of crops) and 1,470 households, the authors find the project increased the adoption of certain agriculture practices sevenfold over a traditional training and visit-based extension approach.

However, the scaling up of these types of interventions might encounter several challenges. In particular, common challenges to using ICTs to enhance farm extension services in Africa include converting the large amounts of farm extension information available in paper form to digital and searchable form, reaching the targeted information quickly, providing information in local language, low population literacy levels, generating research on their cost-effectiveness, and sustainable financing (Payne and Woodard, 2011).

6.3.4 ICTs and service delivery

ICTs also have the potential to enhance service delivery. In particular, ICTs can enhance service delivery by making services more accessible via more than one channel. For example, multichannel service delivery can include access to government and private firm websites via mobile phone or an internet-connected computer, rather than in-person offices in distant towns. Because such a system would benefit only those who have access to a mobile phone, service delivery alternatives could also include equipping community centres with computers, and facilitating knowledge sharing and capacity building. Examples of projects that extend access to information include multipurpose community centres (MPCCs), public internet access points (PIAPs), and telecommunications networks to remote communities in rural areas, such as Nteletsa (Botswana), Kitsong centres (Botswana), knowledge sharing initiatives (Egypt), Marwan Project (Morocco), community multimedia centres (Mozambique), and eBrain (Zambia) (Yonazi et al., 2012).

Early warning systems are another example of services that can be enhanced through ICTs. An early warning system is one in which the government receives advance information on poor harvest crops that are likely to lead to famines. For example, USAID has developed such systems in Africa, including the Niger Famine Early Warning Systems Network. More broadly, ICTs can also enhance the delivery of weather information, one of the most highly requested services by farmers in the developing world (Tolat et al., 2012). Farmers traditionally rely on historical weather patterns for farming, but increasingly unpredictable weather due to climate change has increased farmers' risk and the need for micro-climate systems information. The use of satellites has had a transformative impact on weather information by making weather information globally available at low cost to regional and national meteorological institutions, as well as the private sector. ICTs can then play a crucial role in disseminating this information in Sub-Saharan Africa. For example, the Toto Agriculture regional initiative uses satellite and weather station data from FORECA (a weather forecasting company that provides digitised weather services) to create weather feeds, and weather information is delivered through SMS, multimedia messaging service (MMS), video, and radio (Tolat et al., 2012). However, the benefits of such systems may be limited by the ability of farmers to understand the weather data, even when they do receive it, and the lack of technical knowledge needed to minimise the risk of expected weather patterns.

ICTs can extend other public services, such as public recording of land rights, inheritance, identity documents, social welfare programs, and money transfers (Aker et al., 2016b). ICTs can enhance the transparency of these services; for example, cash transfers through mobile phones might be less prone to corruption if money flows are more transparent with ICTs. However, service delivery would need to be tailored to the target population because its effectiveness might also depend on the literacy and numeracy levels of the target population. In Niger, literacy levels are very low (19% among adults 15 years old and older in 2015; CIA, n.d.), and recipients might not benefit as much from service delivery through certain ICTs.

6.4 Discussion

A review of the existing evidence points to substantial heterogeneity in effects across settings: not all ICT interventions are effective, and even if they are effective in some settings, they are not necessarily effective in all settings nor for all beneficiaries. However, the literature currently lacks systematic evidence on why ICT interventions are effective in some contexts rather than others. As such, ICT interventions should focus on particular populations that plausibly have the largest potential gains from receiving the information or the ones that are most vulnerable (such as females or young farmers). We provide some thoughts on conducting such a needs assessment in the following section.

Moreover, the particular technology used as a channel of dissemination of information is important and needs to be tailored to the beneficiaries. For example, videos, such as in the case of *Digital Green* described above (Gandhi *et al.*, 2009), may be more appropriate for farmers who cannot benefit from other ICTs due to low levels of literacy or numeracy. Alternatively, programs that teach farmers the necessary ICT usage might enhance the effectiveness of ICT interventions. We discuss the choice of ICT in a following section. Finally, we also turn to some newer developments in the coverage and availability of ICTs in Niger and discuss implications of these.

6.4.1 Conduct a needs assessment to identify beneficiaries

Given the existence of heterogeneous effects, Aker *et al.* (2016a) suggest that before designing and implementing a system that uses ICTs to promote agriculture initiatives, a thorough needs assessment should be implemented for the particular context in which the project is supposed to be implemented.[8] In particular, a needs assessment could take into account network coverage, general affordability, and the maintenance of 'low-tech' technologies that have demonstrated the ability to transmit information in a cost-effective manner. We provide an example of using publicly accessible information to partially understand beneficiary needs and opportunities by examining descriptive statistics from Niger's Living Standards Measurement Study survey.

Based on the literature review, there are settings under which ICTs are effective and others in which they are not. To understand the potential welfare effects of increased availability of price information, it is important to understand the proportion of households that produce and purchase crops. For example, there could be a limited scope for price information to substantially affect producer welfare if the proportion of households selling food crops is low. In Niger, most households surveyed as part of the Niger's Living Standards Measurement Study in 2011

---

[8] For example, given that the average female labour share in crop production is 24% in Niger (Palacios-Lopez *et al.,* 2017) and that studies have shown that there are differential effects of ICTs on agricultural outcomes by gender (Aker and Ksoll, 2016), an information system targeted to female farmers could have 'room' to increase this share. Similarly, another potential target population that could benefit from ICTs is young farmers (Fafchamps and Minten, 2012) because they are likely to be more inexperienced or have a smaller network of support and guidance.

and 2014 did not sell any part of their production (see Table 6.2 for information on sales and purchases of important food crops). Although 2011 was a drought year in Niger (and the Sahel region) with poor harvest and high food prices (World Bank, 2012), 2014 was a year of more plentiful harvests (FEWS NET, 2014). In this survey, 96% of respondents in 2011 had lost part of their production before the harvest and 72% of them said the loss was due to drought. In 2014, 60% of respondents had lost part of their production before the harvest. Among these, 47% said the loss was due to drought.

As a result of insufficient production few households are able to sell crops so ICT may only benefit a minority of households in their capacity as producers. In 2011, only 31% of households sold part of their harvest, while in 2014, 43% did. Although the percentage of households

Table 6.2. Summary statistics of agricultural production, sales, and purchases by year (Niger National Survey on Household Living Conditions and Agriculture, 2011 and 2014).

Variable	2011	2014
Crops produced (4 main crops produced in at least one parcel in 2011 and 2014)		
Household produces millet	93%	91%
Household produces cowpeas	72%	81%
Household produces sorghum	54%	62%
Household produces peanuts	24%	15%
Sale of production		
Household reports selling at least part of its harvest	31%	43%
Household sold cowpeas[1]	55%	57%
Household sold millet[1]	19%	19%
Household sold peanuts[1]	19%	14%
Household sold sesame[1]	11%	10%
Crop purchases		
Household purchased any staple crop[2] in the past seven days	100%	100%
Household purchased rice in the past seven days (overall)	66%	74%
Household purchased rice in the past seven days, conditional on consuming rice	96%	98%
Household purchased maize in the past seven days (overall)	40%	54%
Household purchased maize in the past seven days, conditional on consuming maize	94%	98%
Household purchased millet in the past seven days (overall)	50%	51%
Household purchased millet in the past seven days, conditional on consuming millet	59%	61%
Household purchased sorghum in the past seven days (overall)	11%	13%
Household purchased sorghum in the past seven days, conditional on consuming sorghum	43%	49%

[1] These percentages are based on households that sell their production.
[2] Staple crops are maize, millet, rice and sorghum.

who sold part of their production increased between 2011 and 2014, the overall percentage is relatively low, suggesting that most of the agricultural production is consumed and not sold. As a reason for not selling, 98% of respondents in 2014 said that production was not enough for the household, and only 2% said it was because prices were low. Because most households do not sell their production and because most farmers do not report prices as the main reason for not selling, there seems to be a limited scope for ICTs to play a major role in reducing poverty in this setting.[9] However, specific subgroups producing specific crops might still benefit, for example those producing cash crops who can use the proceeds in turn to purchase food crops.

Similarly, ICTs might play a role in increasing consumer welfare because all households in the survey declare purchasing some staple crop such as maize, millet, rice, and sorghum in the last seven days. In particular, among households that consumed the crops in 2014, 98% of households purchased rice, 98% purchased maize, 61% purchased millet, and 49% purchased sorghum. Table 6.2 presents summary statistics for crops produced, sold, and purchased by households in Niger in 2011 and 2014. Given the evidence in Niger of price dispersion in the retail markets, providing price information might have a role in shaping outcomes for consumers. Essam's (2013) study, however, suggests that the lack of integration in millet markets in Niger is smallest when harvests are below average, suggesting that the provision of additional price information may have limited effects during droughts, at least for millet.

Since livestock sales contribute 15% of rural households' income and 25% of their food consumption requirements, a similar exercise could be undertaken for livestock production. Qualitative research is also important to complement this analysis by providing hypotheses for groups that might be particularly constrained by a lack of price information.

6.4.2 Selection of a specific information and communications technology in Niger

In addition to effectively targeting beneficiaries, the type of information and the way in which the information is delivered also matters. In particular, specific information and communications technologies should be matched to the constraints (Aker *et al.*, 2016a). For example, the information delivered might be price information, weather information, or information about crops. It is possible to deliver all of these types of information, but this option would have to be carefully studied, taking into account the characteristics of the target population, in particular literacy and numeracy. Price information can be delivered through a public MIS (for example, the radio as is currently done in Niger for a small number of markets and goods), a private MIS (for example, through a subscription) or through a facilitated informal system that allows people to communicate with contacts in the local market. Fafchamps and Minten (2012) discuss a relatively

---

[9] This might reflect the particularly bad years in which the survey was conducted.

low take-up of a market and weather information system delivered to mobile phones of farmers in India, suggesting that tailoring the information and its access to the population is key.[10]

In addition, heterogeneity in access to ICTs can play an important role. For example, female farmers and poorer households might have less direct access to mobile phones, so that a program that targets females might need to incorporate the distribution of mobile phones. Similarly, some services, such as weather applications, might be useful only to those who have access to the internet. This heterogeneity in access and the ability to use the technology should be taken into account when considering a specific technology.

Due to poor ICT infrastructure, some ICT technologies, such as internet, face particular challenges in Niger. In some cases it may be possible to work around the constraints in order to achieve the desired outcomes for a particular setting. For example, the Horticultural Remote Irrigation System developed by an entrepreneur in Niger allows the remote control of a solar-powered low-water-use irrigation system from a mobile handset (The Observers, 2015). In a developed country context this would likely be an internet or application based system. Because of the lack of access to the internet in Niger, this purpose-designed platform relies on SMS to start and stop irrigation. While this removes a significant restriction to the usefulness of the technology, widespread adoption among poorer households is likely to be low due to the high upfront costs.

6.4.3 Access to internet and future developments

Some of the approaches for delivering more information described in previous sections include using village kiosks or cyber cafes, using promotional videos, or conducting site visits. Agricultural extensions might be able to include information delivered through YouTube channels, although this medium would have to be tailored to the specific context. Similarly, as the gender of the person delivering the message may increase the effectiveness of the messages in some contexts, female extension workers – who are limited in numbers due to the much lower female educational outcomes in Niger – could be shown in online videos to deliver information to female farmers (FAO, 2011).

While some of these possible approaches seem unfeasible with current internet access rates in Niger, they might be mechanisms to improve agricultural outcomes in the medium and long run as several rural internet access initiatives are developed by major technology companies.[11]

---

[10] Reasons farmers offered for service refusal included the belief they would be charged for service later on or that they were illiterate households who could not read SMS messages. Other reasons for non-usage included never activating the service (subscribers were required to select three crops and markets, and some subscribers never completed the activation sequence), changing phone numbers, or migration.

[11] Rural electrification rates in Niger are also a concern (14% in 2014, one of the lowest in the region; World Bank, n.d.-b), though Niger is included in the Power Africa initiative, a U.S. government initiative created with the goal of doubling access to electricity in Sub-Saharan Africa by increasing installed generation capacity by 30,000 megawatts and adding 60 million new household and business connections by 2030.

For example, Google's Project Loon initiative is meant to bring internet access to rural and remote areas across the globe, using high-altitude balloons that create a wireless network. In 2017, Google provided emergency internet services in Peru after a flood, though the transfer speeds limit the connection to basic services. Similarly, Facebook has initiated projects to expand internet access in developing countries and, in many cases, making that access free. For example, since September 2015, the Facebook-launched Free Basics app gives users free access to a limited number of websites, Facebook-owned messaging service WhatsApp, and Facebook itself, without charging data costs in Africa. In November 2016, Facebook partnered with Airtel Africa to provide basic websites and services to introduce people to the internet. The initiative includes providing free health, education, and finance-related information to people in 17 African countries, including Niger. In addition, Facebook has previously tested drone-delivered internet and is investing in satellite-based technology. However, the effectiveness of these approaches to providing sufficiently high internet download speeds to be useful in poor and remote areas where low literacy necessitate video or audio has not yet been proven, and rigorous analysis would be needed before relying on these services as an alternative to other lower technology solutions.

6.5 Conclusions

In this paper, we provided a review of the literature on ICT in rural agricultural settings with a particular focus on Niger. The review of the literature shows that ICTs can have a substantial effect on agricultural price dispersion, prices, and crop choice, thereby having the potential to play a role in poverty reduction. However, the results vary by setting. Studies on the effects of ICTs on agricultural outcomes do not point to a unique, most effective approach. Instead, the evidence suggests that the approach to be used will depend on the constraint that will be addressed, the population experiencing the constraint, and the ability to tailor the system to address the needs of the specific population. To inform the design and choice of the approach, a needs assessment should be undertaken, based on high-quality quantitative and qualitative information from surveys and discussions with local stakeholders.

Acknowledgements

We thank the editor and an anonymous referee and Abbie Turiansky for useful comments, Mathematica Policy Research for funding, and Christina Phelps for research assistance.

References

Aker, J.C., 2010. Information from markets near and far: mobile phones and agricultural markets in Niger. American Economic Journal: Applied Economics 2: 46-59.

Aker, J.C. and Fafchamps, M., 2015. Mobile phone coverage and producer markets: evidence from West Africa. World Bank Economic Review 29: 262-292.

Aker, J.C. and Ksoll, C., 2016. Can mobile phones improve agricultural outcomes? Evidence from a randomized experiment in Niger. Food Policy 60: 44-51.

Aker, J.C. and Mbiti, I.M., 2010. Mobile phones and economic development in Africa. Journal of Economic Perspectives 24: 207-232.

Aker, J.C., Boumnijel, R., McClelland, A. and Tierney, N., 2016b. Payment mechanisms and antipoverty programs: evidence from a mobile money cash transfer experiment in Niger. Economic Development and Cultural Change 65: 1-37.

Aker, J.C., Ghosh, I. and Burrell, J., 2016a. The promise (and pitfalls) of ICT for agriculture initiatives. Agricultural Economics 47, S1: 35-48.

Andersson, C., Bezabih, M. and Mannberg, A., 2017. The Ethiopian commodity exchange and spatial price dispersion. Food Policy 66: 1-11.

Asad, S., 2016. The crop connection: impact of cell phone access on crop choice in rural Pakistan. World Bank, Washington, DC, USA. Available at: http://tinyurl.com/yacq9alb.

Birner, R. and Anderson, J.R., 2007. How to make agricultural extension demand-driven?: the case of India's agricultural extension policy. IFPRI Discussion Paper 00729. Available at: http://tinyurl.com/y8zu43gk.

Buys, P., Dasgupta, S., Thomas, T.S. and Wheeler, D., 2009. Determinants of a digital divide in Sub-Saharan Africa: a spatial econometric analysis of cell phone coverage. World Development 37: 1494-1505.

Casaburi, L. and Kremer, M., 2017. Management information systems and firm performance: experimental evidence from a large agribusiness company in Kenya. PEDL, UK. Available at: http://tinyurl.com/y7cyxd2x.

Casaburi, L., Kremer, M., Mullainathan, S. and Ramrattan, R., 2014. Harnessing ICT to increase agricultural production: evidence from Kenya. Working paper. Available at: http://tinyurl.com/yal88y6d.

Central Intelligence Agency (CIA), n.d. The world factbook – Niger. Available at: http://tinyurl.com/2nwbno.

Cole, S.A. and Fernando, A.N., 2016. Mobile'izing agricultural advice: technology adoption, diffusion and sustainability. Harvard Business School Finance Working Paper No. 13-047. Available at: http://tinyurl.com/ycfunax9.

Domínguez-Torres, C. and Foster, V., 2011. Niger's infrastructure: a continental perspective. IACD Africa Infrastructure Country Diagnostic, Country Report. Available at: http://tinyurl.com/ya6mxqu5.

Essam, T.M., 2013. Analyzing millet price regimes and market performance in Niger with remote sensing data. Dissertation, University of Maryland, College Park, MD, USA.

Fafchamps, M. and Gabre-Madhin, E., 2006. Agricultural markets in Benin and Malawi. Working paper. Available at: https://web.stanford.edu/~fafchamp/afjae.pdf.

Fafchamps, M., Gabre-Madhin, E. and Minten, B., 2005. Increasing returns and market efficiency in agricultural trade. Journal of Development Economics 78: 406-442.

Fafchamps, M. and Minten, B., 2001. Social capital and agricultural trade. American Journal of Agricultural Economics 83: 680-685.

Fafchamps, M. and Minten, B., 2012. Impact of SMS-based agricultural information on Indian farmers. World Bank Economic Review 26: 383-414.

Famine Early Warning Systems Network (FEWS NET), 2014. Overall crop and pasture production expected to be average to above-average. October 2014 to March 2015. Available at: http://tinyurl.com/y7ns58o4.

Famine Early Warning Systems Network (FEWS NET), 2017. Niger: staple food and livestock market fundamentals. September 2017. Available at: http://tinyurl.com/ybfx72vy.

Food and Agriculture Organization of the United Nations (FAO), 2011. The state of food and agriculture: 2010-2011. Women in agriculture: closing the gender gap for development. Available at: http://tinyurl. com/4p8ukhc.

Ford, J.D., Tilleard, S.E., Berrang-Ford, L., Araos, M., Biesbroek, R., Lesnikowski, A.C., MacDonald, G.K., Hsu, A., Chen, C. and Bizikova, L., 2016. Big data has big potential for applications to climate change adaptation. Proceedings of the National Academy of Sciences of the USA 113: 10729-10732.

Funk, C.C., Rowland, J., Eilerts, G., Adoum, A. and White, L., 2012. A climate trend analysis of Niger. U.S. agency for international development (USAID) famine early warning systems network –informing climate change adaptation series. Fact Sheet 2012-3080. Available at: http://tinyurl.com/y9qhlsge.

Gandhi, R., Veeraraghavan, R., Toyama, K. and Ramprasad, V., 2009. Digital green: participatory video for agricultural extension. Information and Communication Technologies and International Development 5: 1-15.

Goundan, A. and Tankari, M.R., 2016. A dynamic spatial model of agricultural price transmission: evidence from the Niger millet market. IFPRI Discussion Paper 01536. Available at: http://tinyurl.com/ybnkfsp9.

Goyal, A., 2010. Information, direct access to farmers, and rural market performance in Central India. American Economic Journal: Applied Economics 2: 22-45.

International Telecommunication Union (ITU), n.d. ITU/World Telecommunication/ICT development report and database. Available at: http://tinyurl.com/y7amxvzb.

Jahan, S., Jespersen, E., Mukherjee, S., Kovacevic, M., Abdreyeva, B., Bonini, A., Calderon, C., Cazabat, C., Hsu, Y-C, Lengfelder, C., Luongo, P., Mukhopadhyay, T., Nayyar, S. and Tapia, H., 2016. Human development for everyone: briefing note for countries on the 2016 Human Development Report: Niger. Human Development Report 2016. Available at http://tinyurl.com/ybsptvrc.

Jensen, R.T., 2007. The digital provide: information (technology), market performance, and welfare in the South Indian fisheries sector. Quarterly Journal of Economics 122: 879-924.

Jensen, R.T., 2010. Information, efficiency, and welfare in agricultural markets. Agricultural Economics 41 S1: 203-216.

Labonne, J. and Chase, R.S., 2009. The power of information: the impact of mobile phones on farmers welfare in Philippines. World Bank working paper 4996. Available at: http://tinyurl.com/yb6rpybz.

Miguel, E., Satyanath, S. and Sergenti, E., 2004. Economic shocks and civil conflict: an instrumental variables approach. Journal of Political Economy 112: 725-753.

Mitra, S., Mookherjee, D., Torero, M. and Visaria, S., 2018. Asymmetric information and middleman margins: an experiment with Indian potato farmers. Review of Economics and Statistics 100: 1-13.

Nakasone, E. and Torero, M., 2016. A text message away: ICTs as a tool to improve food security. Agricultural Economics 47, S1: 49-59.

Niger National Institute of Statistics, 2011. Niger-National Survey on Household Living Conditions and Agriculture Reference No. NER_2011_ECVMA_v01_M. Available at: http://tinyurl.com/yc8c2fwz.

Niger National Institute of Statistics, 2014. National Survey on Household Living Conditions and Agriculture Reference No. NER_2014_ECVMA_v01_M. Available at: http://tinyurl.com/yc8c2fwz.

Palacios-Lopez, A., Christiaensen, L. and Kilic, T., 2017. How much of the labor in African agriculture is provided by women? Food Policy 67: 52-63.

Payne, J. and Woodard, J., 2011. ICT to enhance farm extension services in Africa. Briefing paper. Available at: https://pdf.usaid.gov/pdf_docs/PA00J7P8.pdf.

Svensson, J. and Yanagizawa, D., 2009. Getting prices right: the impact of the market information service in Uganda. Journal of the European Economic Association 7: 435-445.

Tack, J. and Aker, J.C., 2014. Information, mobile telephony and traders search behavior. American Journal of Agricultural Economics 96: 1439-1454.

Tata, J.S. and McNamara, P.E., 2016. Social factors that influence use of ICT in agricultural extension in Southern Africa. Agriculture 6: 15.

The Observers, 2015. How mobile phones are improving irrigation in Niger. Available at: http://tinyurl.com/ycwvaf3s.

Tolat, M., Tulchin, D. and Reiff, D.S., 2012. Using ICT to provide weather information for agriculture. Briefing paper. Available at: http://pdf.usaid.gov/pdf_docs/PA00J7PX.pdf.

World Bank, 2012. New World Bank push to tackle drought in the horn of Africa and Sahel. Available at: http://tinyurl.com/yb5q35f2.

World Bank, 2013. Agricultural sector risk assessment in Niger: moving from crisis response to long-term risk management. World Bank, Washington, DC, USA. Agriculture and Environment Services (AES) Department and Agriculture, Rural Development, and Irrigation (AFTAI) Unit in the Africa Region, Report No. 74322-NE. Available at http://tinyurl.com/y7gnxdkk.

World Bank, n.d.-a. The World Bank in Niger. Available at: http://www.worldbank.org/en/country/niger/overview.

World Bank, n.d.-b. World Bank sustainable energy for all database. Available at: https://data.worldbank.org/data-catalog/sustainable-energy-for-all.

Yanagizawa-Drott, D. and Svensson, J., 2012. Estimating impact in partial vs. general equilibrium: a cautionary tale from a natural experiment in Uganda. Working paper. Available at http://tinyurl.com/y8aathyo.

Yonazi, E., Kelly, T., Halewood, N. and Blackman, C., 2012. The transformational use of information and communication technologies in Africa. World Bank, Washington, DC, USA. Available at: https://52.21.52.208/handle/10986/26791.

Appendix 6.

Table 6.A1. Summary of primary analysis papers.[1]

Setting (reference)	Methodology	Primary outcomes analysed and findings
Grain markets and traders in Niger during the 1999-2007 period (Aker, 2010).	Difference in-differences model that exploits the exogenous variation of mobile phone rollout to identify its impact on agricultural market performance in Niger. The sample includes 415 traders located in 35 markets across 6 geographic regions of Niger.	• The introduction of mobile phones is associated with a 10 to 16% reduction in price dispersion across markets, with a larger impact for those market pairs with higher transport costs. The effect is also larger when a higher percentage of markets have mobile coverage, which is suggestive of network externalities. • Mobile phones are more likely to be useful as network coverage increases, since traders are able to search over a larger number of markets. By 2004/2005, mobile phone coverage reached 31% of all market pairs, and was associated with a 2.98 CFA/kg and statistically significant reduction in price dispersion across markets, compared to a not statistically significant reduction during the initial years of mobile coverage. • Paper also examines alternative explanations for the empirical results by studying spill-over effects and collusive behaviour among traders, but finds little evidence of such mechanisms.
Program recipients in a cash transfer program (all of whom were women) in villages from one region of Niger (Aker et al., 2016).	Cluster RCT with 1,082 program recipients in 96 clusters (villages) with three treatment arms (there is not pure control group): 32 villages were assigned to the Cash group, 32 to the Mobile group, and 32 to the Zap group. In the Cash group, households receive an unconditional cash transfer. In the Mobile group, the intervention mirrored the manual cash intervention, but program recipients also received a mobile-money-enabled mobile phone and training on how to use it. In the Zap group, program recipients receive their cash transfer via an m-transfer in a mobile phone (recipients have to take the mobile phone to an m-transfer agent to obtain their transfer).	• Households in the Zap (m-transfer) group used their cash transfer to buy more diverse types of goods and were more likely to purchase protein and energy-rich foods. • Transfers resulted in a 9-16% improvement in diet diversity, primarily due to increased consumption of beans and fats, and children consumed an additional one-third of a meal per day. • M-transfer program recipients travelled shorter distances to obtain their transfer as compared with their manual cash counterparts (2.5 days less over a 5-month period). • No evidence that m-transfer households reduced their ownership of other durable and nondurable goods.
Producer price dispersion of cowpeas, millet, and sorghum in markets across Niger from 1999 to 2009 (Aker and Fafchamps, 2015).	Difference-in-difference strategy comparing market pairs with and without mobile phone coverage. Tests a theoretical model using market-level panel data sets on producer prices for millet, sorghum, and cowpea in Niger between 1999 and 2009; a panel survey of traders and farmers in 32 markets and 37 villages across six geographic regions in Niger between 2005 and 2007; and a 2009 survey of 1,038 farm households from 100 Niger villages.	• Results suggest that mobile phone coverage reduces spatial producer price dispersion by 6% for cowpea, a semi-perishable commodity. These effects are strongest for remote markets and during certain periods of the year. • The extension of mobile phones coverage has no effect on producer price dispersion for millet and sorghum, two staple grains that are less perishable and are commonly stored by farmers. • There are no impacts of the introduction of mobile phones on producer price levels.

Fostering transformation and growth in Niger's agricultural sector

Table 6.A1. Continued.

Setting (reference)	Methodology	Primary outcomes analysed and findings
Farmers in rural Niger during the 2009-2011 period (Aker and Ksoll, 2016).	RCT where the treatment is the delivery of a mobile phone module on agricultural production and prices of agricultural goods. The control is the delivery of a standard adult education intervention. 113 villages were first stratified by administrative division before being randomly assigned to a year cohort (e.g. 2009 or 2010), and were then assigned to either a mobile-phone 'enhanced' (ABC) adult education treatment program or a basic (non-ABC) control program. Fifty-eight villages were assigned to the ABC intervention and 55 to the non-ABC intervention. Difference-in-difference strategy is used to compare outcomes of treatment and control villages before and after the program.	• Farm households living in treated villages cultivated 0.34 more crops as compared to their non-treated counterparts. This change represents an 8% increase in the number of crops cultivated as compared to the mean of non-ABC households during the baseline. • The treatment did not increase the likelihood of households cultivating most staple food and cash crops, such as millet, sorghum, cowpea or sesame. However, households in the treated villages were 9% more likely to cultivate okra than those in non-ABC villages. • Households in ABC villages with female literacy participants produced 0.24 to 0.46 more types of crops. ABC households with male literacy participants also cultivated more types of crops, but not with a statistically significant effect. • No evidence that the program affected the quantities produced.
How price spreads between regional markets in Ethiopia were affected by the Ethiopian Commodity Exchange (ECX) in combination with regional warehouses from 2007 to 2012 (Andersson et al., 2017).	Difference in-differences model that exploits differences in the opening date of warehouses.	• Results show that when two markets both have access to an operating warehouse, the average price spread is 0.86-1.78 ETB lower than it is for markets where at least one part lacks warehouse access. This is a substantial reduction given that the average price spread over the full period is 3.33 ETB. • Main results are robust to various econometric specifications (e.g. OLS, fixed effects and Prais-Winsten (PCSE) estimates).
Villages and farmers in rural Pakistan in 2008 and 2013 (Asad, 2016).	Fuzzy Regression Discontinuity Design (spatial regression discontinuity design) to estimate the causal impact of cell phone access on crop choice at the village level. Sharp Regression Discontinuity Design to estimate the impact of cell phone access on crop choice at the household level. Paper exploits a unique policy that restricts cell phone coverage in Pakistan from villages that lie within 10 km of the Indian border. 450 households in the data where 225 were sampled from within restriction zone (5-10 km from border) while the other 225 households were sampled from outside the restriction zone (10-15 km from the border).	• Cell phone access causes a 23-27% increase in the probability of producing perishable crops. • Cell phones access increases the share of land allocated to extremely perishable and highly perishable crops by 23-27% and 16-18% respectively. • Cell phones access decreases the number of days between harvest and sale date by 5-7 days for extremely perishable crops and 4-6 days for highly perishable crops. • Cell phones access decreases the percent of output lost in the post-harvest period by 21-35% for extremely perishable crops and 16-20% for highly perishable crops. Results are statistically and economically insignificant for the less perishable crops. • Cell phones access increases farmers' agricultural income and household consumption by 10-15% and 8-10% respectively.

Fostering transformation and growth in Niger's agricultural sector

Table 6.A1. Continued.

Setting (reference)	Methodology	Primary outcomes analysed and findings
Analysis of determinants of cell phone coverage in over 990,000 grid cells in Sub-Saharan Africa from 1999 to 2006 (Buys et al., 2009).	Use a spatially disaggregated econometric approach that allows the investigation of the local determinants of coverage at grid points in Sub-Saharan Africa. Probit techniques are used for over 990,000 grid cells with adjustments for spatial autocorrelation to estimate a probability model that relates the likelihood of cell tower location within a grid square to variables including potential market size, per capita income, and national competition policy.	• The probability of GSM cell tower location in a grid square increases significantly with population, per capita income, and the degree of competition. • The probability of GSM cell tower location in a grid decreases significantly with higher levels of installation and maintenance cost factors (higher elevation, steep slope, longer distance from the main road, and longer travel time to the nearest major city). • Simulations based on the econometric results suggest that improvement in competition policy could lead to vast improvements in cell phone area coverage, and to an overall coverage increase of nearly 100%.
Farmers in Kenya during the 2011-2013 period (Casaburi et al., 2014).	RCT that uses plot-level administrative data to measure the impact of two interventions (receiving agricultural advice via SMS messages and access to a farmer hotline) on two main outcomes (farmers' plot yields and fertiliser deliveries). The unit of randomisation is the field, which is Data includes farmers in 10,000 plots. The unit of randomisation is the field, which is defined as a set of typically three to ten plots.	• Relative to control group with no messages, smallholder farmers who received agricultural advice via SMS messages increased yields by 11.5%. • Effects were concentrated among farmers who had no agronomy training and had little interaction with sugar cane company staff at baseline. • Enabling farmers to report input provision delays to the company reduces the proportion of delays in fertiliser delivery by 21.6%. • There is evidence of significant positive spill-overs on non-eligible farmers in the same field.
Farmers in rural India surveyed in 2012 (Cole and Fernando, 2016).	RCT consisting of 800 farmers across 40 villages in rural India with household level randomisation. Participants were assigned to a control group or treatments with toll-free access to Avaaj Otal (AO), a mobile phone-based technology that allows farmers to call a hotline, ask questions and receive responses from agricultural scientists and local extension workers. Callers can also listen to answers to questions posed by other farmers. The first treatment group (AOE) received toll-free access to AO in addition to traditional extension. The traditional extension component consisted of a single session each year lasting roughly two-and-a-half hours. The second treatment group (AO) received toll-free access to AO, but no offer of the traditional agricultural extension, and the final set of households served as the control group (no intervention). In addition, among the two treatment groups (AO and AOE), 500 were randomly selected to receive bi-weekly reminder calls (reminder group) to use the service while the remaining 300 did not. Difference-in-difference specifications are used to analyse the data.	• 60% of treatment group used service within 7 months of the intervention, and 80% used service after two years. • Receiving advice increased yields in cumin by 28%. • For a subgroup who received reminders, cotton yields increased by 8.6%. • There was approximately a $10 private return for each dollar spent on the service.

Table 6.A1. Continued.

Setting (reference)	Methodology	Primary outcomes analysed and findings
Analysis of staple food prices in Niger leading up to the 2004-2005 food security crisis (Essam, 2013)	Analyses the relationship between normalised difference vegetation index (NDVI) and staple food prices in Niger leading up to the 2004-2005 food security crisis. Spatial price analysis was used to analyse the geospatial economic relationship in millet price data. Price dispersion model was used to analyse how millet market performance varies with NDVI outcomes.	• Inter-market price spreads and levels of market integration can be reasonably explained by deviations in vegetation index outcomes from the growing season. • Negative (positive) NDVI shocks are associated with better (worse) than expected market performance. • Market integration was found to be associated with vegetation index outcomes; below (above) average NDVI outcomes result in more integrated (segmented) markets.
Agricultural traders from Benin and Malawi between 1999 and 2000 (Fafchamps and Gabre-Madhin, 2006).	Comparative analysis of descriptive survey data. The sample consists of 1,371 agricultural traders from 24 markets in Benin and 40 markets in Malawi.	• Many well-known trader features are found in the paper: small size of businesses, lack of equipment, rudimentary business practices, dominant role of transport costs. • Under-documented aspects of traders' operations include the importance of personal travel, bagging practices, short distance over which most traders operate, incidences of theft and contract breaches. • The main purpose of advances from traders to farmers is not to exploit farmers' need for cash in order to finance agricultural production, but rather a means for traders to secure future deliveries. • Quality control requires the presence of the trader at the time of purchase. This raises costs as the trader has to travel a lot, and makes it difficult for trading enterprises to grow. Since enterprises remain very small, personal transport and search time represents a non-negligible share of marketing costs.
Traders of domestic agricultural production from 24-40 markets in both rural and urban areas in Benin, Madagascar, and Malawi (Fafchamps et al., 2005).	Assess whether traders are capable of capturing gains from coordination and of achieving system-wide returns to scale by focusing on trader costs and margins. Uses 1999-2001 surveys of traders of domestic agricultural production to analyse presence of increasing returns in agricultural trade in three recently liberalised countries (Benin, Madagascar, and Malawi).	• Analysis of margins, costs, and value added find very little evidence that returns to scale exist in agricultural trade. • Motorised transport is found more cost effective for large loads on longer distances. There is no evidence that larger trucks are systematically more cost effective than small pickup trucks, although the data indicates that traders switch to large trucks for large transactions and long distances. • Personal travel costs are a source of increasing returns, but the effect is not very large. • Working and network capital are key determinants of value added. Constant returns to scale in all accumulable factors – working capital, labour, and network capital – cannot be rejected.

Table 6.A1. Continued.

Setting (reference)	Methodology	Primary outcomes analysed and findings
Uses 1997, 1999, and 2000 survey data of agricultural traders in Madagascar, Malawi and Benin respectively. Majority of traders surveyed were women (Fafchamps and Minten, 2001).	The role of social capital in explaining differences in trader productivity is investigated by regressing value added on social capital as well as conventional factors of production such as working capital, manpower, and the human capital of the entrepreneur. Samples of 600 to 800 traders were surveyed in each country.	• Results suggest that start-up conditions have a long-lasting effect on agricultural traders' productive resources. Working capital accumulates at 3-4% per year on average, versus 0.7% for social capital. Thus, initial contacts have a determinant role on trader performance. • Family networks and parental experience have no systematic effect on factor accumulation after enterprise creation, but they help determine the initial level of social capital. • Female entrepreneurs appear systematically disadvantaged in spite of the fact that they represent the majority of surveyed agricultural traders.
Farmers from 100 villages in Maharashtra, India were enrolled to receive SMS messages with agricultural advice between 2007 and 2009 (Fafchamps and Minten, 2012).	RCT consisting of 1000 farmers selected from 100 villages in central India. Farmers were assigned to one of two treatment groups or a control group, which was not targeted by marketing campaigns of a commercial service called Reuters Market Light, RML. In the first treatment, all 10 farmers in the selected villages were offered free RML. In the second treatment, three farmers randomly selected among the villages were offered RML (the purpose is to test whether the treatment of some farmers benefit others as well). The treatment (RML) was also offered to randomly selected extension agents covering half of the treatment 1 and treatment 2 villages. Randomisation of treatment across villages was implemented by constructing, in each district, triplets of villages that are as similar as possible along a number of dimensions that are likely to affect the impact of the treatment. Data is analysed using intent to treat analysis and an instrumental variables analysis.	• Treated farmers associate RML information with a number of decisions they have made, and there is some evidence that treatment affected spatial arbitrage and crop grading. But the magnitude of these effects is small. • There are no statistically significant average treatment effect on the price received by farmers, the likelihood of changing cultivation practices and crop varieties, or crop losses resulting from rainstorms. • Based on the available evidence, on average they would have obtained a similar price or revenue, with or without RML.
Farmers across 16 villages in India from 2007-2008 (Gandhi et al., 2009).	RCT which involved 16 villages (8 control and 8 treatment villages balanced for parameters such as size and mix of crops) and a total of 1,470 households during 13-months. The treatment is providing 'Digital Green' (DG), a research project that seeks to disseminate targeted agricultural information to small and marginal farmers in India using digital video. Analysis consisted of primarily quantitative analysis but also included an ethnographic investigation of existing agriculture extension practices, and prototyping of technology and its use in a village context.	• Techniques and practices adopted by farmers were nearly equivalent in both the control and DG villages across the duration of the study. • However, adoption rates, differed significantly. Farmers in control areas adopted practices at a rate of 1-4% while farmers in DG areas adopted practices at a rate of 10-33% in any given month. • On a cost-per-adoption basis, DG was at least 10 times more effective per dollar spent than the classic extension system alone.

Table 6.A1. Continued.

Setting (reference)	Methodology	Primary outcomes analysed and findings
Markets in Niger from January 2000 to December 2012. Monthly commodity price data for millet, sorghum, maize, and rice from the SIMA (System of Agricultural Market Information) (Goundan and Tankari, 2016).	Spatial dynamic panel data model applied to Niger's millet market. Approach attempts to decompose impacts of a price shock into direct effect (origin location self-impact), indirect effect (impact on other locations), and the total effect (cumulated impact).	• Results show that price transmission is stable but that prices are not co-integrated. A change in the price of sorghum was transmitted to millet price. The prices of other cereals were found have no influence on the price of millet. • Past price shocks are highly transmitted to future prices for around 70% of the price variation. • Results show local spill-overs in prices for locally traded commodities, such as millet and sorghum, but no linkage between locally, regionally, or internationally traded products, such as millet, rice, or maize. • Results do not reveal any spill-over or diffusion effects between regions for the millet market.
144 *mandis* (government regulated wholesale agricultural markets) in the central Indian state of Madhya Pradesh for the 1998-2005 period (Goyal, 2010).	The identification strategy exploits interdistrict variation in the timing of the introduction of kiosks and hubs across 23 districts to isolate the impact of the intervention on the price and output of soybean in agricultural *mandis* located in a district. The internet kiosks provide price information and quality-testing (e-choupals').	• The introduction of internet kiosks had a positive effect on *mandi* soybean prices, with a 1-3% increase in markets located in districts where kiosks were introduced. • The introduction of kiosks yielded a 19% increase in soy production, leading to an overall increase of 33% in farmers' net profits.
Fishermen and wholesalers in Kerala, India between 1996 and 2001 (Jensen, 2007).	Compares how changes in the outcomes of interest (price dispersion, waste, and welfare) correspond to the staggered introduction of mobile phones across regions. Weekly survey of 300 randomly selected sardine fishing units in three districts of Kerala, India from 1996 to 2001.	• The introduction of mobile phones dramatically reduced price dispersion. The fisheries sector was transformed from self-sufficient fishing markets to a state of nearly perfect spatial arbitrage. • The mean coefficient of variation of price across markets declined from 60-70 to 15% or less. • There were almost no violations of the Law of One Price once mobile phones were in place, compared to 50-60% of market pairs before. • Waste was completely eliminated. Before mobile phones, it averaged 5-8% of daily catch. • Fishermen's profits increased on average by 8% while the consumer price declined by 4%.

Table 6.A1. Continued.

Setting (reference)	Methodology	Primary outcomes analysed and findings
Plots in fields and farmers across Kenya. The date is not specified (Casaburi and Kremer, 2017).	RCT with two interventions: (1) an integrated mobile-based query system (farmer hotline) aimed at improving a sugar company's performance in the management of the provision of inputs (mostly fertilisers) to the farmers; and (2) text messages with agricultural advice. The pilot targeted 8,081 plots in 1,089 fields. During recruitment, farmers of 3,768 plots out of the 8,081 included in the study recorded their cell phone number and qualified as eligible for the service in the case in which their field was randomised into the treatment group.	• The mobile-based query system reduced by 54% the likelihood that a supplier did not receive fertiliser from the company (from 7.4 to 4%). • Mobile-based query system reduced by 23% the likelihood that a supplier did not receive the fertiliser within the time window recommended by the company agricultural department. • Non-eligible plots in treatment fields experience a reduction of 7.5 percentage points in the fertiliser delivery delays (19.8% of the average for non-eligible plots in control fields). • In contrast to the findings from a previous pilot that found a large, though not always precise, impact of the SMS on yields, the SMS intervention did not have a statistically significant impact on yields.
Farming households in the Philippines in both 2003 and 2006 (Labonne and Chase, 2009).	Spatially coded mobile phone data and household panel data to assess whether changes in consumption can be attributed to mobile phone ownership. Estimation is undertaken through OLS and instrumental variables (IV) with data from 1,231 farming households in the 16 poorest municipalities.	• Purchasing a mobile phone is associated with a 15% increase in the growth rate of per capita consumption. • Controls show that the education level of the household head and the number of household members in the farming industry have little effect on these results. • Ownership of a mobile phone is associated with an increase in trust of traders, and an increase in frequency of visits to the municipal market, which may help account for the increase in consumption.
Potato farmers in West Bengal, India, in 2008 (Mitra et al., 2018).	RCT where villages were randomly assigned to either one of two treatment groups (which received information) or a control group (which did not receive any information). In the first treatment group (private information treatment), four randomly selected farmers in each of 24 villages received the information through phone calls from a team of telecallers. In the second treatment group (public information treatment), the information was posted publicly in 24 villages.	• The gaps between resale prices and farmgate prices are large. Farmgate prices were 44-46% of wholesale prices. Middlemen may earn 50-71% of this gap. • When farmers in randomly chosen villages were informed about wholesale prices, average farm-gate sales and prices were unaffected. The pass-through from retail prices to farmgate prices was a statistically insignificant 2%, while pass-through to wholesale prices was a much larger 81%. • Results imply that ex ante, the information interventions did not change farmers' welfare, and reduced traders' welfare. Ex post, the welfare effects depend on the actual realisations of wholesale prices.

Chantal Toledo and Christopher Ksoll

Table 6.A1. Continued.

Setting (reference)	Methodology	Primary outcomes analysed and findings
Analyses of 2010-2012 household survey data from Ethiopia, Malawi, Niger, Nigeria, Tanzania, and Uganda to understand women's contributions to the agriculture labour force in Africa, and test the premise that women provide 60-80% of Africa's agricultural labour (Palacios-Lopez et al., 2017).	Uses plot-level unit record data of each household member's labour from nationally representative household surveys from Ethiopia (4,000 households), Malawi (12,271 households), Niger (4,000 households), Nigeria (4,716 households), Tanzania (3,924 households), and Uganda (2,716 households).	• Study estimates that the average female labour share in crop production is 40%. It is slightly above 50% in Malawi, Tanzania, and Uganda, and substantially lower in Nigeria (37%), Ethiopia (29%), and Niger (24%). • While there are no systematic differences across crops and activities, female labour shares tend to be higher when women are more educated and in households where women own a larger share of the land. • Controlling for the gender and knowledge profile of the respondents does not meaningfully change the predicted female labour shares.
Farmers in Uganda in 2000 (Svensson and Yanagizawa, 2009).	Differences in-differences between MIS project districts and districts where the project was not implemented, and across households with and without access to a radio.	• Having access to regular market information, proxied by having access to a radio, is associated with a 15% higher farm-gate price. • In the non-MIS areas, the estimated effect is close to zero and insignificant.
Grain traders in Niger operating in markets where mobile phone coverage was introduced between 2001 and 2008 (Tack and Aker, 2014).	Theoretical model of search in which traders engage in sequential search for the optimal sales price. Use a census of all traders conducted between 2000 and 2007 and a panel survey of 395 traders and market resource persons in thirty-two markets across six geographic regions in Niger between 2005 and 2007.	• Confirming the theoretical model, mobile phone coverage increases traders' search behaviour, as measured by the number of markets searched and the number of market contacts. • The effect is dynamic, and increases with the duration of mobile phone coverage.
Extension agents in Madagascar, Malawi, Zambia and Zimbabwe in 2012 and 2013 (Tata and McNamara, 2016).	Identify and categorise the challenges faced by extension agents who received Farmbook training (an ICT application that enables extension agents to help farmers plan their businesses, assess productivity, and profitability of their farming enterprise) in Madagascar, Malawi, Zambia and Zimbabwe and select socio-economic indicators influencing their work. Focus groups and interviews with extension agents who received Farmbook training and document review.	• Women reported facing more farm level challenges compared to their male colleagues. Conversely, women reported lower occurrence of technical challenges to using the Farmbook ICT application compared to their male colleagues. • Extension agents 35 years and above reported experiencing more technical problems compared to those below 35 years old. • Extension agents with advanced degrees faced less technical challenges using Farmbook than their less-educated colleagues. • Agents with internet access in the field and who were proficient at using internet experienced fewer challenges using Farmbook compared to their colleagues who had no internet access in the field and who were not proficient in their use of the internet.

Fostering transformation and growth in Niger's agricultural sector

Table 6.A1. Continued.

Setting (reference)	Methodology	Primary outcomes analysed and findings
Farmers in Uganda in 1999, 2000, 2004 and 2005 (Yanagizawa-Drott and Svensson, 2017).	General equilibrium approach that relaxes the assumption of fixed market price and allows for behavioural responses among farmer without direct access to the intervention (as opposed to a partial equilibrium assumption of unaffected urban market prices from Svensson and Yanagizawa, 2009). Use variation in access to market price information over time, across space, and between crops, and exploit the fact that market prices are set on local (district) markets that are not (fully) integrated. Use three data sets: the Uganda National Household Survey 1999/2000 (7,960 farmers), the Uganda National Household Survey 2004/2005 (5,733 farmers), and data from the Market Information Service (with weekly data on collected urban market prices).	• A 1% increase in number of informed farmers resulted in a 0.36% fall in district market prices. • Access to market information increased the likelihood of selling the crop by about 3 percentage points, or 13%, in the informed group, while market participation among uninformed farmers fell by 6 percentage points (a 9 percentage point difference in market participation between informed and uninformed farmers as a result of the intervention). • Ignoring the general equilibrium effects, the estimated coefficients would suggest a large, positive, effect from the intervention (crop revenue of informed farmers increase by 75%, albeit starting from a low level). However, in general equilibrium, there is a much more modest increase in crop revenue for the informed farmers (13% increase), while uninformed farmers saw their crop income drop by 35%. • The aggregate impact of the intervention on average crop revenue was negligible, but it had large distributional consequences: consumers benefited from lower prices; informed farmers benefited from higher farm revenues, and crop income fell for uninformed farmers.

[1] Results are all statistically significant at the 10, 5 or 1% levels.

Chapter 7.
A dynamic spatial modelling of agricultural price transmission: evidence from the Niger millet market

Anatole Goundan* and Mahamadou Roufahi Tankari
IFPRI-Dakar, Titre 3396, Lot #2, BP 24063 Dakar Almadies, Senegal; a.goundan@cgiar.org

Abstract

Spatial interactions are essential drivers of price transmission mechanisms and may significantly affect any food's policy outcomes. However, spatial aspects seem to be generally overlooked when analysing price transmission. This paper attempts to fill this gap by highlighting the usefulness of spatial interaction and models for market integration analysis. A Spatial Dynamic Panel Data model is presented and applied to Niger's millet market. Empirical results show that (1) the millet market is partly integrated, (2) locally traded commodities (millet and sorghum) are linked by a cross-commodity price transmission, (3) most imported cereals prices, which for Niger is maize and rice, did not affect the millet market, and (4) no cross-regions price transmission occurred for the millet market.

Keywords: spatial econometrics, panel data, agricultural commodities, market integration, Niger

7.1 Introduction

In recent years, agricultural products have undergone large price variation in international markets. Such variation in world markets is not without effect on local markets. The extent of these shocks varies across countries as some are more dependent on international markets than others. Several factors determine the degree of price transmission in a country such as trade flows, transactions costs, trade policies, availability of price information across markets, and infrastructure. For example, if domestic products dominate the local markets, price transmission will be less severe than in markets where foreign goods dominate local goods. In addition, high transaction costs and trade barriers reduce price transmission by limiting trade flows.

Price transmission analysis measures how well different spatially separated markets are connected because a price change in one market affects other markets. If markets are perfectly integrated, price signals are transmitted from a selected location to other locations. This implies a price adjustment in response to the existence of a supply or demand excess in other locations.

There is extensive theoretical and applied research on the mechanisms of price transmission. As applied studies often focus on policy implications, a large portion of the literature deals with methodological improvements in the fields of price transmission analysis. Therefore, various approaches can be found in the literature. Studies initially used correlation coefficients of prices to test market integration between spatially separated markets (Ejiga, 1977; Jones, 1972; Lele, 1967; Loveridge, 1991). Other research employed regression-based models (Gardner and Brooks 1994; Isard, 1977; Monke and Petzel, 1984; Mundlak and Larson, 1992) or time-series analysis techniques, such as dynamic regression (Ravallion, 1986; Timmer, 1987), Granger Causality (Alexander and Wyeth, 1994; Koontz *et al.*, 1990; Mendoza and Rosegrant, 1995; Uri *et al.*, 1993), impulse response functions of vector autoregressive models (VAR) (Goodwin *et al.*, 1999) and cointegration techniques (Barrett, 2001; Baulch, 1997; Goodwin and Piggott, 2001). Furthermore, several studies have proposed nonlinear approaches (Greb *et al.*, 2013; Meyer and Cramon-Taubadel, 2004). The common feature of these approaches is that they are generally based on time-series analysis.

It is important to note that price transmission is an economic phenomenon that takes place across locations that are spatially separated. The failure to take this fact into account can bias the results of an analysis. For example, LeSage (1999) stated that, due to spatial dependence and heterogeneity, the Gauss-Markov assumption is violated. Therefore, an alternative approach to traditional econometrics is needed. Spatial econometrics, which successfully models those issues and draws appropriate inferences is a straightforward solution. However, this tool seems to be rarely used in price transmission analysis. To the best of our knowledge, Keller and Shiue (2007) are the rare authors that used the spatial econometrics to study market integration.

The main aim of this chapter is to add to the literature by highlighting the usefulness of the spatial econometrics approach for analysing price transmission. Another contribution of this research can be called 'cross-commodity' prices transmission in this spatial setting. This chapter argues that the price of substitutes (for example, cereals such as millet, sorghum, maize, and rice) are linked and influence each other. This could be explained by the behaviour of economic agents and by the scarcity of a product in space and time. Indeed, consumer behaviour may explain why the rise in price of one product is passed to that of another product. In response to a price shock, households can move from consumption of millet to sorghum or corn. The scarcity of a given product (shortage, poor harvest, locust invasion, etc.) is also a factor that can lead households to change their consumption behaviour. Under these conditions, economic agents will adapt their preference to available alternatives. Each of these situations can affect prices and therefore demand for products. Therefore, one should consider change in the price of substitute products, at least as exogenous factors, when analysing price transmission of a selected commodity. We will use this model to study the market integration of cereals in Niger with a special focus on the millet market. Niger is a Sub-Saharan African country that tends to face major problems of chronic, seasonal, and acute food insecurity and malnutrition. The attention paid to the millet market is justified because it is the most consumed commodity and represents 78% of cereals consumption and 62% of food consumption in Niger (FAO, 2009).

The remainder of this chapter continues as follows. In Section 7.2, we discuss why spatial interactions matter in price transmission analysis. Section 7.3 and 7.4 set out the spatial model used and derives the computation of direct, and indirect effects of price change. Section 7.5

presents the data used for estimation, which is monthly cereal prices across regions in Niger. We present the empirical findings and interpret these in Section 7.6. Finally, Section 7.7 summarises our conclusions and discusses policy implications.

7.2 Do spatial linkages matter in price transmission analysis?

Price transmission examines how price shocks are conveyed between markets in geographically separated locations and provides information on the existence of market integration. Market integration ensures that price signals and information are transmitted from one market to another (Chirwa, 2001; Ghosh, 2011). When this occurs, the trade flow moves from food surplus regions to food deficit ones (Chirwa, 2001). This leads to more stable prices and more effective trade policies. Market integration is a prerequisite for the success of trade policies, such as price stabilisation of staples (Rashid et al., 2008). If markets are integrated, economic agents (producers and consumers) can benefit from liberalisation policies (Ghosh, 2011; Rashid et al., 2008). In food emergency situations, policy makers need to decide whether to resort to cash transfers or food aid. If markets are well integrated, cash transfers will be more appropriate compared to food aid. Therefore, price transmission analysis may contribute to an improvement in decision making (Beekhuis and Laouali, 2007; Shin, 2010). The level of market integration is closely related to trade flows influenced by transportation cost. However, distance and quality of infrastructure affect the cost of transportation. Policy makers can target some of these factors to achieve better integrated markets.

Price transmission models the dynamics of price levels between two or multiple regions. For studies on price transmission analysis, which involve locational components (countries, states or regions), at least two potential problems exist: (1) spatial dependence and (2) spatial heterogeneity (LeSage and Pace, 2009). These arguments are particularly relevant in market integration analysis. In fact, at a country level, it will be difficult to justify that the price of a selected product (say millet prices) is independent from one region to another. Then, the price dynamic would exhibit a pattern of spatial dependence. In addition, in the context of market integration, it is not unreasonable to imagine that accessibility of a market, existence of a highway, weather and many other factors may influence the price level. Therefore, standard assumptions of the linear model, such as the independence of errors between observation units and between the error and the explanatory variables, are quite strong assumptions for empirical price transmission analysis. These aspects could easily be included in a spatial econometrics model. Spatial econometrics is a branch of econometrics that mainly focuses on spatial interaction and structure. Therefore, spatial econometrics more clearly deals with the two previously stated problems. Spatial features are important as geographical distances influence trade and possible arbitrage. As stated by Tobler's first law of geography, 'Everything is related to everything else, but near things are more related than distant things' (Tobler, 1970). In addition, spill-over effects exist since the price dynamic in one location is influenced by observed prices in its neighbouring regions (Keller and Shiue, 2007). Such spill-over effects could be explained by information sharing between regions. This information sharing is made possible by traders and the rise of mobile phones (Aker, 2010).

By using mobile phones, a consumer or producer can be informed about prices in nearby or remote markets without traveling to these. Moreover, in most developing countries, the costs of communication are decreasing, and people increasingly connected.

Agricultural commodities traders search for arbitrage opportunities in different markets. Due to this information flow, because of higher prices, trade flow should move from surplus to deficit locations. Transaction costs between markets should be the main barriers to trade. In empirical studies, a potential proxy for these costs is the distance between regions. Thus, using spatial econometrics to analyse market integration would provide more reliable results than in the previous studies.

7.3 Methodological framework

To consider the interactions among geographical units, we formulate a Spatial Dynamic Panel Data (SDPD) model. Let Y_t^k be the vector of price for N locations at time t for commodity k and X_t stand for exogenous variables, which could be the price of other products or weather variables. The SDPD setup is:

$$Y_t^k = \tau Y_{t-1}^k + \rho WY_t^k + \eta WY_{t-1}^k + X_t\theta + WX_t\beta + \mu + \alpha_t l_N + V_t \tag{7.1}$$

where:
W is an $N \times N$ spatial weights matrix;
τ is the autoregressive time *home* effect;
ρ is the contemporaneous endogenous interaction effects;
η is the lagged endogenous interaction effects;
θ denotes the contemporaneous exogenous *home* effects;
β denotes the contemporaneous exogenous interaction effects;
μ is a vector of individual fixed effects;
α_t vector of time fixed effects;
l_N is a vector of ones;
V_t is a vector i.i.d error terms.

This framework offers many advantages for price transmission analysis. Indeed, by eliminating all the terms associated to the weight matrix (W), we obtain a time-series econometric model. This model is an example of a *VARX/VECMX* (VAR model with exogenous variables). Assuming ρ is nonzero in the previous model, one explicitly integrates a spatial aspect in the modelling. The resulting model states that the price dynamics in one region depend on the price in other regions but on a different scale. In fact, the weight matrix discriminates the different regions based on some considerations, such as proximity or contiguity and existence of road infrastructure. When the term η is introduced into the model, the assumption is that the price level of a product in a given location is related to the observed prices for the same product in surrounding regions during an earlier period. Another advantage of the model is the presence of X variables (exogenous variables) that could be weather or other variables. When X represents the prices of other products, this model makes it possible to study price transmission across products or cross-commodities price transmission. For example, one can examine the transmission between the rice price and other cereal prices (for example, sorghum, and maize) in a given country.

One issue that may arise with cross-product analysis is the problem of endogeneity between prices. In fact, the price of rice can affect the price of other cereals and *vice versa*. Therefore, it is relevant to treat this problem appropriately. One solution is the use of the instrumental variables or generalised method of moments (IV/GMM) approach. However, Elhorst (2010) found that this method is severely biased in the context of the model in Equation 7.1. Lee and Yu (2014) proposed a suitable GMM estimator for Equation 7.1, which is only consistent when T is small relative to N. This is not the case for our empirical study. Another solution to the endogeneity problem consists of estimating a system of equations where equations for all commodities must be estimated simultaneously. Such an approach is not well developed in the literature[1]. In this chapter, we address the endogeneity issue by using average price over the last three, four or five previous price observations for substitute commodities.[2].

Based on the proprieties of the model, its solution can be classified into three different cases. According to Lee and Yu (2010b), we have: a stable model if: $\tau + \rho + \eta < 1$; a spatial cointegrated model if: $\tau + \rho + \eta = 1$; and an explosive case when $\tau + \rho + \eta > 1$.

To estimate the model specified in Equation 7.1, we follow Yu *et al.* (2008, 2012) and Lee and Yu (2010a,b,c), who used a bias-corrected quasi-maximum likelihood (BC-QML) estimator. This method produces consistent parameter estimates when the model is stable. However, when this stability condition is not satisfied, a data transformation is needed to consistently estimate model 1 using BC-QML. Lee and Yu (2010b) and Yu *et al.* (2012) propose the spatial first-difference transformation using the matrix $(I-W)$ where I denotes the $N \times N$ identity matrix.

$$(I-W)Y_t^k = \tau(I-W)Y_{t-1}^k + \rho W(I-W)Y_t^k + \eta W(I-W)Y_{t-1}^k + (I-W)X_t\theta$$
$$+ W(I-W)X_t\beta + (I-W)\mu + \alpha_t(I-W)l_N + (I-W)V_t \qquad (7.2)$$

It is worth noting that this transformation has three main effects on the model. First, it eliminates the time-fixed effect. Second, similar to the time first-difference transformation, it reduces the cross-section dimension and therefore the number of observations. Third, it modifies the rank of the variance-covariance matrix, which is the number of nonzero eigenvalues of $\Sigma = (I-W)(I-W)'$. Let $[F_n, H_n]$ be the orthonormal matrix of eigenvectors and Λ_n the diagonal matrix nonzero eigenvalues of Σ such that $\Sigma F_n = F_n\Lambda_n$ and $\Sigma H_n = 0$. Note that the transformed weight matrix is $W^* = \Lambda_n^{-\frac{1}{2}}F_n'W_nF_n\Lambda_n^{-\frac{1}{2}}$ which has a $(N-1) \times (N-1)$ dimension. A second model can be specified, when omitting the k index for simplicity, as:

---

[1] Future work should pay more attention to those models.
[2] It means $\frac{1}{n}\sum_{j=1}^n x_{t-j}$, where n=3, 4, or 5 and x the price of other commodities.

$$Y_t^* = \tau Y_{t-1}^* + \rho W^* Y_t^* + \eta W^* Y_{t-1}^* + X_t^* \theta + W^* X_t^* \beta + \mu^* + V_t^* \tag{7.3}$$

Where $Y_t^* = \Lambda_n^{-\frac{1}{2}} F_n'(I-W)Y_t$ and other variables are defined accordingly. This model is estimated using BC-QML.

7.4 Direct and indirect effects

The coefficients of Equation 7.1 cannot be used directly to test for the existence of spill-over effects because this could lead to erroneous conclusions (LeSage and Pace, 2009). One should instead estimate the partial derivatives. Equation 7.1 is rewritten as:

$$Y_t = [(I - \rho W)^{-1}(\tau I + \eta W)]Y_{t-1} + [(I - \rho W)^{-1}(X_t \theta + W X_t \beta)] + [(I - \rho W)^{-1}(\mu I_N + \alpha I_n + V_t)] \tag{7.4}$$

The short-term impacts of a change in the explanatory variable X on the dependent variable can be computed as:

$$\left[\frac{\partial Y}{\partial X}\right] = [(I - \rho W)^{-1}(X\theta + W X\beta)] \tag{7.5}$$

This partial derivative is an $N \times N$ matrix. As noticed in Debarsy *et al.* (2012), the diagonal elements of Equation 7.3 are different for each cross section, the off-diagonal elements differ from zero and the matrix is nonsymmetrical. Diagonal elements represent direct effects while off-diagonal elements are the indirect effects. Thus, the direct effect is defined as the impact of a change of X in a region on Y in the same region. In contrast, indirect effects measure the impact of a change of X on Y on an adjacent region. Therefore, matrix (Equation 7.5) could be used to analyse price change effects (1) between two selected areas, (2) between a region and all regions, or (3) at the aggregate level. In the first case, the researcher will use the element of matrix (Equation 7.5) at the intersection of the two selected regions. While for the second case, one will sum the elements of Equation 7.5 for the row corresponding to the selected area. In the last case, the average of the diagonal elements represents the aggregate direct effect while the average of all off-diagonal elements is used as an estimate of the overall indirect effect. A Monte Carlo simulation is required to assess the significance of different estimates. Clearly, this framework is richer than the traditional linear model. Following Elhorst (2014), the long-term effects can be computed as follow:

$$\left[\frac{\partial Y}{\partial X}\right] = [(1 - \tau)I + (\eta - \rho)W]^{-1}(X\theta + W X\beta) \tag{7.6}$$

As the model is dynamic, one can also calculate convergence effects[3] in the terminology of Elhorst (2014) as

$$\left[\frac{\partial Y}{\partial Y_{t-1}}\right] = [(I - \rho W)^{-1}(\tau I + \eta W)] \tag{7.7}$$

---

[3] As noticed by a reviewer, this term can be linked to what is called serial correlation or persistence term in time-series analysis,

To summarise the information contained in the previous three matrices, LeSage and Pace (2009) proposed three scalar measures: average direct effect, indirect effect and total effect. The direct effect is obtained by the average of the N-diagonal elements while the indirect effect is the average of either the row sums or the column sums of the non-diagonal elements of these matrices. The total effect is the average of all elements of the respective matrix.

7.5 Data

The data used in this study is collected by the System of Agricultural Market Information (SIMA) of Niger. It covers monthly cereals price for all eight regions (Agadez, Diffa, Dosso, Maradi, Niamey, Tahoua, Tillaberi and Zinder, see Figure 7.1) of Niger over the period from January 2000 to December 2012. Commodities of interest are millet, sorghum, maize and rice, which are the main staples in Niger. Established in 1989, SIMA is a specialised service of the government of Niger, which is operated by the Ministry of Trade and Private Sector Promotion. The main mission of SIMA is to collect, process, and disseminate information about agricultural markets for better decision making by policy makers. By doing so, it contributes to a sustainable improvement of food security in Niger by providing better market transparency and a good knowledge of food trade, especially cereals. SIMA monitors a sample of 74 agricultural markets, including 48 regular markets[4], 18 sentinel markets,[5] and 8 cross-border markets.

---

[4] These markets are constituted of collection, aggregation, and consumption markets.
[5] They are selected as a result of an analysis on the vulnerability of areas. These markets are located in structurally vulnerable areas.

Figure 7.1. Map of Niger's regions (DIVA-GIS, 2013).

The dynamics of various cereals prices considered are depicted in Figure 7.2. As seen from this figure, for each cereal market all prices seem to follow a common trend. It can be noted that the trend shifted for rice markets after the 2007-2008 international food price crisis. For other cereals, which are mainly traded locally, dynamics are quite similar. Summary statistics (average and standard deviation) of cereal prices are available in the appendix.

In terms of the linkages between prices in different markets, a high correlation exists between the four commodities we studied (Appendix Table 7.A1). Correlation coefficients vary from 0.69 between rice and maize to 0.99 between millet and sorghum. The results give a preliminary idea about the strong relationship of prices between different commodities. Further analysis will clarify if price transmission takes place between those commodities.

Table 7.1 describes road distances between pairs of regions of Niger. Distance is obtained from the Google Maps website[6]. It is the great-circle distance between the centres of each pair of regions. Pairwise distances between regions vary between 115 km and 1,479 km with an average of 694 km and about 349 km as standard deviation. The average distance between a selected region and other regions is between 559 km (for Maradi) and 1,030 km (for Diffa). The entire pairwise distance matrix between Niger's regions is available in the appendix.

---

[6] https://www.google.com/maps.

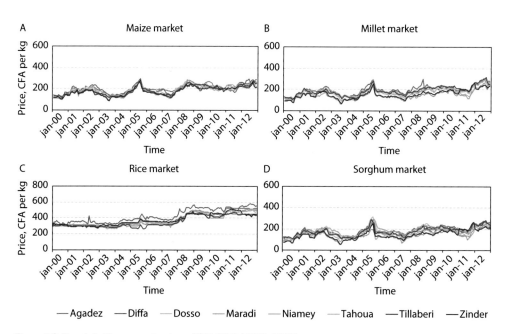

Figure 7.2. Trends in Niger cereals prices, 2000-2012 (SIMA, 2013).

CFA = Communauté Financière Africaine (West African Economic Monetary Union currency unit).

Fostering transformation and growth in Niger's agricultural sector

Table 7.1. Distance summary statistic between regions (km) using SIMA data.

	Minimum	Average	Standard deviation	Maximum
Agadez	406	754	235	1,064
Diffa	475	1,030	333	1,479
Dosso	139	589	346	1,228
Maradi	235	559	190	775
Niamey	115	667	416	1,365
Tahoua	328	565	218	1,032
Tillaberi	115	765	439	1,479
Zinder	235	623	251	1,004
All regions	115	694	349	1,479

Following Elhorst *et al.* (2013), we use the weight matrix based on the inverse of the distance between regions with a defined threshold. In other words, we assume that there is a threshold distance beyond which the interaction between two regions is zero. This means that if the distance between two regions is lower than the threshold distance, the weight matrix is set to the inverse of that distance. However, if the distance is greater than the threshold, the corresponding matrix element is set to zero, which means there is no interaction). The best threshold is such that every region has at least one neighbour region and the estimated model shows the highest value of the log-likelihood function. Therefore, the candidate thresholds are between 500 and 1000 km. The selected threshold is 850 km.

7.6 Application to Niger's millet market

In this section, the model previously presented is applied to analyse the price transmission of millet, the most consumed cereal in Niger. Two competing models are estimated; the first considers only spatial fixed effects (Model 1), and the second examines spatial and time fixed effects (Model 2).[7] As in Elhorst *et al.* (2013), the model choice is made using a Fisher test. The null hypothesis of that test is that the restricted model (Model 1) is preferred to the unrestricted one (Model 2). Another important characteristic of the selected model is its stability. If the selected model is not stable, further transformation is needed before interpreting findings. The stability condition is tested using a Wald test.

Table 7.2 presents the results of price transmission analysis on Niger's millet market when accounting for other cereal prices. It is worth noting that results presented here are ones where we consider the three lags average of other cereals (maize, rice and sorghum) as independent variables. We also had tested four and five lags average and the results were found to be consistent.

---

[7] For estimation, we use the Matlab routine of Jihai Yu available on Elhorst's homepage.

Table 7.2. Millet market integration results using dynamic spatial approach.

Parameters	Model 1		Model 2	
	Estimate	t-stat	Estimate	t-stat
τ	0.81	29.69	0.70	24.99
η	-0.23	-5.95	-0.16	-3.05
ρ	0.59	27.90	0.20	5.32
Maize price	0.04	1.10	0.04	0.88
Rice price	0.05	1.64	0.02	0.67
Sorghum price	-0.02	-0.89	0.07	3.20
W × maize price	-0.03	-0.92	0.01	0.16
W × rice price	-0.02	-0.54	-0.08	-1.45
W × sorghum price	-0.20	-7.23	0.01	0.23
Log likelihood	2,133.7		2,101.4	
Observations	1,208		1,057	

Model stability test	$\tau + \rho + \eta$	Wald stats	P-value
Model 1	1.17	63.71	0.00
Model 2	0.74	27.10	0.00
Model selection (Model 1 vs Model 2)	Fisher Stat[1] = 1.6873		0.000

[1] Fisher test reveals that the unrestricted model (Model 2) is preferred.

Results for those specifications are available upon request. According to the Fisher test, the null hypothesis cannot be accepted, then Model 2 is preferred. A Wald test reveals that the selected model is stable[8].

Since Model 2 is found to be stable, it can be used for further analysis. Even though estimated coefficients cannot be directly interpreted, they give insights on the necessity of including spatial aspects or not in the regression. In our case, the first parameter of Model 2 is significantly positive and equals 0.7, which implies that the previous observed price of millet had a positive and high impact on the current price. The second and third parameters (-0.23 and 0.59) are both significant. These parameters reveal the existence of a spatial price transmission among various millet markets. It also transpires that only the price of sorghum in neighbouring regions (-0.2) had some influence on the price of millet. As stated in the methodological section, to quantitatively evaluate the effect of a price change in spatial setting, one needs to compute the direct, indirect, and total effects.

---

[8] The row named 'τ+ρ+η' reported the sum of the first three parameters of the model (see the first three rows of Table 7.2). This amount is tested to be equal to one using the Wald test.

Table 7.3 presents at the national level, the direct, indirect, and total effects associated with every explanatory variable. The convergence effect, the effect due to the temporal or spatial lag of the dependent variable, which is the millet price, showed a positive and significant direct effect and a negative and insignificant indirect effect. The direct convergence effect is equal to 0.7. This means that an increase in the price of millet in the previous period is transmitted to its current level for about 70%. This parameter is the price transmission elasticity of the millet price from one period to the next.

Concerning the impact of the price of millet's substitute commodities (maize, sorghum, and rice), we found that a change in the price of maize or rice in any region of Niger had no direct or indirect impact on the millet price. Price dynamics in maize and rice markets did not significantly affect the demand for millet. In contrast, an increase in the price of sorghum significantly increased the price of millet. In fact, the coefficient associated with sorghum (0.08) implies that about 8% of a change in the price of this commodity is transmitted to the price of millet. This finding could be seen as evidence that sorghum is a substitute for millet.

These results can be explained by the production structure of millet and sorghum. In fact, these commodities are not only the most consumed cereals in Niger but also the most produced. According to the figures of the Niger's National Institute of Statistics (INS-Niger, 2013), millet is produced in all regions of Niger. The major regions of production are Maradi, which contributed 22.6% of the national production in 2012, Tahoua (19.6%), Tillaberi (19.5%), Dosso (17.8%), and Zinder (17.8%). Sorghum is produced in almost all regions in Niger (seven out of eight). The main regions of sorghum production are Maradi, which contributed 29.2% of the national production in 2012, Zinder (29.2%), and Tahoua (28.2%). Other cereals are marginally produced in Niger. In addition, according to the USDA database, in 2012 the local demand of millet and sorghum was mainly satisfied by national production in contrast to the demands for rice and maize. In fact, the import-consumption ratio for 2012 are 0% for millet, 2% for sorghum, 84% for rice and 90% for maize (USDA, 2016).

This data sheds light on our findings, especially about the existence of price transmission between cereal markets in Niger. Even though each of the aforementioned cereals were natural substitutes,

Table 7.3. Price change effects estimates.

	Direct effect		Indirect effect		Overall effect	
	Estimate	t-stat	Estimate	t-stat	Estimate	t-stat
Millet (convergence)	0.70	14.94	-0.02	-0.19	0.68	5.50
Maize	0.04	0.70	0.02	0.31	0.06	0.54
Rice	0.01	0.31	-0.08	-1.05	-0.07	-0.63
Sorghum	0.08	1.83	0.03	0.46	0.11	1.09

their availability on local markets and the associated prices influence consumer choices. Millet and sorghum, which are locally produced and consumed, are likely to be the first choices of the population. Results also confirmed that Niger's most important cereal imports, rice and maize, are not substitutes for locally traded commodities such as millet and sorghum.

Consumption habits are likely to be a key factor in consumer choice. In fact, it is difficult to explain why the maize market does not have any influence on the millet market by the price differential between millet and other cereals. Over the period of study, the average price differential between maize and millet was 10.6 CFA per kg, -9.2 CFA between sorghum and millet, and 198.9 CFA between rice and millet. Consequently, the lack of price transmission from maize to millet is likely due to availability and consumer behaviour. For rice, this could be explained by the price gap – rice price is about 2 to 4 times the price of millet (SIMA, 2013) – and the fact that in many West African countries, rice is considered a luxury good, and is generally only consumed during dedicated events (FAO, 2009).

Concerning the cross-regions price transmission, results show that none are significant when spatial fixed effects and time fixed effects are taken into account in the model. Therefore, there is no spatial price transmission for the millet market. This means that a price change in any market (millet, maize, sorghum, or rice) had no effect on the price level for other, adjacent markets. Therefore, price signals that originated from one region (for any cereals commodities) are not transmitted to other regions when region and time unobservable characteristics are considered. Many reasons can be given to explain this finding. We highlight the role of high transportation cost, poorly functioning transport (lagged transmission), imperfect substitution of goods, lack of price information and infrastructure (Badiane and Shively, 1998; Ghosh, 2011; Minot, 2010; Rashid *et al.*, 2008). Even though each of these factors could explain the lack of price transmission across regions, transport-related factors and infrastructure would be the most important factors in Africa in general and Niger specifically. Only limited road infrastructure exists in Africa. Therefore, transport costs are high compared to other regions of the world (Macchi and Raballand, 2009; Teravaninthorn and Rabelland, 2009). Due to a lack of adequate infrastructure, the transportation of commodities takes a long time. This situation could constitute a caveat for price transmission since traders cannot access readily available price information.

7.7 Conclusion and policy implications

Price transmission is an important research topic from a scientific and policy perspective. The recurring commodity price spikes, especially the recent food price crisis, have revived the debate on the issue of market integration and the appropriate policy response. Price transmission occurs from one period to another and between separate locations. This chapter proposes the use of a dynamic spatial econometrics framework for the analysis of price transmission and thus the integration of markets. The spatial econometrics approach, especially its dynamic version, has some appealing features for price transmission analysis. As an application, the dynamic spatial model presented has been used to analyse the price transmission on the millet market and the linkage of this market with other cereals markets. Our results show that price transmission is stable but that markets are not cointegrated. Past price shocks are strongly transmitted to future prices for around 70% of the price variation. Cross-commodities price transmission has also been shown between selected cereals, especially from the sorghum market to the millet market. A change in the price of sorghum was transmitted to the millet price for around 10%. The prices of other cereals were found to have no influence on the price of millet. These results revealed a relationship between locally traded commodities such as millet and sorghum but no linkage between locally, regionally or internationally traded products such as millet, rice, or maize. Conversely, our results did not reveal any spill-over or diffusion effects between regions for the millet market. One interesting lesson from those findings is that our approach can decompose impacts of a price shock into a direct effect (origin location self-impact), an indirect effect (impact on other locations) and a total effect (cumulated impact). Traditional approaches do not allow for this distinction. Therefore, results show that only region specific self-transmission occurred for the millet market.

These findings have some policy implications. First, the absence of inter-region price transmission reveals that a unique market-based price policy in Niger might not be effective in terms of mitigating the impact of a food crisis. To be effective, the government must design region-specific interventions. However, such options come at an elevated cost. Therefore, strategic investments are required to create conditions for price transmission between regions and ensure market integration. For example, investments in road infrastructure, which are essential for transport costs reduction, could be a good starting point. Second, since there is price transmission only between locally produced and consumed cereals (millet and sorghum), it would be interesting for the government to promote growth in their production, which may be a good resilience strategy for consumers. In fact, these cereals constitute the major portion of households' food baskets and are mainly produced in Niger (less than 2% of millet and sorghum consumed is from imports). The country has a limited connection with the international market and results show that a price change for other cereals (rice and maize) is not transmitted. In addition, the government could promote efficient trading of agricultural commodities by providing storage facilities to reduce postharvest losses.

Even though this chapter and its empirical application showed that spatial dynamics econometrics could be very useful in the analysis of price transmission and market integration, some aspects of this work could be improved going forward. First, the issue of price endogeneity needs to be addressed. The use of a vector auto-regressive-like spatial model may be a satisfactory solution. Second, here we only considered one lag for the model. In a future version of the model, it would be interesting to investigate the use of further lags. Third, it may be useful to test a dynamic weights matrix as interactions (trade and trade related infrastructures) between locations could change over time. If available, this matrix could be based on average trade costs or an index of road infrastructure quality between selected regions.

References

Aker, J.C., 2010. Information from markets near and far: mobile phones and agricultural markets in Niger. American Economic Journal: Applied Economics 2: 46-59.

Alexander, C. and Wyeth, J., 1994. Cointegration and market integration: an application to the Indonesian rice market. Journal of Development Studies 30: 303-334.

Badiane, O. and Shively, G.E., 1998. Spatial Integration, transport costs, and the response of local prices to policy changes in Ghana. Journal of Development Economics 56: 411-431.

Barrett, C.B., 2001. Measuring integration and efficiency in international agricultural markets. Review of Agricultural Economics 23: 19-32.

Baulch, B., 1997. Testing for Food market integration revisited. Journal of Development Studies 33: 512-534.

Beekhuis, G. and Laouali, I., 2007. Cross-border trade and food markets in Niger: why market analysis is important for humanitarian action. Humanitarian Exchange Magazine 38: 25-27.

Chirwa, E.W., 2001. Food pricing reforms and price transmission in Malawi: implications for food policy and food security. Unpublished. University of Malawi, Zomba, Malawi.

Debarsy, N., Ertur, C. and LeSage, J.P., 2012. Interpreting dynamic space-time panel data models. Statistical Methodology 9: 158-171.

DIVA-GIS, 2013. Niger country data. Available at: http://www.diva-gis.org/datadown.

Ejiga, N., 1977. Economic analyses of storage, distribution and consumption of cowpeas in Northern Nigeria. Ithaca, NY, US: Cornell University.

Elhorst, J.P., 2010. Dynamic panels with endogenous interaction effects when T is small. Regional Science and Urban Economics 40: 272-282

Elhorst, J.P., 2014. Spatial panel models. In: Fischer, M.M. and Nijkamp, P. (eds.) Handbook of regional science. Springer-Verlag, Berlin, Germany, pp. 1637-1652.

Elhorst, J., Zandberg, E. and de Haan, J., 2013. The impact of interaction effects among neighbouring countries on financial liberalization and reform: a dynamic spatial panel data approach. Spatial Economic Analysis 8: 293-313.

FAO (Food and Agriculture Organization of the United Nations), 2009. Profil Nutritionnel du Niger. Division de la Nutrition et de la Protection des Consommateurs. FAO, Rome, Italy.

Gardner, B.L. and Brooks, K.M., 1994. Food prices and market integration in Russia: 1992-93. American Journal of Agricultural Economics 76: 641-646.

Ghosh, M., 2011. Agricultural policy reforms and spatial integration of food grain markets in India. Journal of Economic Development 36: 15-37.

Goodwin, B.K., Grennes, T.J. and McCurdy, C., 1999. Spatial price dynamics and integration in Russian food markets. Journal of Policy Reform 3: 157-193.

Goodwin, B.K. and Piggott, N.E., 2001. Spatial market integration in the presence of threshold effects. American Journal of Agricultural Economics 83: 302-317.

Greb, F., Von Cramon-Taubadel, S., Krivobokova, T. and Munk, A., 2013. The estimation of threshold models in price transmission analysis. American Journal of Agricultural Economics 95: 900-916.

INS-Niger (Institut National de la Statistique du Niger), 2013. Annuaire Statistique 2008-2012. Niamey, Niger.

Isard, P., 1977. How far can we push the law of one price? American Economic Review 67: 942-948.

Jones, W.O., 1972. Marketing staple food crops in Tropical Africa. Cornell University Press. Ithaca, NY, USA.

Keller, W. and Shiue, C.H., 2007. The origin of spatial interaction. Journal of Econometrics 140: 304-332.

Koontz, S.R., Garcia, P. and Hudson, M.A., 1990. Dominant-satellite relationships between live cattle cash and futures markets. Journal of Futures Markets 10: 123-136.

Lee, L.-F. and Yu, J., 2010a. Estimation of unit root spatial dynamic panel data models. Econometric Theory 26: 1332-1362.

Lee, L.-F. and Yu, J., 2010b. Some recent developments in spatial panel data models. Regional Science and Urban Economics 40: 255-271.

Lee, L.-F. and Yu, J., 2010c. A spatial dynamic panel data model with both time and individual fixed effects. Econometric Theory 26: 564-597.

Lee, L.-F. and Yu, J., 2014. Efficient GMM estimation of spatial dynamic panel data models with fixed effects. Journal of Econometrics 180: 174-197.

Lele, U.J., 1967. Market integration: a study of sorghum prices in Western India. Journal of Farm Economics 49: 147-159.

LeSage, J.P., 1999. The theory and practice of spatial econometrics. University of Toledo. Toledo, OH, USA.

LeSage, J. and Pace, R.K., 2009. Introduction to spatial econometrics. Boca Raton, FL, USA, CRC Press/Taylor & Francis Group.

Loveridge, S., 1991. Marketing in Rwanda imports and infrastructure. Food Policy 16: 95-104.

Macchi, P. and Raballand, G., 2009. Transport prices and costs: the need to revisit donors policies in transport in Africa. Bureau for Research & Economic Analysis of Development Working Paper no. 190. World Bank, Washington, DC, USA. Available at: http://ssrn.com/abstract=1511190.

Mendoza, M.S. and Rosegrant, M.W., 1995. Pricing behavior in Philippine corn markets: implications for market efficiency. International Food Policy Research Institute, Washington, DC, USA.

Meyer, J. and Cramon-Taubadel, S., 2004. Asymmetric price transmission: a survey. Journal of Agricultural Economics 55: 581-611.

Minot, N., 2010. Transmission of world food price changes to markets in Sub-Saharan Africa. International Food Policy Research Institute, Washington, DC, USA.

Monke, E. and Petzel, T., 1984. market integration: an application to international trade in cotton. American Journal of Agricultural Economics 66: 481-487.

Mundlak, Y. and Larson, D.F., 1992. On the transmission of world agricultural prices. World Bank Economic Review 6: 399-422.

Rashid, S., Gulati, A. and Cummings Jr., R., 2008. Grain marketing parastatals in Asia: why do they have to change now? In: From parastatals to private trade: lessons from Asian agriculture, John Hopkins University Press, Baltimore, USA, pp. 51-76.

Ravallion, M., 1986. Testing market integration. American Journal of Agricultural Economics 68: 102-109.

Shin, M., 2010. A geospatial analysis of market integration: the case of the 2004/5 food crisis in Niger. Food Security 2: 261-269.

SIMA (Système d Information sur les Marchés Agricoles du Niger), 2013. Cereals price data. Available at: http://www.simaniger.net.

Teravaninthorn, S. and Raballand, G., 2009. Transport prices and costs in Africa: a review of the international corridors. Directions in Development; Infrastructure. World Bank, Washington, DC, USA. Available at: https://openknowledge.worldbank.org/handle/10986.

Timmer, C.P., 1987. Corn marketing. In: The corn economy of Indonesia. Cornell University Press, Ithaca, NY, US, pp. 201-234.

Uri, N.D., Chomo, G., Hoskin, R. and Hyberg, B., 1993. The integration of the market for soybeans and soybean products. Food Policy 18: 200-213.

USDA (United States Department of Agriculture), 2016. Market and trade data. Available at: https://apps.fas.usda.gov/psdonline/psdDownload.aspx.

Yu, J., de Jong, R. and Lee, L.-F., 2008. Quasi-maximum likelihood estimators for spatial dynamic panel data with fixed effects when both N and T are large. Journal of Econometrics 146: 118-134.

Yu, J., de Jong, R. and Lee, L.-F., 2012. Estimation for spatial dynamic panel data with fixed effects: the case of spatial cointegration. Journal of Econometrics 167: 16-37.

Appendix 7.

Table 7.A1. Cross commodities correlation matrix (SIMA data, 2013).

Commodity	Rice	Maize	Millet	Sorghum
Rice	1			
Maize	0.77	1		
Millet	0.7	0.92	1	
Sorghum	0.69	0.95	0.99	1

Table 7.A2. Commodity prices per kg, in CFA (SIMA data, 2013).[1]

Region	Millet	Maize	Sorghum	Rice
Agadez	190.69	205.22	181.4	388.23
	(40.13)	(41.87)	(38.36)	(83.22)
Diffa	193.65	196.04	177.34	426.83
	(42.06)	(40.77)	(40.63)	(85.82)
Dosso	174.66	178.69	176.18	358.32
	(36.97)	(42.05)	(44.2)	(66.35)
Maradi	144.49	181.69	137.11	374.57
	(39)	(44.49)	(38.56)	(78.62)
Niamey	188.98	180.63	185.58	361.15
	(44.21)	(42.07)	(41.66)	(78.05)
Tahoua	177.44	196.85	160.29	371.59
	(41.48)	(44.21)	(38.02)	(77.54)
Tillaberi	188.67	183.5	177.11	350.88
	(45.02)	(41.94)	(41.23)	(71.27)
Zinder	155.98	176.58	146.22	374.37
	(41.46)	(41.63)	(42.48)	(67.88)

[1] The numbers between brackets show the standard deviation.

Table 7.A3. Matrix of road distances between regions in Niger.[1]

	Agadez	Diffa	Dosso	Maradi	Niamey	Tahoua	Tillaberi	Zinder
Agadez		920	814	680	950	406	1,064	446
Diffa	920		1,228	710	1,365	1,032	1,479	475
Dosso	814	1,228		524	139	414	253	753
Maradi	680	710	524		661	328	775	235
Niamey	950	1,365	139	661		551	115	891
Tahoua	406	1,032	414	328	551		665	557
Tillaberi	1,064	1,479	253	775	115	665		1,004
Zinder	446	475	753	235	891	557	1,004	

[1] Based on Google Maps, https://www.google.com/maps.

Table 7.A4. Matrix of great circle distances between regions in Niger.[1]

	Agadez	Diffa	Dosso	Maradi	Niamey	Tahoua	Tillaberi	Zinder
Agadez		648	673	401	736	370	763	368
Diffa	648		1,037	616	1,152	826	1,226	411
Dosso	673	1,037		423	128	303	228	633
Maradi	401	616	423		536	252	613	211
Niamey	736	1,152	128	536		372	105	744
Tahoua	370	826	303	252	372		418	420
Tillaberi	763	1,226	228	613	105	418		815
Zinder	368	411	633	211	744	420	815	

[1] Based longitude and latitude coordinates of regions' centre.

Chapter 8.
Recent trends and future prospects of cross-border agricultural trade in Niger

Sunday Odjo[1]* and Ousmane Badiane[2]

[1]International Food Policy Research Institute, West and Central Africa Office, Lot #2 Titre 3396, BP 24063, Dakar-Almadies, Senegal; [2]International Food Policy Research Institute, 1201 Eye Street NW, Washington DC 20005, USA; s.odjo@cgiar.org

Abstract

High rainfall variability, resulting in frequent floods, droughts and locus infestations, undermines Niger's efforts to ensure its food security. This paper deals with the role of regional trade in fostering the resilience of domestic food markets in Niger. Current trends in agricultural trade between Niger and its regional neighbours reveal that the regional market plays a crucial role in stabilising domestic supplies of staple food crops, in addition to serving as the major export outlet for Niger's cash crops and live animals. An economy-wide multimarket and multi-country model of the West Africa region is used to explore likely changes in cross-border trade flows. Assuming a continuation of current trends in cultivation areas, crop yields, population and non-agricultural income, the projection of future prospects of cross-border agricultural trade reveals that Niger's participation in regional trade will continue to expand both in terms of net imports and exports. Simulation results suggest that the level of participation in the future could be affected considerably by potential changes in policy and productivity such as a modest reduction in general trading costs, the removal of cross-border trade obstacles, or a slight increase in yields. Such policy changes would have important implications not just for the country's trade with the rest of the region but also for it ability to improve food security for its population.

Keywords: rainfall variability, domestic food supply, cross-border trade, multimarket model

8.1 Introduction

Rainfall variability, frequent floods, droughts and locus infestations, prevalence of rudimentary production techniques and exposure to external shocks hamper Niger's development efforts. The country frequently faces food shortages and relies on food purchases or aid. Regional trade plays a key role in Niger, both in terms of domestic food supply as well as a source of export earnings. In addition to helping to increase local supplies, cross-border trade in agricultural commodities also helps stabilise supplies in the context of highly variable production patterns. Several factors such as transport costs, foreign exchange availability, responsiveness of the import sector, and dietary preferences provide valid economic justification for country efforts to boost regional trade as part of a wider supply stabilisation strategy that would also include increased trade with extra-regional markets.

The purpose of this chapter is to assess the structure, past trends and prospects of agricultural trade between Niger and the rest of the region. The chapter starts with an analysis of cross border trade data since 2000, covering Niger's most important imported as well as exported commodities. This is followed by a projection of likely changes in traded quantities, both imports and exports, assuming a continuation of current trends in production, population and non-agricultural income. The final section of the chapter looks at how potential changes in policy and technology could affect the country's future trade patterns with its regional neighbours. This is done by simulating the effects of reducing overall costs of trading in general, removing harassment and other obstacles to cross-border trade and raising crop yields, on the country's ability to participate in regional agricultural markets.

8.2 Geographic and socio-economic context

Located in the heart of West Africa, Niger is a landlocked country, bordered by Libya to the northeast, Algeria to the northwest, Mali and Burkina Faso to the west, Nigeria and Benin to the south and Chad to the east. It has a total area of 1.267 million km2, four fifths of which are covered by the Sahara Desert. The non-desert parts are prone to periodic droughts, floods and locust infestations, which result in chronic food insecurity. In 2011, agricultural land represented 35.1% of land available, including 12.3% for arable land, 0.1% for permanent crops and 22.7% for permanent pasture (FAOSTAT online database). The available arable land is confined to the southern fringes of the country along the border with Nigeria and Benin. Within this zone, annual rainfall varies significantly and its seasonal distribution is erratic. Some 600 mm of rain are generally expected on average between June and September, though rainfall can reach 700-900 mm within an area of about 1% of the country, in the surroundings of Gaya along the border with Benin.

Niger has a fragile economy largely based on smallholder subsistence farming, livestock rearing, small informal trading, and uranium and petroleum oil mining. The country's population was estimated in 2012 at about 17.2 million inhabitants, 84% of which reside in rural areas (INS-Niger, 2016). Niger is one of the fastest growing nations in the world with a population growth rate estimated at 3.9%. Most of the rural population is involved in agriculture, which contributed 42% of the country's gross domestic product on average between 2012 and 2014, including 28% generated by crop production activities and 10% by the livestock sector (INS-Niger, 2017). Almost all cultivated land is rain-fed and mainly devoted to drought-resistant cereals – millet and sorghum – and cowpeas and groundnuts. Rice and vegetables, mostly onions, are irrigated and grown mainly in the Niger river valley. Cassava, sweet potato, maize and wheat are cultivated on a small scale under rainfed and/or irrigated conditions. Livestock raising is based on extensive grazing and involves camels, cattle, goats, sheep, chickens and guinea fowl. Fishing activities are primarily conducted in Niger river and Lake Chad.

Given the predominance of rainfed crop production in the economy, rainfall variability has often had some direct bearing on the overall economic growth of Niger. A near-average level of rainfall as in 2008, 2010 and 2012, always led to an acceleration in the real GDP growth rate while below average rainfall as in 2009, 2011 and 2013, generally triggered a deceleration in the economic growth rate (Figure 8.1). Between 2007 and 2014, the growth rate fluctuated but often remained above 3%, climbing to 9.8% in 2010 and 11.9% in 2012 and falling to -0.7% in 2009 and 2.3% in 2011. Fluctuations in crop production were the major source of volatility in Niger's economic growth (Figure 8.2). For instance, growth in agriculture contributed 71% of real GDP growth achieved in 2010 while a decline in the sector accounted for 54% as a source of the contraction of the economy in 2009.

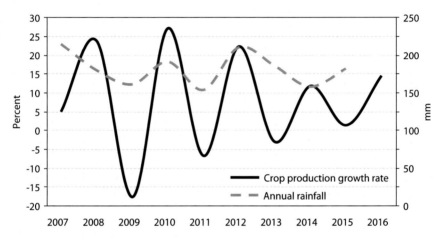

Figure 8.1. Rainfall variability and crop production fluctuations, 2007-2015 (based on national accounts data from the National Institute of Statistics, 2010-2017).

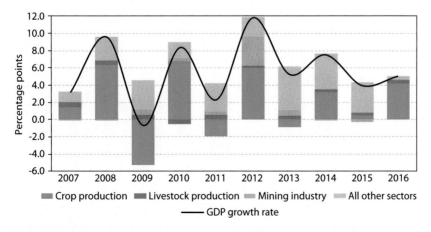

Figure 8.2. Economic growth and sectoral contributions, 2007-2016 (based on national accounts data from the National Institute of Statistics, 2010-2017).

In addition to strong dependence on rainfall, the recent growth performance of Niger's economy appears to be very sensitive to external shocks that affected the mining industry and foreign trade sectors, such as security threats in the northern part of the country, fluctuations in the world prices of uranium and crude oil and changes in Nigeria's economy. The mining sector's contribution to economic growth increased from an average of 6.1% in 2009-2011 to 28% in 2012, reflecting the start of petroleum oil production, then collapsed to 10% in 2013, following a terrorist attack that damaged the largest uranium mine of the country in May 2013 (Figure 8.1).

Niger runs a structural trade deficit. Exports to world markets consist basically of mining products, with France and China as major destinations. The share of mining products in Niger's exports increased from an average of 49.1% between 2006 and 2008 to an average of 53.1% between 2009 and 2011, then decreased to an average of 43.8% between 2012 and 2014, in response to declining world commodity prices, especially the prices of uranium ore and petroleum oil, which constitute the major mineral exports (Figure 8.3). Exports to regional markets essentially comprise raw foodstuffs, mainly livestock, onions, cowpeas and hides and skins, Nigeria being the main destination. From an average of 32.8% between 2006 and 2008, the average share of foodstuffs in Niger's trade fell to an average of 20.9% between 2012 and 2014.

Niger's imports from rest of the world are more diversified, including, notably, cereals, machinery, vehicles and parts, cement and petroleum. Food and capital goods accounted on average for 51% of all imports between 2006 and 2014 (Figure 8.4). Their average share diminished from 57% in

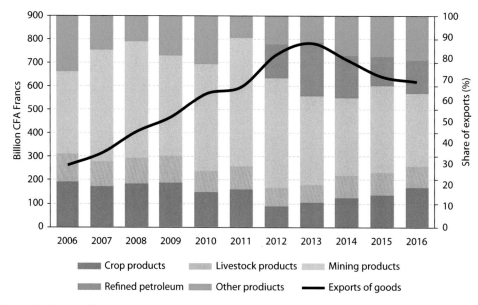

Figure 8.3. Merchandise exports value and composition, 2006-2016 (based on national accounts data from the National Institute of Statistics, 2010-2017).

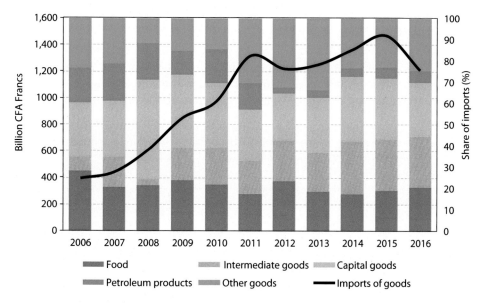

Figure 8.4. Merchandise imports value and composition, 2006-2016 (based on national accounts data from the National Institute of Statistics, 2010-2017).

2006-2011 to 46% in 2012-2014. The share of petroleum products fell from 17 to 3.4% between the two periods, reflecting the new trend of substituting refined oil imports with domestic production since 2012. In contrast, the average share of intermediate goods increased from 8 to 21% between the two periods. France, China and Belgium are Niger's major import partners. Imports from the regional market are relatively more modest and consist of raw foodstuffs mostly from Nigeria, Togo and Benin.

Given its exposure to rainfall variability and external shocks, Niger's economy is upheld by foreign financial assistance and food aid. To reduce the economy's vulnerability and avoid food shortfalls, the government has encouraged off-season production through investments in small-scale irrigation operations. Government efforts are also targeted at promoting agricultural trade with neighbouring countries. The next section is devoted to analysing recent trend in Niger's agricultural trade with its neighbours and exploring the potential for domestic supply stabilisation through regional trade expansion.

8.3 Profile of agricultural trade between Niger and the West Africa region

Cross-border agricultural trade flows in West Africa involve several commodities that are either imported or exported or cross-hauled by Niger. To give a picture of Niger's position in the regional market, bilateral trade of specific commodities between the country and its neighbours are aggregated into net-import or net-export quantities and values by commodity groups. The results of this aggregation are summarised in the Appendix Tables 8.A1-8.A4 and plotted in Figure 8.5 and 8.6.

The commodities that are generally net-imported by Niger are basically food products as shown in Figure 8.5. They include cereals, vegetable oils, fish and animal products, sugar and other food products. Cereals represent the highest volumes of net cross-border imports between 2000 and

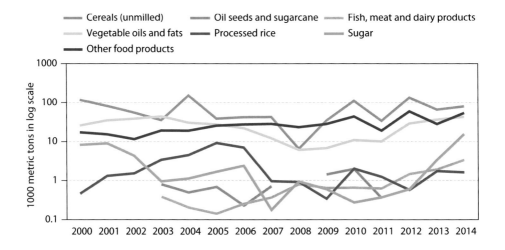

Figure 8.5. Historical trends in cross-border agricultural trade by Niger, 2000-2014: net-imported products (1000 metric tons) (Based on bilateral trade flows between Niger and West African countries from COMTRADE database).

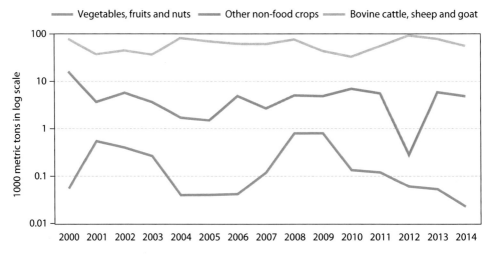

Figure 8.6. Historical trends in cross-border agricultural trade by Niger, 2000-2014: net-exported products (1000 metric tons) (Based on bilateral trade flows between Niger and West African countries from COMTRADE database).

2014. Over that period the net-import of cereals amounted to an average of 69 thousand tons with a minimum of 7 thousand tons in 2008 and a maximum of 152 thousand tons in 2004. Thus, Figure 8.5 illustrates the persistent dependency of Niger on the regional market for its food security.

In contrast, Figure 8.6 shows the commodities that are consistently net exported from Niger to the region between 2000 and 2014. These include vegetables, fruits and nuts as well as other non-food crops and live animals. Vegetables, including onions, tomatoes and pulses, account for the greatest quantities of net cross-border exports from Niger. Over the 2000-2014 period, net exports of vegetables, fruits and nuts amounted to 61 thousand tons on average with a minimum of 33 thousand tons in 2010 and a maximum of 93 thousand tons in 2012. In sum, Niger participates in the regional market not only as a net-importer of major staple food crops but also as a net-exporter of a few cash crops and live animals.

8.4 Regional trade simulation model

Simulations of prospects of Niger's cross-border agricultural trade are carried out using the regional Economywide Multimarket Model of the International Food Policy Research Institute (IFPRI) described below (Diao *et al.*, 2007; Nin-Pratt *et al.*, 2010). The original model has been augmented in this study to account for intra- versus extra-regional trade sources and destinations, as well as informal versus formal trade costs in intra-regional trade transactions (see Badiane and Odjo, 2016). In its original version, the model solves for optimal levels of supply QX_{rc}, demand QD_{rc} and net trade (either import QM_{rc} or export QE_{rc}) of different commodities c for individual member countries r of the ECOWAS region.

Supply and demand balance at the national level determines domestic output prices PX_{rc} as stated by Equation 8.1, while Equation 8.2 connects domestic market prices PD_{rc} to domestic output prices, taking into account an exogenous domestic marketing margin $margD_{rc}$. The net trade of a commodity in a country is determined through mixed complementarity relationships between producer prices and potential export quantities, and between consumer prices and potential import quantities. Accordingly, Equation 8.3 ensures that a country will not export a commodity ($QE_{rc} = 0$) as long as the producer price of that commodity is higher than its export parity price, where pwe_{rc} is the country's free on board (FOB) price and $margW_{rc}$ is an exogenous trade margin covering the cost of moving the commodity from and to the border.

$$QX_{rc} + QM_{rc} - QE_{rc} = QD_{rc} \qquad (8.1)$$

$$PX_{rc} \cdot (1 + margD_{rc}) = PD_{rc} \qquad (8.2)$$

$$PX_{rc} \geq pwe_{rc} \cdot (1 - margW_{rc}) \qquad \perp \qquad QE_{rc} \geq 0 \qquad (8.3)$$

$$pwm_{rc} \cdot (1 + margW_{rc}) \geq PD_{rc} \qquad \perp \qquad QM_{rc} \geq 0 \qquad (8.4)$$

If the domestic market balance constraint in Equation 8.1 requires that the country exports some excess supply of a commodity ($QE_{rc} > 0$), then the producer price will be equal to the export parity price of that commodity. Additionally, Equation 8.4 governs any country's possibility to import a commodity, where pwm_{rc} is its cost, insurance, and freight (CIF) price. There will be no imports ($QM_{rc} = 0$) as long as the import parity price of a commodity is higher than the domestic consumer price. If the domestic market balance constraint requires that the country imports some excess demand of a commodity ($QM_{rc} > 0$), then the domestic consumer price will be equal to the import parity price of that commodity.

In the version of the model used in this chapter, the net export of any commodity is an aggregate of two output varieties differentiated according to their (regional and extra-regional) market outlets, assuming an imperfect transformability between the two export varieties. Similarly, the net import of any commodity is modelled as a composite of two varieties differentiated by their (regional and extra-regional) origins, assuming an imperfect substitutability between the two import varieties.

To implement export differentiation by destination, the mixed complementarity relationship in Equation 8.3 is replaced with two new equations that specify the price conditions for export to be possible to both destinations. Equation 8.5 indicates that, for export to extra-regional market outlets to be possible ($QEZ_{rc} > 0$), suppliers should be willing to accept a price for that destination, PEZ_{rc}, that is not greater than the export parity price. Similarly, Equation 8.6 assures that export to within-region market outlets is possible ($QER_{rc} > 0$) only if suppliers are willing to receive a price for that destination, PER_{rc}, that is not more than the regional market clearing price, PR_c, adjusted downward to account for exogenous regional trade margins, $margR_{rc}$, incurred in moving the commodity from the farm gate to the regional market (see Equation 8.17 below for the determination of PR_c).

$$PEZ_{rc} \geq pwe_{rc} \cdot (1 - margW_{rc}) \qquad \perp \qquad QEZ_{rc} \geq 0 \qquad\qquad (8.5)$$

$$PER_{rc} \geq PR_c \cdot (1 - margR_{rc}) \qquad \perp \qquad QER_{rc} \geq 0 \qquad\qquad (8.6)$$

Subject to these price conditions, Equations 8.7 through 8.10 determine the aggregate export quantity and its optimal allocation to alternative destinations. Equation 8.7 indicates that the aggregate export of a commodity by individual countries, QE_{rc}, is obtained through a constant elasticity of transformation (CET) function of the quantity QEZ_{rc} sold on extra-regional market outlets and the quantity QER_{rc} sold on intra-regional market outlets, where ρ^e_{rc}, δ^e_{rc} and α^e_{rc} represent the CET function exponent, share parameter, and shift parameter, respectively. Equation 8.8 is the first-order condition of the aggregate export revenue maximisation problem, given the prices suppliers can receive for the different export destinations and subject to the CET export aggregation function. It says that an increase in the ratio of intra-regional to extra-regional destination prices will increase the ratio of intra-regional to extra-regional export quantities – that is, a shift toward the export destination that offers the higher return. Equation

8.9 helps identify the optimal quantities supplied to each destination. It states that aggregate export revenue at a producer price of export, PE_{rc}, is the sum of export sales revenues from both intra- and extra-regional market outlets at supplier prices, whereas Equation 8.10 sets the producer price of export to be the same as the domestic output price, PX_{rc}, which is determined through the supply and demand balance Equation 8.1 as previously explained.

$$QE_{rc} = \alpha_{rc}^e \cdot \left(\delta_{rc}^e \cdot QER_{rc}^{\rho_{rc}^e} + (1 - \delta_{rc}^e) \cdot QEZ_{rc}^{\rho_{rc}^e} \right)^{\frac{1}{\rho_{rc}^e}} \tag{8.7}$$

$$\frac{QER_{rc}}{QEZ_{rc}} = \left(\frac{PER_{rc}}{PEZ_{rc}} \cdot \frac{1 - \delta_{rc}^e}{\delta_{rc}^e} \right)^{\frac{1}{\rho_{rc}^e - 1}} \tag{8.8}$$

$$PE_{rc} \cdot QE_{rc} = PER_{rc} \cdot QER_{rc} + PEZ_{rc} \cdot QEZ_{rc} \tag{8.9}$$

$$PE_{rc} = PX_{rc} \tag{8.10}$$

Import differentiation by origin is implemented following the same treatment as described above for export differentiation by destination. Equation 8.4 is replaced with Equations 8.11 and 8.12. Accordingly, import from the extra-regional origin will occur (QMZ_{rc} >0) only if domestic consumers are willing to pay for the extra-regional variety at a price, PMZ_{rc}, that is not smaller than the import parity price. Furthermore, import from the intra-regional origin is possible (QMR_{rc} >0) only if domestic consumers are willing to pay for the intra-regional variety at a price, PMR_{rc}, that is not smaller than the regional market clearing price, PR_c, adjusted upward to account for exogenous regional trade margins, $margR_{rc}$, incurred in moving the commodity from the regional market to consumers.

$$pwm_{rc} \cdot (1 + margW_{rc}) \geq PMZ_{rc} \quad \bot \quad QMZ_{rc} \geq 0 \tag{8.11}$$

$$PR_c \cdot (1 + margR_{rc}) \geq PMR_{rc} \quad \bot \quad QMR_{rc} \geq 0 \tag{8.12}$$

Under these price conditions, Equation 8.13 represents an aggregate import quantity, QM_{rc}, as a composite of intra- and extra-regional import variety quantities, QMR_{rc} and QMZ_{rc}, respectively, using a constant elasticity of substitution (CES) function, with ρ_{rc}^m, δ_{rc}^m and α_{rc}^m standing for the CES function exponent, share parameter, and shift parameter, respectively. The optimal mix of the two varieties is defined by Equation 8.14, which is the first-order condition of the aggregate import cost-minimisation problem, subject to the CES aggregation Equation 8.13 and given import prices from both origins. An increase in the ratio of extra- to intra-regional import prices increases the ratio of intra- to extra-regional import quantities – that is, it effects a shift away from the import origin that becomes more expensive. Equation 8.15 identifies the specific quantities imported from each origin. It defines the total import cost at the consumer price of imports, PM_{rc}, as the sum of intra-regional and extra-regional import costs, while Equation 8.16

sets the consumer price of imports to be the same as the domestic market price, PD_{rc}, which is determined through Equation 8.1 and 8.2 as previously explained.

$$QM_{rc} = \alpha_{rc}^m \cdot \left(\delta_{rc}^m \cdot QMR^{-\rho_{rc}^m} + (1 - \delta_{rc}^m) \cdot QMZ^{-\rho_{rc}^m} \right)^{-\frac{1}{\rho_{rc}^m}} \tag{8.13}$$

$$\frac{QMR_{rc}}{QMZ_{rc}} = \left(\frac{PMZ_{rc}}{PMR_{rc}} \cdot \frac{\delta_{rc}^m}{1 - \delta_{rc}^m} \right)^{\frac{1}{1+\rho_{rc}^m}} \tag{8.14}$$

$$PM_{rc} \cdot QM_{rc} = PMR_{rc} \cdot QMR_{rc} + PMZ_{rc} \cdot QMZ_{rc} \tag{8.15}$$

$$PM_{rc} = PD_{rc} \tag{8.16}$$

Having determined export quantities and prices by destination and import quantities and prices by origin, the regional market clearing price, PR_c, can now be solved. Equation 8.17 imposes the regional market balance constraint by equating the sum of intra-regional export supplies to the sum of intra-regional import demands, with $qdstk_c$ standing for discrepancies existing in observed aggregate intra-regional export and import quantity data in the model's base year. Thus, PR_c is determined as the price that ensures the regional market balance:

$$\Sigma_r QER_{rc} = \Sigma_r QMR_{rc} + qdstk_c \tag{8.17}$$

Calibration is performed so as to replicate, for every member country within the region, the same production, consumption, and net trade data observed for different agricultural subsectors and two non-agricultural subsectors in 2007-2008. Baseline trend scenarios are then constructed such that, until 2025, changes in crop yields, cultivated areas, outputs, and GDP reflect the same observed changes. Although the model is calibrated to the state of national economies seven years earlier, it closely reproduces the countries' current growth performance.

Four different scenarios are simulated using the model. The first is the baseline scenario described above, which assumes a continuation of current trends to 2025 and is used as a reference to evaluate the impact of changes under the remaining three scenarios. These other scenarios introduce three different sets of changes to examine their impacts on regional trade levels:
1. a 10% reduction in the overall cost of trading across the economy;
2. removal of all harassment costs (that is, a reduction of their tariff equivalent to zero); and
3. a 10% increase in yields across the board.

These changes occur between 2008 (the base year) and 2025. The change in cross-border exports is used as an indicator of the impact on intra-regional trade. In the original data, large discrepancies exist between recorded regional export and import levels, with import levels often being a multiple of export levels. The more conservative export figures are therefore the preferred indicator of intra-regional trade.

8.5 Cross-border trade flows under business-as-usual scenario

Under the baseline scenario net cross-border trade by Niger is expected to expand steadily as presented in Tables 8.A5 and 8.A6 in the Appendix and plotted in Figure 8.7 and 8.8. Figure 8.7 shows the commodities that will remain net-imported from 2008 to 2025 under a continuation of current trends in cultivation areas, yields, population and non-agricultural income in Niger. Net cross-border imports of cereals will increase from 53 thousand tons in 2008 to 89 thousand tons in 2025 with an average of 70 thousand tons over the period. Roots, palm oil, animal products and other food and non-food crops will also continue to be net-imported under the baseline scenario as under historical trends.

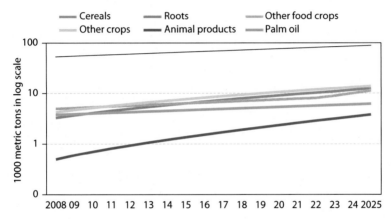

Figure 8.7. Baseline trends in cross-border agricultural trade by Niger, 2008-2025: net-import products (1000 metric tons) (based on the regional Economy-wide Multimarket Model). The graph depict future prospects of net import quantities under continuation of current cultivation, yield and population trends.

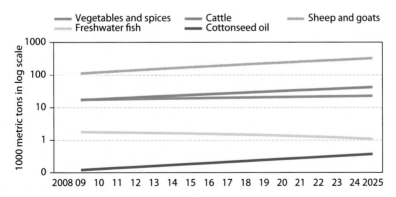

Figure 8.8. Baseline trends in cross-border agricultural trade by Niger, 2008-2025: net export products (1000 metric tons) (based on the regional Economy-wide Multimarket Model). The graph depict future prospects of net export quantities under continuation of current cultivation, yield and population trends.

As under historical trends, Niger will conversely sustain some net cross-border exports of the commodities shown in Figure 8.8, including vegetables and spices, cattle, sheep and goats, freshwater fish and cottonseed oil. Sheep and goats will account for the highest levels of net exports from 2008 to 2025 increasing steadily from 113 thousand tons to 344 thousand tons.

8.6 Cross-border trade projection under cost and yield scenarios

The results under cost and yield scenarios are plotted in Figure 8.9 and 8.10 that show the percentage changes from average baseline net-import quantities and net export quantities, respectively. Figure 8.9 shows that all net-import products will respond positively to the cost reduction scenarios. Removal of cross-border trade barriers will on average have a stronger impact across all imported commodities than would a general reduction in trading cost, although effects under the latter scenario are also important ranging from 5 to more than 15%. Animal products will be the most responsive to cost reduction. A 10% reduction in general trading costs in Niger will increase the average baseline net-imported quantity of animal products by 30%. The corresponding increase will be 16% in the case of a removal of cross-border trade barriers. Cross-border cereal imports tend to least responsive to reductions in trading cost and obstacles to cross-border commodity movement. On the other hand, increases in productivity levels, will have different effects across different commodities. While cross-border imports of animal products and palm oil would continue to grow, these imports will fall strongly for roots and tubers and to a lesser extent for other food and non-food crops. Cross-border imports in cereals would not be affected by the size of the productivity change that is implied by our simulations.

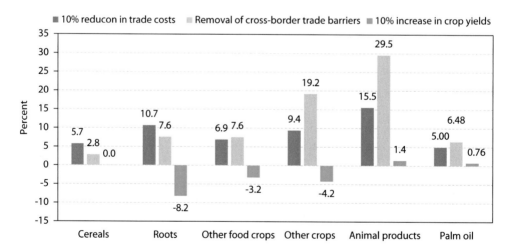

Figure 8.9. Change from baseline net imports of agricultural products under alternative scenarios (%) (based on the regional Economy-wide Multimarket Model). The bars depict the percentage change from the average baseline quantities of net imports under alternative scenarios.

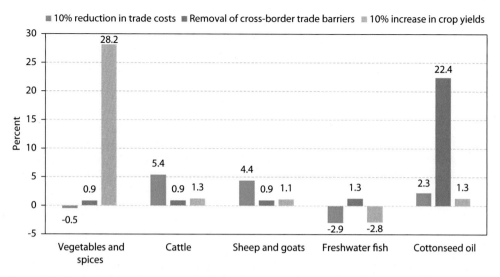

Figure 8.10. Change from baseline net exports of agricultural products under alternative scenarios (%) (based on the regional Economy-wide Multimarket Model). The bars depict the percentage change from the average baseline quantities of net imports under alternative scenarios.

Compared to cross-border imports, the effect of a reduction in general cost of trading or the removal of cross-border trade obstacles on net export quantities is more modest (Figure 8.10). Animal exports would be most affected with the highest impact on net exports of cattle, projected to rise by 5.4% if general trading costs are cut by 10%. Cross-border exports of sheep and goats would also jump by 4.4%, under the scenario of lower trading cost. Changes for all other exported commodities would remain modest. In contrast, an improvement in crop yields would have considerable impact but only on net exports of vegetables and spices, which would increase by nearly 30%. Similarly, a removal of cross-border trade barriers would have a major impact on net exports of only one commodity, in this case cottonseed oil, for which cross border export would increase by more than 20%.

8.7 Conclusions

Niger continues to play a key role in regional agricultural trade in West Africa. It is not only a main net-importer of staple food products, including cereals, vegetable oils, fish and livestock products and sugar but also a net-exporter of cash crops, including vegetables, fruits and nuts as well as live animals. Assuming a continuation of current trends in cultivation areas, crop yields, population and non-agricultural income, the projection of prospects of cross-border agricultural trade reveals that the country's participation in regional trade will continue to expand both in terms of net imports and exports. The level of participation in the future could be affected considerably by potential changes in policy and productivity. For instance, the simulation results presented here suggest that a modest reduction in general trading costs, the removal of cross-border trade obstacles, or a slight increase in yields, all realistic changes, would increase cross-border trade between Niger and its neighbours. A modest reduction in trade costs or a removal of cross-border trade barriers will increase not only net imports of cereals and other staple food products but also the net-exports of live animals. Moreover, a modest improvement in crops yield will reduce the levels of the country's net imports of food products and enhance the potential for net-exporting vegetables and spices to the regional market. In sum, policy changes along the lines of the scenarios that are simulated above would have important implications not just for the country's trade with the rest of the region but also for its ability to improve food security for its population. This would happen through improved and more stable domestic food supplies as well as higher incomes.

References

Badiane, O. and Odjo, S., 2016. Regional trade and volatility in staple food markets in Africa. In: Kalkuhl, M., Von Braun, J. and Torero, M. (eds.) Food price volatility and its implications for food security and policy. Springer International Publishing, Heidelberg, Germany, pp. 385-412.

Diao, X., Fekadu, B., Haggblade, S., Taffesse, A., Wamisho, K. and Yu, B., 2007. Agricultural growth linkages in Ethiopia: estimates using fixed and flexible price models. IFPRI Discussion Paper 695. International Food Policy Research Institute, Washington, DC, USA.

INS-Niger, 2016. Tableau de Bord Social. Institut National de Statistique du Niger. Edition 2016. Available at: http://tinyurl.com/y8gyjv9f.

INS-Niger, 2017. Comptes economiques de la Nation. Institut National de Statistiques du Niger. Avril 2017.

Nin-Pratt, A., Johnson, B., Magalhaes, E., You, L., Diao, X. and Chamberlain, J., 2011. yield gaps and potential agricultural growth in West and Central Africa. International Food Policy Research Institute, Washington, DC, USA.

Appendix 8.

Table 8.A1. Volumes of cross-border agricultural trade by Niger, 2000-2014: net-import quantities (1000 metric tons) (based on bilateral trade flows between Niger and its West African neighbours from COMTRADE database).

	Paddy rice	Wheat	Other unmilled cereals	Oil seeds	Sugar cane	Other animal products	Fishing	Bovine meat products	Other meat products	Vegetable oils and fats	Dairy products	Processed rice	Sugar	Other food products
2000		0.050	118.407		0.231		0.003			25.749	0.074	0.460	8.260	17.233
2001	0.967	0.606	79.843		0.100					34.794	0.172	1.315	9.007	15.384
2002	0.090	0.073	54.918	0.151	0.002					38.410	0.308	1.526	4.321	11.521
2003	0.036	0.039	35.196	0.851			0.118		0.003	43.968	0.302	3.419	0.951	19.090
2004	0.042	0.130	152.097	0.495			0.245		0.013	30.610	0.164	4.521	1.125	18.985
2005	0.121	1.331	37.340	1.287			0.145			27.569	0.265	9.198	1.674	25.495
2006	0.063	0.015	42.328	0.169	0.060		0.135			22.105	0.386	7.069	2.389	27.518
2007		0.022	42.757	0.740	0.014		0.166		0.009	12.170	0.227	0.967	0.177	28.365
2008	0.016	0.025	6.528		0.009		0.516			6.124	0.414	0.915	0.941	23.336
2009		0.065	34.328	0.754	0.676	0.169	0.233		0.004	6.812	0.240	0.342	0.601	28.149
2010		0.019	110.195	0.489	1.512		0.237		0.032	10.872	0.464	2.007	0.274	43.707
2011	0.033	0.272	33.604		1.070		0.275		0.010	10.063	0.388	1.234	0.372	19.003
2012	0.040	0.173	133.051		0.751	0.254	0.432		0.055	28.915	0.742	0.575	0.598	59.217
2013	0.329	0.134	65.584		1.423	0.868	0.161	0.007	0.046	36.378	0.854	1.736	3.391	28.218
2014		3.141	76.720	11.089	4.467	0.968	0.177	0.002	0.119	43.004	2.103	1.612	15.574	53.911
Average	0.174	0.406	68.193	1.781	0.860	0.564	0.219	0.004	0.032	25.169	0.473	2.460	3.310	27.942

Table 8.A2. Volumes of cross-border agricultural trade by Niger, 2000-2014: net-export quantities (1000 metric tons) (based on bilateral trade flows between Niger and its West African neighbours from COMTRADE database).

	Paddy rice	Vegetables, fruits and nuts	Oil seeds	Plant-based fibres	Other crops	Bovine cattle, sheep and goat	Other animal products	Fishing	Bovine meat products	Other meat products
2000	0.062	79.356	4.011	0.177	16.093	0.054	0.569		0.017	0.045
2001		37.527	0.656		3.687	0.546	0.578	0.915	0.004	0.035
2002		45.247		0.641	5.757	0.400	0.245	0.075	0.001	0.004
2003		36.533		0.056	3.667	0.264	0.032		0.007	
2004		82.317			1.728	0.039	0.205		0.013	
2005		69.960		0.600	1.496	0.040	0.237		0.028	0.003
2006		62.126			4.910	0.042	0.258		0.001	0.007
2007	0.059	61.273		0.039	2.685	0.118	0.035		0.000	
2008		76.832	0.241	0.146	5.023	0.798	0.115		0.000	0.007
2009	0.005	43.540			4.857	0.799				
2010	0.014	32.827		0.030	6.945	0.133	0.069		0.011	
2011		55.249	0.720	0.000	5.569	0.120	0.048			
2012		93.120	1.253	0.514	0.280	0.060			0.019	
2013		78.678	1.883	0.338	5.861	0.053				
2014	0.168	55.446			4.819	0.023				
Average	0.062	60.669	1.461	0.254	4.892	0.233	0.217	0.495	0.009	0.017

Table 8.A3. Values of cross-border agricultural trade by Niger, 2000-2014: net-import values (1000 USD) (based on bilateral trade flows between Niger and its West African neighbours from COMTRADE database).

	Paddy rice	Wheat	Other unmilled cereals	Oil seeds	Sugar cane	Plant-based fibers	Fishing	Bovine meat products	Other meat products	Vegetable oils and fats	Dairy products	Processed rice	Sugar	Other food products
2000		3.67	4,326.28		24.14					17,169.53	90.08	113.46	2,531.95	5,251.59
2001	252.24	195.72	4,894.66		17.48	110.54				19,498.15	209.40	318.05	2,447.29	4,818.06
2002	18.58	9.39	2,848.75		0.23					26,051.40	230.87	351.06	984.27	6,175.58
2003	3.49	4.10	2,470.52			62.86	85.31			34,601.88	602.88	852.84	361.62	7,140.12
2004	11.14	12.24	17,249.59			0.29	107.85		9.12	22,227.40	183.31	1,366.72	284.76	7,377.18
2005	24.28	713.76	7,336.46	97.88			63.15			19,898.56	409.13	2,910.38	610.53	10,124.33
2006	179.40	1.50	4,398.36		7.42	0.24	35.05			12,053.87	510.81	3,392.00	861.06	14,805.76
2007		4.14	4,253.96		1.93		101.21			7,136.92	421.27	317.76	91.84	20,274.35
2008		7.81	1,207.41		1.34		176.64			3,612.48	1,127.93	310.42	295.54	16,394.02
2009	1.42	16.99	1,300.02	21.95	65.66	0.70	137.61		2.41	3,384.81	483.75	112.79	213.99	19,921.06
2010		1.41	25,387.96	17.78	87.30		126.31		0.45	5,730.58	627.04	1,176.34	77.51	16,382.27
2011	7.09	128.42	4,322.31		31.94	0.75	95.71		1.25	5,883.72	913.77	480.54	120.18	14,230.71
2012	16.00	17.93	27,324.95		73.96		85.89		11.62	20,842.45	1,385.38	199.93	522.26	26,408.57
2013	220.88	30.30	11,208.92		34.79		68.05	4.06		29,460.82	1,573.05	1,192.06	2,273.83	27,256.10
2014		1,441.79	10,908.97	410.24	99.56		53.63	0.62	15.71	39,205.73	3,305.12	631.43	9,509.38	23,844.48

Table 8.A4. Values of cross-border agricultural trade by Niger, 2000-2014: net-export values (1000 USD) (based on bilateral trade flows between Niger and its West African neighbours from COMTRADE database).

	Paddy rice	Vegetables, fruits and nuts	Oil seeds	Plant-based fibres	Other crops	Bovine cattle, sheep and goat	Other animal products	Fishing	Bovine meat prods	Other meat products
2000	31.64	26,381.98	954.02	158.05	4,345.65	48,888.87	3,490.03	11.41	29.83	17.56
2001		16,207.26	268.35		1,417.75	40,484.74	2,991.19	207.48	2.89	12.18
2002		20,316.34	81.26	272.36	1,487.16	31,957.15	341.10	198.05	2.13	5.51
2003		21,968.26	234.91		1,057.40	38,958.11	107.16		8.60	3.62
2004		28,853.62	196.76		752.95	38,048.96	406.64		15.22	
2005		24,978.18		227.54	555.54	32,136.09	931.08		2.78	2.05
2006		20,959.60	151.28		1,024.79	36,598.84	2,000.46		0.10	6.04
2007	30.02	26,376.14	0.68	8.15	1,246.51	33,390.33	1,495.34		0.36	2.11
2008	7.54	33,801.35	128.21	23.80	1,842.72	15,6322.11	10,106.17		0.10	1.05
2009		33,203.18			1,166.71	124,373.80	8,130.60			
2010	4.24	6,833.40		45.58	2,145.32	44,703.25	2,270.90		12.35	
2011		44,599.62	372.14		1,814.12	38,543.73	3,123.81			
2012		21,505.84	365.16	390.86	1,252.91	30,685.95	3,803.46		8.23	
2013		16,087.06	886.19	404.10	2,270.18	16,344.77	1,429.08			2.17
2014	106.97	13,182.57			1,953.03	13,444.08	1,193.86			

Table 8.A5. Baseline projection of cross-border agricultural trade by Niger, 2008-2025: net-import quantities (1000 metric tons) (based on the regional Economy-wide Multimarket Model).

	Cereals	Roots	Other food crops	Other crops	Meat	Milk	Skin	Sea fish	Soybean oil	Palm oil
2008	53.4	3.3	5.0	4.2	0.04	0.42	0.00	0.028	0.141	3.786
2009	55.1	3.7	5.2	4.7	0.05	0.44	0.08	0.029	0.145	3.904
2010	56.8	4.1	5.3	5.2	0.07	0.44	0.16	0.029	0.149	4.019
2011	58.6	4.5	5.5	5.7	0.08	0.44	0.26	0.030	0.154	4.137
2012	60.4	5.0	5.7	6.1	0.09	0.45	0.36	0.031	0.158	4.259
2013	62.2	5.4	5.9	6.6	0.10	0.45	0.48	0.032	0.163	4.384
2014	64.2	5.9	6.1	7.2	0.12	0.46	0.60	0.033	0.168	4.513
2015	66.1	6.4	6.4	7.7	0.13	0.46	0.74	0.034	0.173	4.646
2016	68.1	6.9	6.6	8.2	0.14	0.46	0.89	0.035	0.178	4.783
2017	70.2	7.4	6.8	8.8	0.16	0.46	1.05	0.036	0.183	4.924
2018	72.4	7.9	7.1	9.4	0.17	0.46	1.23	0.037	0.188	5.069
2019	74.6	8.5	7.3	10.0	0.19	0.46	1.43	0.038	0.194	5.219
2020	76.8	9.0	7.6	10.6	0.20	0.46	1.64	0.039	0.199	5.372
2021	79.2	9.6	7.8	11.2	0.22	0.46	1.87	0.040	0.205	5.530
2022	81.6	10.2	8.1	11.9	0.24	0.46	2.13	0.042	0.211	5.692
2023	84.0	10.9	8.9	12.5	0.25	0.45	2.40	0.043	0.218	5.858
2024	86.5	11.7	10.1	13.2	0.27	0.45	2.70	0.044	0.224	6.027
2025	89.0	12.5	11.3	14.0	0.29	0.44	3.03	0.045	0.230	6.200
Average	70.0	7.4	7.0	8.7	0.16	0.45	1.24	0.036	0.182	4.907

Table 8.A6. Baseline projection of cross-border agricultural trade by Niger, 2008-2025: net-export quantities (1000 metric tons) (EMM model projections).

	Pulses	Cotton seed	Vegetables	Spices	Cattle	Sheep and goats	Freshwater fish	Cotton seed oil	Groundnut oil
2008	0.000	0.033	17.498	0.158	17.102	112.651	1.782	0.121	
2009		0.031	17.685	0.135	18.097	121.506	1.750	0.130	
2010		0.028	17.979	0.111	19.201	131.031	1.723	0.139	
2011		0.025	18.274	0.088	20.357	141.025	1.693	0.149	
2012		0.021	18.573	0.063	21.569	151.509	1.662	0.159	
2013		0.018	18.875	0.038	22.838	162.504	1.628	0.171	0.000
2014		0.014	19.180	0.012	24.169	174.033	1.592	0.183	0.022
2015		0.009	19.489		25.564	186.120	1.553	0.196	0.047
2016		0.005	19.802		27.026	198.790	1.512	0.210	0.074
2017			20.120		28.557	212.067	1.467	0.226	0.103
2018			20.439		30.160	225.969	1.420	0.242	0.136
2019			20.765		31.839	240.534	1.371	0.259	0.172
2020			21.099		33.599	255.791	1.318	0.278	0.211
2021			21.443		35.444	271.773	1.262	0.298	0.253
2022			21.800		37.379	288.512	1.204	0.320	0.300
2023	2.103		22.181		39.414	306.068	1.143	0.343	0.351
2024	6.199		22.598		41.559	324.496	1.080	0.368	0.407
2025	10.706		23.055		43.820	343.832	1.015	0.394	0.468
Average	6.336	0.020	20.047	0.086	28.761	213.790	1.454	0.233	0.196

Chapter 9.
Taking stock of Niger's existing regional and global trade agreements

Fousseini Traore

IFPRI-Dakar, Titre 3396, Lot #2, BP 24063 Dakar Almadies, Senegal; fousseini.traore@cgiar.org

Abstract

This chapter examines the global and regional trade agreements signed by Niger, their implementation status, and the main obstacles to their full implementation. For the agreements that involved strong commitments by Niger, the results are mixed in terms of implementation. For tariff related measures, Niger has implemented all its commitments with the exception of the recent violations of its WTO bound tariffs following the introduction of the ECOWAS Common External Tariff (CET). As for non-tariff commitments, Niger has made considerable progress although there is room for improvement. It has put in place most of the institutions needed to implement the agreements and adapted its legislation accordingly, in particular to comply with the Sanitary and Phytosanitary Measures, the Technical Barriers to Trade Agreement and the sub-regional regulations under both ECOWAS and WAEMU. The creation of the National Standardisation Council (CNN) as well as the National Board for Ensuring Conformity with Standards (AVCN) are in pursuit of this objective. With regard to custom valuation, with a few exceptions, the country applies the transaction value principle, in accordance with the WTO custom valuation agreement, and WAEMU and ECOWAS regulations. The main challenges for customs are related to the new Trade Facilitation Agreement (TFA) adopted at the Bali Conference in 2013. The private sector needs support in building capacities to comply with international norms and standards. Also supply-side constraints (poor road and transport infrastructure, ineffective telecommunication services) should be addressed so that the country can take advantage of the liberalisation process.

Keywords: Niger, trade agreements, supply side constraints, trade facilitation

9.1 Introduction

Niger is a landlocked developing country that has gone through major changes over the past decade. The country tripled its gross domestic product (GDP) from 2000 to 2015, but its growth path is still unstable (Figure 9.1). The robust growth of the last two years driven by the start of crude oil production in the country, has been dampened by poor performance in agriculture. Niger's trade pattern highlights a large concentration around a few commodities (e.g. uranium,

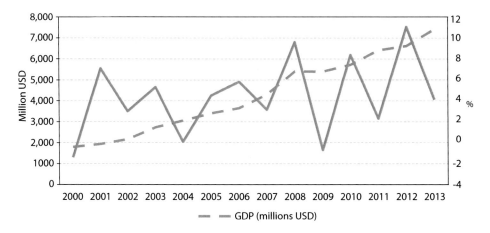

Figure 9.1. Niger's gross domestic product (GDP) and GDP growth rates, 2000-2013 (World Bank, 2015).

oil, and livestock) and a move towards limited numbers of external markets. The trade openness ratio (67% in 2013) is however reasonable and the persistent current account deficit is improving.[1]

As a member of many international and regional organisations, Niger has signed various agreements that affect its trade and under which it has made commitments. The aim of this chapter is to assess the commitments of Niger with regards to these regional and global trade agreements, their current status of implementation and the main obstacles to their implementation. The chapter also gives some recommendations on the international support needed to assist Niger with the implementation process. Regarding non-tariff measures, the chapter focuses on international (global) agreements as most of the regional measures are being aligned with these international standards. The chapter covers both the symmetric and reciprocal agreements (World Trade Organisation (WTO), West African Economic and Monetary Union (WAEMU), Economic Community of West African States (ECOWAS)) and the reciprocal but asymmetric ones (economic partnership agreements (EPAs) with the European Union) or the preferential non-reciprocal ones (African Growth and Opportunity Act (AGOA) with the USA).

The chapter is organised as follows. We first present the evolution of Niger's economy over the past decade. The main macroeconomic features are highlighted with a focus on economic growth issues. The next section focuses on trade issues by giving an overview of the trade patterns in terms of commodities, geographical orientation and nature, i.e. formal versus informal trade. We also analyse in this section the tariff profile of Niger. In Section 9.3 we provide a description of the institutional framework governing Niger's trade policy. We provide an inventory of the global and regional trade agreements signed by Niger as well as their status of implementation in Section 9.4. At the multilateral level, we focus on the new Trade Facilitation Agreement

[1] (Exports + Imports) / GDP.

Fostering transformation and growth in Niger's agricultural sector

(TFA) that will bring new challenges for Niger. In Section 9.5 the agreements active for Niger's key trading partners, which could affect Niger's trade, are analysed. An important issue here is the erosion of preferences for Niger. The political will and the risks to meet trade liberalisation commitments of Niger's key trading partners are assessed in Section 9.6. Niger's capacity to implement the commitments and the main obstacles to implementation are analysed in Section 9.7. Section 9.8 concludes with recommendations for international support.

9.2 Niger's key macroeconomic features

Niger is the biggest country in West Africa in terms of land area. It is a mainly arid country with two thirds of its land area made up of desert and steppes, which triggers problems related to water scarcity and the need for agricultural irrigation. With 40.8% of its population living below $1.25 a day, Niger is one of the poorest countries in the world. In 2013, the country had the lowest Human Development Index of 0.337, ranking last out of 187 countries. The country also holds the highest fecundity rate in the world with an average of 7.6 children per women.

Between 2000 and 2013, Niger's GDP tripled despite volatile GDP growth rates during this period. Niger's economic growth has been very unsteady over the past fifteen years, as shown in Figure 9.1. GDP growth is largely characterised by peaks and troughs year after year, showing a vulnerable economic performance and structure. The country entered a recession in 2009 as GDP grew at a negative -0.71%.

More recently, after strong growth of 11.1% in 2012, driven by the start of crude oil production and a good harvest, real GDP growth declined to 4.1% in 2013. The decline was due to lower agricultural production following poor rains and a slowdown in mining following temporary stoppages that occurred in some uranium and gold mines.

Niger's primary sector (agriculture, hunting, forestry and fishing) makes up the largest share of the country's economy with 39.6% of the GDP in 2013, followed by wholesale and retail trade activities and mining (Table 9.1). It is noteworthy that the share of Niger's mining sector doubled between 2007 and 2013, rising from 4.8 to 11.4%, 10 times higher than the share in 2005. Niger's economy is characterised by a large informal sector, which contributed more than 67% of GDP during 1990-2010. Apart from the informal nature of its GDP and the predominance of the primary sector, the weakness and volatility of Niger's economic growth is also due to a business climate that is unfavourable to private sector development and more generally a lack of competitiveness. The underlying factors for this include: (1) a weak institutional framework; (2) limited infrastructure; (3) weak human capital (in terms of health, primary education, and higher education); (4) narrow and non-competitive goods and labour markets combined with a weak industrial sector, an undeveloped financial market, and the absence of technological innovations.

With production rising in the mining sector, good growth prospects are foreseen and growth is likely to show a significant rebound. However, several factors still threaten the stability of

Table 9.1. Niger's gross domestic product (GDP) composition by sector shares (ASY, 2014).

	2007	2013
Agriculture, hunting, forestry and fishing	44.2%	39.6%
Mining and quarrying	4.8%	11.4%
Manufacturing	5.6%	6.6%
Electricity, gas and water	1.2%	1.3%
Construction	2.7%	2.6%
Wholesale and retail trade, restaurants and hotels	15.2%	14.4%
Finance, insurance, real estate	5.7%	5.1%
Transport and communication	7.1%	6.7%
Public administration	9.5%	9.4%
Education	1.7%	1.5%
Health and social work	1.9%	1.6%
Other services	1.5%	0.7%
GDP at factor cost (billions CFA)	1,908.225	3,380.106

the economy's performance, and these include the country's exposure to climate shocks, the recurrence of food crises, and weaknesses of the natural resource management policy and the business environment. Programs have been launched to mitigate vulnerability to climate change and to strengthen natural resource management. Niger has launched several programs under the 2012-15 Economic and Social Development Plan aimed at driving sustained and inclusive growth and developing the private sector. These include the implementation of the 3N (Nigeriens nourish Nigeriens) initiative which has contributed to increasing crop production under irrigation. The country has adopted a national good governance charter for the management of mineral resources. However, private sector development needed for economic diversification and inclusive growth remains a challenge. Niger has not undertaken significant reforms to improve the business environment, and the formal private sector's share in the economy has eroded over the past two decades in favour of the informal sector. The private sector also suffers from high supply side constraints that undermine its overall competitiveness.

9.3 Recent trade patterns

9.3.1 Global patterns

Figure 9.2 shows the evolution of Niger's exports, imports and trade balance from 2009 to 2013. The trade openness index remained stable at about 67% during this period. The negative trade balance has been improving, in particular since 2012 due to a rise in exports (from CFAF 482.8 billion in 2008-2010 to CFAF 706 billion in 2011-2013) and a smaller decrease in imports (from CFAF 1,445.2 billion in 2011 to CFAF 1,395.2 billion in 2012). The trade balance has now

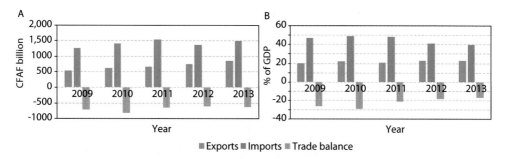

Figure 9.2. Evolution of trade; (A) in CFAF Billion, (B) in % of gross domestic product (GDP) (BCEAO, 2014).

stabilised at about 17% of GDP, compared to 26% in 2009 (Figure 9.2B). The increase in exports is essentially due to an increase in uranium exports, Niger's main source of exports. It also due to a sharp increase in refined oil exports, while the decrease in imports is due to hydrocarbon, which is no longer the main import and is now the second largest export product. However, this fall in imports has been dampened by the increase in rice imports, fertiliser and capital goods to satisfy the demand from the mining sector. Despite the relative success of exports that are highly concentrated, the trade sector is still hampered by an unfavourable business environment and supply side constraints (trade, transport and telecommunication infrastructure), limited warehousing and processing capacities, inadequate transportation infrastructure and the informal nature of trade. However, there are opportunities that could be exploited for investing in the following major areas: agriculture, livestock, mines, and handicrafts.

9.3.2 Trade by product

With exports valued at CFAF 302.8 billion in 2013 (representing 39% of total exports), uranium remains Niger's main export product (Figure 9.3A). However, uranium's share in exports has decreased (from 52.9% 2011 to 38.6% in 2013; Figure 9.4) due to significant exports of hydrocarbon starting in 2012 by Niger, the terrorist attack that occurred in 2013 on the site of the Société des Mines de l'Air (SOMAIR), and social conflicts in the Société des Mines d'Azelik (SOMINA) (BCEAO, 2013). Total uranium exports thus declined from 4,623 tons in 2012 to 4,382 tons in 2013. The other main export commodities which make up a sizeable share of total exports are refined oil products, starting in 2012 (25%), livestock (8.5%) and black eyed peas (4.5%). The remaining export products consist of leather and reexports of cigarettes and clothes to Nigeria. Regarding imports, as we already mentioned, due to increased production in the mining and oil sectors, raw materials and equipment are the main imported products (69% of total imports) followed by food (25%) and energy products (4%) (Figure 9.3B). Raw materials consist mainly of cement, steel, and chemicals. However, despite the increase in mining products, imports of hydrocarbon products remain important (CFAF 11 billion in 2012).

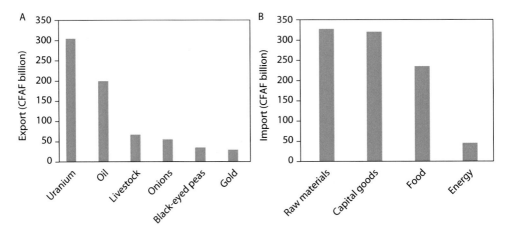

Figure 9.3. (A) Main exports in 2013 and (B) main imports in 2013 (BCEAO, 2014).

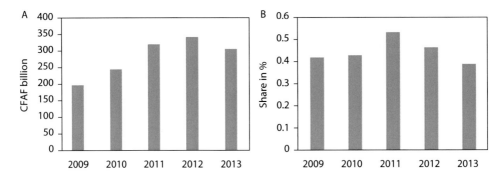

Figure 9.4. Uranium exports; (A) in CFAF Billion, (B) share in % (BCEAO, 2014).

9.3.3 Directions of trade

On the export side, the main destination for Niger's products is the EU (38% of exports) followed by ECOWAS (non WAEMU) (20% of exports) and WAEMU (17% of exports). The regional share (WAEMU+ECOWAS) is almost the same as the EU share. The USA accounts for 9% and all other destinations account for 16% of Niger's exports (Figure 9.5). The EU's huge share is largely due to uranium and gold exports. Within the EU, France is the main export market with 87% of total exports to the region and 30% of Niger's total exports. Niger's exports to WAEMU countries represent the second largest share and significantly increased from CFAF 37 billion in 2009 to CFAF 124 billion in 2013. Within WAEMU, Burkina Faso and Mali made up the largest export destinations, with 44% and 32% of total exports to WAEMU from Niger, respectively (Figure 9.6). Refined oil is the main commodity exported by Niger to WAEMU countries. Exports to ECOWAS (non WAEMU) countries also represent a large share of Niger's trade (18% in 2013)

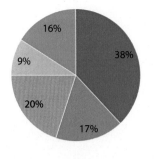

EU ■ WAEMU ■ ECOWAS ■ USA ■ Others

Figure 9.5. Destination of exports in 2013 (BCEAO, 2014).

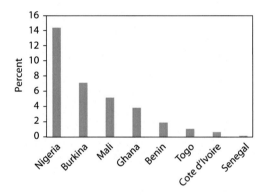

Figure 9.6. Sub-regional exports in % in 2013 (BCEAO, 2014).

and have strongly increased since 2009 (+69%) due to the rise in production of hydrocarbons and black-eyed peas[2]. In the region Nigeria is the main destination (78%), followed by Ghana (21%).

Regarding imports, Niger's main suppliers are in Asia, with China being the biggest supplier (22%), followed by India (5.4%) and Japan (4%). The position of China is explained by the fact that the country has been Niger's main partner in the mining industry. The products imported from Asia consist of capital goods, electronic devices, and clothes. The West Africa sub-region is Niger's second largest supplier with 26% of total imports (Figure 9.7). The main commodities imported by Niger from the sub-region are cement, cereals, and fruits and vegetables. Niger's principal partners in the sub-region are Togo, which supplies 7% of Niger's total imports, followed by Benin (4.8%) and Nigeria with 4.6% (Figure 9.8). The EU is the third largest supplier of Niger's imports, with 18% of its total imports. The imports mainly consist of petroleum and

[2] Black eyed pea exports are part of a large informal trade to Nigeria that is underestimated in official statistics.

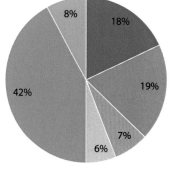

Figure 9.7. Origin of imports in % in 2013 (BCEAO, 2014).

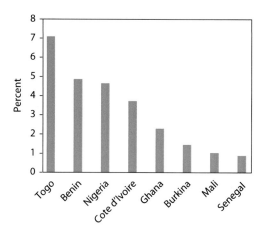

Figure 9.8. Sub-regional imports in % (BCEAO, 2014).

pharmaceutical products, dairy products, cigarettes, telecommunication devices, and used cars. Within the EU, half of the imports come from France.

9.3.4 Cross border and informal trade

Like many African countries, Niger has a large proportion of informal cross border trade. The trade flows correspond to commodities that may be legal imports or exports on one side of the border and illicit on the other side and *vice versa*, and commodities that have not been subjected to statutory border formalities such as customs clearance. In Niger the informal cross border trade flows consists mainly of food staples (cereals) and livestock products.

Evaluating cross border trade flows is a challenging task as it requires a good knowledge of the corridors used by traders. The Central Bank of West African States (BCEAO) uses a reweighting method to come up with global cross border flows. Based on surveys conducted in villages along the border and from the Chamber of Commerce, Agriculture, Industry and Crafts of Niger (CCIAN), a reweighting coefficient of 20% is applied to exports and 5% to imports. The extent to which these surveys are representative is questionable as the methodology (survey sampling design) is not publicly available. However, they provide a rough estimate of the volume of informal trade flows.[3]

Figure 9.9 and 9.10 give estimates of cross border informal trade between Niger and its WAEMU neighbouring countries. Exports (CFAF 11 billion) and imports (CFAF 40 billion) are mainly oriented towards Benin, Mali, and Togo. Benin and Mali are Niger's main trading partners and they represent more than 50% of cross border trade with Niger (Figure 9.9 and 9.10). It is worth noting that the aforementioned numbers cover only the WAEMU region, and Nigeria, which is also a key trading partner, is not a WAEMU member. Data on cross border trade with Nigeria are scarce. The Permanent Interstate Committee for Drought Control in the Sahel (CILSS) in partnership with USAID and professional national and regional organisations provide useful intra-regional trade flows in West Africa but only for agricultural products. Based on data collected on a daily basis at the borders and in strategic markets in the region, monthly reports are published to highlight cross border flows.[4] Figure 9.11 shows that these flows are dominated by millet/sorghum and maize.[5] The main sources of Niger's imports are Nigeria with 46% of maize imports and 92% of millet/sorghum imports and Burkina Faso with 40% of maize imports (Figure 9.12). Exports were valued at FCFA 2.83 billion in 2013 and are largely made up of cattle going to Nigerian markets.

---

[3] Official and informal.
[4] As a consequence, they do not reflect necessarily informal flows.
[5] These figures are based on 8 months and may be subject to some seasonal bias.

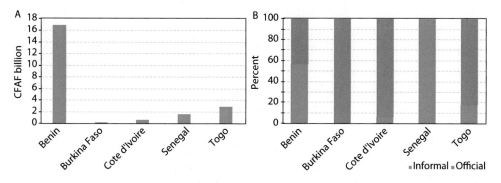

Figure 9.9. Exports to WAEMU; (A) informal flows, (B) formal and informal export flows in % (BCEAO, 2014).

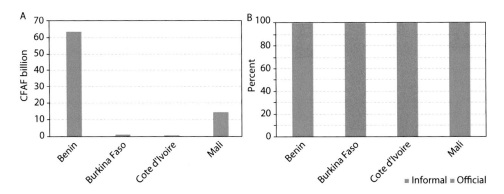

Figure 9.10. Imports from WAEMU; (A) informal flows, (B) formal and informal import flows in % (BCEAO, 2014).

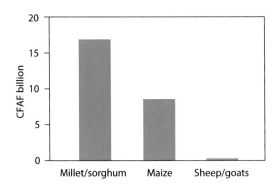

Figure 9.11. Cross border imports of agricultural products in 2013 (CILSS, 2013).

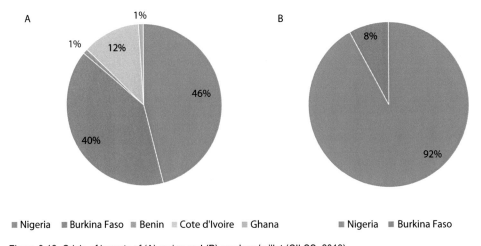

Figure 9.12. Origin of imports of (A) maize and (B) sorghum/millet (CILSS, 2013).

9.3.5 Tariff profile

Niger's tariff profile is similar to that of other developing countries. During the Uruguay Round and in its Schedule of Concessions LIII attached to the 1994 GATT, Niger bound all its tariff lines for agricultural products at 50 or 200% and for most non-agricultural products at 50%. The binding coverage is 96.7% of total tariff lines and 96.2% for non-agricultural products (Table 9.2). As a consequence, the average bound rates are particularly high (44.7%), especially for agricultural products (85.7%). However, like for almost all other countries, the applied Most Favoured Nation (MFN) rates are on average much lower: 11.9% and 14.6% for agricultural products.[6] Niger's binding coverage is however much higher than its neighbouring countries, in particular within WAEMU, with the exception of Senegal whose binding coverage is full.[7] There are no commodities in the schedule of agricultural concession covered by tariff quotas (Table 9.2). In terms of frequency distribution, most of the tariff lines (58.6%) are concentrated in the 15-25% range for agricultural commodities and in the 25-50% range for non-agricultural products (68.2%). Also, most of the bound tariffs fall in the 25-50% range and above 100% for agricultural products that are bound at 200% (Table 9.3). There is also a positive correlation between the level of imports and the level of tariffs, presuming a revenue maximising strategy.

For export markets and for its main trading partners, Niger does not face high tariffs (Table 9.4 and 9.5). In particular, as an Least Developed Country (LDC) it benefits from the 'everything but arms' initiative in EU markets. This situation will continue with the incoming EPAs. In the sub-region, as part of the WAEMU trade agreement, Niger's commodities enter duty-free and quota-free in WAEMU countries and now in ECOWAS countries. Niger benefits from the AGOA initiative of the USA. The low level of applied tariffs is confirmed in terms of commodities

---

[6] One should however be careful when comparing bound and applied tariffs as the binding coverage is not full.
[7] Share of HS six-digit subheadings containing at least one bound tariff line.

Table 9.2. Niger's tariff summary (WTO, 2014).

	Year	Total	Agricultural	Non-agricultural
Simple average final bound		44.7%	85.7%	38.2%
Simple average MFN applied[1]	2013	11.9%	14.6%	11.5%
Trade weighted average	2012	11.5%	13.9%	10.5%
Binding coverage	Total		96.7%	
	Non-agricultural		96.2%	
Agricultural tariff quotas (in %)			0%	
Agricultural special safeguards (in %)			0%	

[1] MFN = most favoured nation.

Table 9.3. Frequency distribution (WTO, 2014).[1]

		Tariff lines and import values (in %)							NAV
		Duty-free [0,5]	[5,10]	[10,15]	[15,25]	[25,50]	[50,100]	[100]	in %
Agricultural products									
Final bound		0	0.4	1.4	0	0.2	73.2	0.8	24.1	0
MFN applied	2013	0	26.2	15.2	0	58.6	0	0	0	0
Imports	2012	0	13.6	36.1	0	50.2	0	0	0	0
Non-agricultural products									
Final bound		0.7	11.8	6.4	5.2	4.0	68.2	0	0.0	0
MFN applied	2013	1.9	0.1	20.9	0	37.2	0	0	0	0
Imports	2012	6.8	29.8	34.3	0	29.1	0	0	0	0

[1] MFN = most favoured nation.

exported. With the exception of vegetables, Niger faces low tariffs. The preference margins are heterogeneous with respect to the main trading partners (Table 9.4) but they should be analysed with caution since a low preference margin (EU for instance) in a particular market may not necessarily indicate that Niger does not benefit from a lot of preferences in that market, but just the fact that the MFN rate applied by the trading partner is low.

Since April 2015 Niger has been applying the ECOWAS Common External Tariff (CET) which consists of five bands: 0% (essential social goods), 5% (goods of primary necessity, raw materials and specific inputs), 10% (intermediate goods), 20% (final consumption goods), and 35% for

Table 9.4. Duties faced and preference margins in main export markets (based on Laborde, 2014).

	Applied tariff	Preferential margins (MFN[2] - applied tariff to Niger)
EU	0	1.40
Nigeria[1]	27.48	6.83
Burkina Faso	0	16.27
Benin	0	17.25
Mali	0	17.47
USA	0.96	3.27
Japan	0.08	0.38

[1] Before ECOWAS CET.
[2] MFN = most favoured nation.

Table 9.5. Duties faced for main groups of commodities exported (based on Laborde, 2014).

	Live animals-	Vegetables	Ores (uranium)	Mineral oil and fuels	Precious metals
Applied tariff	3.12	30.57	0.00	1.17	0.01

some products to protect domestic infant industries.[8] The average tariff is 12.25% and is not significantly different from the WAEMU CET which was 12.1% (Table 9.6). However, with the introduction of the ECOWAS CET, Niger has violated some of its WTO commitments and in particular the 619 tariff lines that require Niger to either negotiate under articles XXIV: 6 and XVIII: 7 of GATT 1994 or ask for a special waiver under article IX: 3 or a negotiation at the regional level with a mandate given to ECOWAS.[9]

9.4 Trade institutional framework

The formulation and implementation of Niger's trade policy involves many actors and institutions. These institutions interact in a complex manner and it is not always easy to disentangle the responsibility of each one of them. There are however some general rules that can be mentioned. The Ministry of Trade and the Promotion of the Private Sector is Niger's main institution responsible for the country's trade policy. The ministry is mainly in charge of multilateral trade negotiations (WTO), plurilateral agreements (such as the EPAs with EU), regional trade agreements (WAEMU and ECOWAS)[10] and bilateral ones (such as the AGOA with the USA). The ministry serves as the focal point for the follow up on trade negotiations

---

[8] The difference relies on the introduction of the fifth band and some line rearrangements.
[9] See Section 9.5.1 about WTO.
[10] However, these two agreements – and particularly WAEMU – go beyond trade and the country is represented by the Ministry of Finance.

Table 9.6. Average ECOWAS CET rate for main commodities imported (based on Laborde, 2014).

	Average CET rate
Cereals	5.71
Machinery and mechanical appliances	6.75
Mineral products (lime and cement)	6.69
Sugars and sugar confectionery	13.50
Tobacco and manufactured tobacco substitutes	14.09
Animal or vegetable fats and oils	15
Worn clothing and worn textile articles	19.35

and is assisted by inter-institutional subcommittees on various topics (such as WTO follow up, trade facilitation and the Integrated Framework Steering Committee). Within the ministry, the General Directorate of trade and its subdivision (the Directorate of External Trade and Economic Partnership) are the key entry points for trade policy. The Ministry of Trade does not handle all aspects of Niger's trade policy. For example, in the case of most non-tariff measures, other ministries are involved. For sanitary and phytosanitary measures, the alignment of the domestic legislation with international standards recommended by the WTO agreement and by regional organisations is under the responsibility of the Ministry of Agriculture (Directorate of Plant Protection) for aspects related to plant protection and the Ministry of Livestock (Directorate for the Safety of Products of Animal Origin) for products of animal origin. In the same vein, the National Standardization Council (CNN) and particularly its executing body, the new National Board for Ensuring Conformity with Standards (AVCN) are responsible for standardisation, technical regulations and conformity issues for import and exports that could be raised under the Technical Barriers to Trade Agreement. The Ministry of Finance is also involved through its General Directorate of Customs. This Directorate is responsible for the implementation of the WTO custom valuation agreement and the regional regulations under WAEMU and ECOWAS related to the agreement. The General Directorate of Customs is also the administration that will be the most impacted by the TFA signed at the Bali Conference in 2013. Finally, the CCIAN is a key institution, which coordinates all legal and fiscal operations between authorities and economic agents. It is also the main interlocutor of the Importers and Exporters Union of Niger. The CCIAN also serves as the headquarters of the Single Window for Foreign Trade Formalities (GUFCE) and the Single Window for the Establishment of Enterprises. At these single windows, economic operators obtain registration forms needed for their custom clearance operations or for establishing a new enterprise.

9.5 Inventory of global and regional trade agreements signed by Niger

This section presents the main trade agreements signed by Niger that are governing its trade policy. International technical assistance issues are not addressed here, nor are bilateral agreements – the main one providing duty-free entry for Nigerien goods being with Tunisia.[11] Bilateral agreements are either not working or are being replaced by agreements between WAEMU and third countries.[12] The government of Niger has signed several trade agreements both at the international and at the regional level. The global level is dominated by the WTO but Niger also benefits from non-reciprocal preference agreements with the European Union (about to be replaced by the EPAs) and with the USA. At the regional level, Niger is a member of WAEMU and ECOWAS. We will first discuss multilateral level agreements and then discuss the regional agreements.

---

[11] Most of these agreements with other members of the WTO provide for the MFN regime.
[12] In addition to Tunisia, negotiations concern preferential trade agreements with Morocco and Algeria.

9.5.1 (Global) multilateral agreements – WTO

At the global (multilateral) level, Niger's trade policy is governed by the various agreements it has signed within the WTO framework. We focus here on the agreements that raise implementation challenges for Niger and those by which Niger can benefit from technical assistance, mainly through Technical Barriers to Trade (TBT), Sanitary and Phytosanitary (SPS) measures, custom valuation and the new TFA. It is also worth noting that due to lack of capacity to follow all the negotiations, there are only a few notifications done by Niger at the WTO and its last trade policy review goes back to 2009.

GATT-goods

Niger joined the WTO in 1996, after being a contracting party to the GATT starting in 1947 as a French overseas territory. For WTO negotiations, Niger is a member of the African, Caribbean and Pacific (ACP) Group, i.e. the least developed countries group, the African Group, the G-90 and the 'W-52' sponsors. Niger benefits from special and differential treatment provisions from its LDC status and from the generalised system of preferences (GSP). It applies the MFN tariffs to its WTO trading partners and has bound most of its tariff lines (more than 90%) but with no commitment in terms of domestic support regarding agriculture. As such, Niger is just committed to not exceed the *de minimis* level of the value of production in terms of domestic support. The country states that it does not grant any production subsidy (WTO, 2009).

With regards to prohibitions and products subject to licensing, according to Niger's 1998 WTO notification, following the liberalisation of trade in Niger in 1990, the licensing system was abolished with the exception of hydrocarbons trade and protected animal species and their by-products under CITES.[13] Niger also has an Import Verification Program (PVI) that it notifies the WTO on. Niger does not have domestic legislation on anti-dumping, countervailing or safeguard measures. These provisions are at the WAEMU level and comply with the provisions of the WTO Agreement. On the export side, Niger has not notified the WTO of any export subsidies but it introduced an export ban on seed cotton in 1998 to promote the development of the sector. Likewise, in the wake of the food crisis of 2005/2006, since 2005 Niger has (provisionally) banned the re-export of milled rice, millet, sorghum, maize, cassava flour, and cattle feed. However, these kinds of measures create uncertainties in the trading sector with potential harmful effects to consumers because of the disincentives that may reduce future supplies and raise domestic prices. Niger is not a member of the plurilateral agreements (such as the Agreement on Trade in Civil Aircraft and the Agreement on Government Procurement). Regarding disputes at WTO, no cases involved Niger as complainant, respondent or as a third party.

---

[13] The *Convention on International Trade in Endangered Species* of Wild Fauna and Flora.

Technical barriers to trade

The agreement on TBT, to which Niger is party to (in Annex 1A of the agreement establishing the WTO), entered into force with the establishment of the WTO in 1995. It contains provisions that ensure that regulations, standards, and testing and certification procedures do not create obstacles to trade. It is thus part of the broader non-tariff measures covered by the WTO. The agreement is based on the non-discrimination principle (between foreign and domestic products and between foreign producers) and strongly encourages members to use relevant international standards, guides or recommendations as the basis for their regulations and standards. Like many other agreements, the TBT agreement contains provisions for special and differential treatment for developing countries (article 12) and for technical assistance in implementation of the agreement, in particular the establishment of national harmonisation bodies and a system to help producers meet technical regulations (article 11). Transparency is the cornerstone of the agreement and it requires members to notify the WTO on how they intend to regulate a particular sector (at the draft stage) in order to achieve specific policy objectives and on the possible trade implications of their regulations. The agreement also requires the establishment of a point of contact which would answer enquiries from other WTO members.

According to its last trade policy review, Niger has a National Standardization Council (CNN) which adopted a new procedure for developing standards in 2002.[14] The Council is comprised of representatives of various government departments, the CCAIAN, consumer associations, importers and exporters and professional associations. Before adopting a technical regulation of the regime, the following steps are required: preparation of a draft standard by a technical committee, a public enquiry of the draft (two months), submission of the draft to the CNN for approval, submission of the draft to the Minister of Trade for endorsement, and the publication of the order approving the standard in Niger's official journal. However, it seems that no technical regulation was adopted in Niger under this regime and Niger's total number of notifications during the 1995-2014 period was zero.

In addition to the CNN, Niger also created AVCN in 2008 to facilitate compliance with the WAEMU regulatory framework that established the West African Accreditation Scheme.[15] This agency's role is to control the quality of imports and exports and attests their compliance with technical regulations. However, AVCN only started operating in April 2015 due to a lack of resources and application decrees. It ensures that international norms are applied when applicable, for example the International Organization for Standardization (ISO) norms, despite Niger being just a correspondent member of the ISO. Indeed, as an observer, Niger may adopt ISO's international standards nationally. When no international standards exist for a particular case, the AVCN applies sub-regional standards.

---

[14] Conseil national de normalisation.
[15] Agence nationale de vérification de conformité aux normes.

The AVCN does not handle the inspections itself. Due to Niger's low capacity to implement the controls, AVCN has two international subcontractors (SGS and Intertek) that act on its behalf. These two international private companies issue certificates jointly with the AVCN. Misunderstandings regarding the provisions of the system have often occurred between Nigerien importers and the AVCN on the cost of the certification which is ideally supposed to be paid by the provider based abroad. The Importers and Exporters Union of Niger is trying to solve this issue with Nigerien authorities but no agreement has been reached. The fact that only two companies are authorised to issue certificates is also a matter of contention between economic actors and national authorities.

Sanitary and phytosanitary measures

The SPS agreement is closely related to the TBT agreement since they are both related to non-tariff measures that could be an obstacle to trade. Given this closeness, Article 1.5 of the TBT agreement excludes SPS measures from its coverage. The SPS agreement applies in cases where the objective of the measure is related to specific risks related to the protection of human health (food safety) and animal/plant health or life. The agreement recognises the right of governments to apply sanitary and phytosanitary measures, but only for the aforementioned objective and in a non-discriminatory basis. Also, as for TBT, governments are strongly encouraged to base their measures on international standards, guidelines, and recommendations if they exist. This includes the *Codex Alimentarius* for food; the standards, guidelines, and recommendations developed under the auspices of the International Office of Epizootics for animals and the standards and recommendations of the Secretariat of the International Plant Protection Convention for plant health. If there is a scientific justification, a WTO member may introduce higher SPS standards. The SPS agreement contains provisions for control, inspection and approval procedures and for Special and Differential Treatment for least developed countries (article 10) as well as for technical assistance (article 9). LDCs such as Niger benefit from longer time-frames to comply with new measures when a concern is on a product of interest to the country (a significant share of its exports). LDCs are also granted a five year delay in the application of the agreement (article 14).

To date Niger has not made any notification to the WTO on its sanitary or phytosanitary regime. However, it established a national committee on SPS measures in 2010 under the authority of the Ministries of Agriculture and Livestock. Niger participates in the annual meetings in Rome held at FAO where SPS standards are discussed and revised. The sanitary controls for imports and exports and the quality of foodstuff consumed in Niger are under the 1993 Public Hygiene Code and under the 2004 framework law on livestock which deals with the sanitary control of animals and animal products to be imported, in transit or exported. Under the law, health certificates are required for imports and are issued for exports. The phytosanitary protection measures for plants, plant products, and seeds are decided by the Ministry of Agriculture (Direction of Plant Protection). Niger is a signatory to the International Plant Protection Convention and it recently adopted a new regulation for plant health, which modifies the 1995 law on plant health in compliance with international and sub-regional standards. The move towards international standards is also promoted at the sub-regional level by WAEMU Regulation No. 07/2007/CM/UEMOA of 6 April 2007 which defines a framework for plant and animal health and food safety. This regulation was transposed at the ECOWAS level in 2010 by regulation No 021. Regulation No 021 calls on ECOWAS member states to align their sanitary measures with international standards and recommendations, such as those of the *Codex Alimentarius* (recommended by the SPS agreement) and the Cartagena Protocol on Biosafety. As a consequence, Niger adopted a decree (No 617) in 2011 to align its national legislation accordingly. This decree defines the new legal framework and was followed by three orders that specify the official government agencies that oversee the sanitary controls and the official control posts.

It is worth noting that despite the efforts made by Niger on SPS issues, the country has had difficulties in complying with SPS measures applied by its trading partners, in particular specifications regarding its exports of agricultural products (mainly livestock products). Some attempts to export livestock products to Asia and South Africa have failed due to Niger's inability to comply with these measures. With the creation of the AVCN which relies on the *Codex Alimentarius* as recommended by the SPS agreement, the issue is now how exporters will be able to comply with the standards.

As with TBT issues, since April 1, 2015 the AVCN has been in charge of the certification process for exports and imports for sanitary issues in collaboration with the international subcontractors. The challenges observed for the technical quality of products are also present in the case of SPS measures in terms of misunderstandings between economic agents and the AVCN.

Custom valuation

Custom valuation deals with the implementation of article VII of GATT 1994 and in particular how to estimate the value of goods at customs. The objective of GATT 1994 is to define a fair and uniform valuation system of goods in order to avoid arbitrary custom values. Article VII stipulates that the primary basis for customs valuation of imported goods should be 'the transaction value' which is given by 'the price actually paid or payable for the goods when sold for export to the country of importation' with potential adjustments for some specific costs incurred by the buyer but not included in the price actually paid or payable for the imported goods. It also makes provisions for differing methods of valuing goods when the customs value of the imported goods cannot be determined by the transaction value defined above.

As a developing country, Niger has benefited from a delay in the implementation of the Customs Valuation Agreement (Article 20.1 and Paragraph 1 of Annex III of the Agreement). Although Niger started applying the Customs Valuation Agreement in 2001, it has had some difficulties in implementing it and has instead opted for WAEMU's reference values, minimum values for cross-border trade, and export and re-export unit values. However, the application of the minimum values is only for small values at cross border offices. For the remaining (large) operations, Niger relies on WAEMU regulation 5-99 which conforms to the Customs Valuation Agreement signed in 2001. The ECOWAS regulation of 9/2/2013 is also largely inspired by the WAEMU regulation and complies with the Agreement.[16] The main issue is that Niger's cross border offices do not have the necessary telecommunications infrastructure to connect with the central office.

GATS-services

Regarding the services sector, Niger has made specific commitments in the hotel and restaurant services, travel agency services, tour operator services, tourist guide services, and some transport services but not in telecommunication services or financial services. It has made commitments for consumption abroad of lodging establishments, restaurants, travel agencies and tour guides (WTO, 2009). The supply of services (commercial presence and the presence of natural persons) is subject to some limitations defined by the ministries involved on a discretionary basis.[17] Professional services are also excluded from Niger's commitments under GATS.

Trade-related aspects of intellectual property rights

With regards to the Trade-Related Aspects of Intellectual Property Rights (TRIPS) Agreement, Niger has signed the revised Bangui Agreement on the African Intellectual Property Organization (OAPI) that entered into force in 2002 and whose terms of protection are defined in accordance with the WTO TRIPS Agreement and have been notified at the WTO. Niger has taken advantage of the transition period granted to LDCs under Article 66 of the TRIPS Agreement and which was extended in 2005. For copyright matters, which are governed by Niger's domestic laws, the regime for copyrights has not yet been aligned with the TRIPS agreement.

Trade facilitation agreement

At the Bali ministerial conference in 2013, WTO members concluded negotiations on a TFA. The new agreement was then inserted into Annex 1A of the WTO Agreement following the protocol of an Amendment adopted in November 2014. The agreement, which is still under the legal review process by countries, will enter into force once two-thirds of members have ratified it. The TFA consists of three sections and contains numerous provisions regarding expediting the movement, release and clearance of goods, and cooperation between customs (Section I). This will require the publication and the availability of information (in particular through the internet) about procedures for importation, exportation and transit; applied rates of duties and taxes; import, export or transit restrictions or prohibitions; penalty provisions for breaches of import, export, or transit formalities; and rules for the classification or valuation of products for customs purposes. The other measures are related to advance rulings, procedures for appeal or review, disciplines on fees and charges, and control and inspections. The second section – which

---

[16] According to Custom authorities, in case of a minor conflict between WAEMU and ECOWAS regulations, the latter prevails.
[17] Otherwise referred to as Mode 4.

is important for Niger – contains provisions on the special and differential treatment (SDT) that allow developing and least developed countries to determine first when they will implement individual provisions of the Agreement (Category A and B provisions) with a transitional period for category B provisions. It also identifies provisions that will be implemented once the countries have received technical assistance and support for capacity building (Category C provisions).

The last section contains provisions on the establishment of a permanent committee on trade facilitation at the WTO, but also requires members to have a national committee to facilitate domestic coordination and implementation of the provisions of the Agreement. As an LDC, Niger will benefit from additional flexibilities in implementing the provisions of the agreement once they enter into force. These four additional flexibilities consist of:

1. An early warning mechanism. This allows a country to request an extension from the WTO Trade Facilitation Committee if it experiences difficulties in implementing a provision in Category B or C by the date it notified to WTO. The required extension would be automatic if the additional time requested does not exceed 3 years.
2. An expert group. In case a requested extension has not been granted and the country lacks capacity to implement the agreement, the Trade Facilitation committee will establish an Expert Group to examine the issue and to make a recommendation on the way forward.
3. A shifting between categories. This allows the country to shift provisions between Categories B and C.
4. A grace period. This protects LDCs during disputes. Once the agreement enters into force, the LDC will not be subject to the Dispute Settlement Understanding for a period of 6 years for Category A provisions and 8 years for Categories B and C.

Niger is interested in trade facilitation and the country created a national trade facilitation committee in April 2009. It has already determined, with the assistance of the WTO, the different categories for trade facilitation measures. Of the 41 measures that the agreement will require, 8 have been classified under the A category, 10 under the B category and 23 under the C category (See Table 9A.2 in the Appendix for a detailed analysis). The time required to implement the B category measures has been estimated at 3 years. For the C category measures that will formally require assistance before implementation, the necessary time varies from 1 to 5 years: two measures will require 1 year, 12 will require 3 years and the remaining 9 measures will require 5 years. Out of all the measures, Niger is requiring assistance in terms of human resources for 18 measures, infrastructure and equipment for 13 measures, and information and communications technology for 19 measures.

It is worth noting that the lack of human and financial resources has held back Niger's effective participation in all WTO related activities. Thus, Niger and other West African countries are trying to coordinate their positions on several topics (such as agriculture) within WAEMU which has an ad hoc observer status at WTO and ECOWAS trade negotiations. This is a crucial issue as each country was negotiating unilaterally. This lack of coordination has had practical consequences; for instance, with the introduction of the ECOWAS CET, Niger has violated its WTO commitments (a total of 619 violations).[18] This will require Niger to negotiate under articles XXIV: 6 and XVIII: 6 of GATT 1994 or a special waiver under article IX: 3 or to negotiate at the regional level under the mandate given to ECOWAS.[19] At the country level, the renegotiation seems possible with regards to Niger's LDC status.[20] The country is also seeking further technical assistance in the implementation of the agreements in various areas, including the harmonisation of laws, regulations and rules with WTO obligations and those covering notifications. Even though Niger participated in the Integrated Framework program, it has not made any noteworthy progress due to domestic political problems and the lack of coordination among Nigerien participants (WTO, 2009).

9.5.2 Regional agreements

At the regional level, Niger is a founding member of various organisations whose rules govern its trade policy. These organisations include the African Union, ECOWAS and WAEMU.

African Union

Niger is a founding member of the Organization of African Unity (OAU), the predecessor of the African Union (AU). The AU does not govern Niger's trade policy, but the African Economic Community instituted by the AU Treaty of Abuja in 1991 (and entered into force in 1994) aims at integrating all the sub-regional economic communities of the continent by 2034. The process is designed to go through six stages: (1) the strengthening of existing regional economic communities and the creation of regional blocs where they do not exist; (2) the stabilisation of tariff and non-tariff barriers and internal taxes; (3) at the level of each regional economic community, the establishment of a free trade area and then a customs union with a CET; (4) co-ordination and harmonisation of tariff and non-tariff systems among the various regional economic communities with a view to establishing a customs union at the continental level; (5) the establishment of an African common market; and (6) consolidation of the common market for the setting up of an African Monetary Union, the establishment of a single African Central Bank and the creation of a single African currency. Under ECOWAS, Niger has already reached the third stage which is expected to become effective in 2017 for all sub-regions in Africa. The fourth stage is expected to become effective in 2019 at the continental level (African Union, 1991).

The Economic Community of West African States

Niger is also a founding member of ECOWAS, a group of 15 countries, founded in 1975 with the aim of promoting economic integration among its member states. The main institutions

---

[18] This is not the case for Niger only. Other countries such as Mali, Burkina Faso and Côte d'Ivoire have the same problem.
[19] This raises other issues. See Section 9.5.2 on ECOWAS.
[20] Niger could build on Gabon's experience on this issue which managed to renegotiate in 2008 its schedules of commitment, invoking its 'small and vulnerable economy' status.

governing ECOWAS are the Commission, the Parliament, the Court of Justice and the Bank of Investment and Development. ECOWAS' goal is to start with a free trade area and end with a common market with a common currency.

With regards to trade, in the wake of the ECOWAS Trade Liberalization Scheme (ETLS) that started in 1979, the process of moving from a free trade area towards a custom union in the region is ongoing and Niger is following this pattern. The process started with agricultural products and was extended to industrial products in the 1990s. To that end, a common certificate of origin was approved in 2003, harmonised with that of WAEMU to address the issue of industrial products entering the region. Thus, it provides a preferential treatment of unprocessed local and handicraft products from other ECOWAS countries. For processed products, provided that they have been sufficiently developed and fulfil the rules of origin, they can benefit from preferential treatment (WTO, 2009). The free trade area scheme is, however, not fully operational as some barriers are still present in terms of cross border regulation, customs clearance processes and roadblocks.

In the case of the customs union, Niger and other ECOWAS countries were supposed to start applying the CET of the region on January 1, 2015. However, due to some technical issues, Niger only started applying it in April. After a series of adjustments, the last version of the CET was adopted by ECOWAS Heads of State at a summit in October 2013 in Dakar and was officially launched on December 15, 2014 during the Abuja summit of ECOWAS Heads of States. The ECOWAS CET is in essence modelled after the previous WAEMU CET and its extension to include a fifth tariff band of 35%. In the same vein, Niger will adopt a 10-digit Regional Tariff and Statistical Nomenclature based on the World Customs Organization Harmonized System. Thus, the CET is defined at the HS-10 digit level and includes 5,899 products. Also, before the harmonisation of community levies takes place, Niger will continue to apply the CET under WAEMU. As previously mentioned, with the introduction of the CET, Niger registered 619 violations of its WTO commitments that will require further negotiations at the WTO (see section 1 on WTO). In addition to the custom duties and the community levy, a statistical tax of 1% will also be applied.

To ease the transition towards the CET, some Supplementary Protection Measures (SPM) designed to help members to adjust to a lower tariff structure and to serve as safeguard measures were adopted by ECOWAS member states in 2013. These measures consist of an Import Adjustment Tax (IAT) and a Supplementary Protection Tax (SPT) that can be applied to non-ECOWAS trading partners. The maximum rate of the IAT is the difference between the MFN rate applied by the country and the CET and can be applied to a maximum of 3% of tariff lines, for five years. Since the IAT is notified, in force for a period of less than 10 years and should not exceed the bound tariffs, it complies with WTO rules. The SPT can be applied if (1) 'the increase in volume of imports of a product entering the customs territory of a member state during any year equals or exceeds 25% of the average import volume during the last three preceding years for which data are available', and (2) 'the average cif import price during any month, priced in domestic currency, falls below 80% of the average cif import price of the last three years' (ECOWAS, 2013). Member states can freely choose the SPT rate according to their commitments at the WTO; however, the maximum MFN duty (including the IAT) should not exceed 70% and cover a period not exceeding two years.

The objective of ECOWAS is to create a monetary union using a common currency, the Eco. However, this requires, first, the creation of a West African Monetary Zone (WAMZ) for countries that do not belong to WAEMU. The creation of WAMZ has not yet materialised. The other important challenge has been the effective coordination of a regional trade policy between ECOWAS countries and with the WAEMU group of countries. In particular, the introduction of the fifth band at 35% resulted in violations of WTO commitments by many WAEMU countries. As previously mentioned, Niger, like other countries, will have to either renegotiate its commitments or give ECOWAS the mandate to negotiate on its behalf and come up with bounds defined at the regional level. The latter option is problematic as it requires that ECOWAS be formally identified as a customs union at WTO, which in turn requires the application of the principle of free circulation, only taxing commodities at the point of entry into the union, and having a redistributive system of tariff revenues such that landlocked countries are not significantly hurt by the removal of tariffs. The other challenge with this option is due the different statuses of ECOWAS countries in terms their stage of economic development. While Niger is an LDC, other countries such as Côte d'Ivoire or Nigeria are not. So it would be difficult to operate under an LDC status for ECOWAS as a whole (Article XXIV of GATT 1994 and Enabling clause). Due to these issues, Niger, like other West African countries, has already started the renegotiation process of its bound tariffs at the WTO.

The West African Economic and Monetary Union

Niger is a founding member of the WAEMU and has been a member since 1994. WAEMU is a customs and currency union between members of ECOWAS that share the same currency, the CFA franc. In addition to the convergence of national macroeconomic and sectorial policies, one of the main objectives of WAEMU is the establishment of a common market with free movement of goods, labour, services, and capital. The institutions governing WAEMU are the Council of Ministers, the Commission (the executive branch), the Court of Justice, the Court of Auditors, the Inter-Parliamentary Committee, and two specialised institutions: the BCEAO and the West African Development Bank.

With regard to trade, WAEMU started operating as a customs union on January 1, 2000; the union has a bearing on Niger's trade policy. As such, unprocessed local products from the union going to Niger are exempt from customs duties and taxes, and so are processed goods as long as they fulfil the common rules of origin adopted in 2003. The same free trade regime applies to quantitative restrictions. In addition to the WAEMU CET, Niger applies the harmonised taxation scheme at its borders to VAT, excise duty and petroleum products (WTO, 2009). The CET applied by Niger consists of four bands: 0, 5, 10, and 20% and is applied to import commodities from other WAEMU countries based on custom values.[21] In addition to the CET, Niger also applies a 1% Community Solidarity Levy that goes toward the union's budget as well as a 1% statistical charge. A Community Solidarity Levy of 0.5% is also levied by Niger within ECOWAS. In addition, Niger may subject commodities from other WAEMU members to a special import tax and to a Degressive Protection tax that is determined by the Council of Ministers. However, except for rice from 2000 to 2002 for which Niger applied a special import tax, these measures have never been applied and the degressive tax regime ended in 2006 (WTO, 2009). Also, the special import tax was not compatible with the WAEMU agreement on agriculture (Article 5).

It is important to note that Niger's trade policy is largely governed by WAEMU, which has a strong influence over its group of countries' common trade policy. Thus, the agreements signed by WAEMU impact Niger's economy. As such, Niger is part of the trade and investment agreement between the WAEMU Commission and the United States of America that was signed in 2002. It will also be a part of the ongoing negotiations between WAEMU and Morocco, Tunisia and Algeria on various preferential agreements.

In addition to trade, Niger's WAEMU membership implies the harmonisation of most of its national legislation (both government and the private sector) and its agricultural, mining, energy and competition policy with those of the Union. For instance, WAEMU's quality program aimed at developing a regional accreditation, standardisation and quality promotion system will imply that Niger aligns its sanitary measures to international standards, and in particular, the *Codex Alimentarius,* and the SPS and TBT Agreements of the WTO (Section 9.5.1 on WTO). In addition, Niger participates in trade negotiations with the EU through the WAEMU Commission and ECOWAS (e.g. in concluding the EPA).

9.5.3 Relations with the USA

Niger receives a non-reciprocal preferential treatment from the USA under the AGOA that was established in 2000 and under its subsequent extensions (AGOAI-IV). Under AGOA, almost all commodities (theoretically more than 6,000) from Niger are granted duty-free and quota-free access to the US market with the noticeable exception of apparel. AGOA actually expands the benefits under the Generalized System of Preferences Program (GSP) by covering more products and by including additional eligibility criteria beyond those in GSP. Niger is also eligible for the special provision (Third Country Fabric) allowing it to source inputs for apparel from countries other than AGOA beneficiaries. Although this provision expired in 2012, it was extended for three years up to September 2015.

The legislation establishing AGOA is due to be reviewed this year by the US government and is expected to be renewed. It may appear as though Niger is not taking advantage of the provisions of AGOA given its exports valued at less than US$89,000 in 2009 (WTO, 2009). The

---

[21] The same four bands adopted by ECOWAS.

exports mainly consist of arts and crafts. However, Niger temporarily lost its AGOA eligibility in 2010 after an alleged undemocratic change of government in the country. Moreover, the main challenge cited by Nigerien exporters to the USA has to do with their inability to comply with quality measures and standards of the US market. US importers often require various tests for impurities and that are be conducted only in a selected number of reference laboratories (often outside Niger). Niger's ability to export traditional apparel to the USA is also limited by this requirement. The fact that preference is unilaterally granted at the discretion of the USA makes exporting to the USA somewhat unpredictable for Nigerien exporters. This has been raised by Niger's exporters union as a major challenge affecting their investment plans.

9.5.4 Agreement with the European Union: from the Lomé conventions to the EPAs

Niger is part of the African, Caribbean and Pacific (ACP) group of countries with which the European Union (EU) concluded the ACP-EU Partnership Agreement, signed in Cotonou in 2000 to replace the Lomé Convention which dates back to the 1970s. The agreement was designed to cover a 20-year period (2000-2020). The Cotonou agreements are aimed at replacing the non-reciprocal trade preferences under the Lomé Convention with new WTO compatible trading arrangements (through EPAs) with a period of transition that ended on December 2007. However, because Niger is an LDC, it has benefited from the Everything But Arms (EBA) initiative since the end of the period of transition, starting in January 2008. Under EBA, all its products (mainly uranium) enter EU markets duty-free and quota-free except for arms and ammunition.[22] By signing on to the EPAs, Niger may not be much better off, given the loss of tariff revenue it may face. In turn, this will likely result in Niger reducing its public expenditures or increasing domestic taxes with possible welfare losses and no preference margin for its exports to EU.

With regard to signing a regional EPA, Niger relies on the ongoing negotiations between the EU with both ECOWAS and WAEMU. The three parties reached a final agreement in 2014 that is currently under consideration by West African policymakers. Nonetheless, the agreement was formally endorsed at a summit of ECOWAS Heads of State and Government held in Abuja, Nigeria on December 15, 2014.[23]

Niger has not yet ratified the EPA. However, this may be only a matter of time as the agreement has been endorsed by ECOWAS Head of State. In its current version, the EU has agreed to open its market to all West African products as soon as the agreement enters into force. The EU has also committed itself not to subsidise any of its agricultural exports to West Africa. In exchange, West African countries will gradually remove tariffs over a 20-year period for 75% of their trade with EU. They will also have more flexibility in terms of foreign components in their exports to Europe by using materials sourced from other countries without losing the benefit of free access

---

[22] The exceptions which were bananas, sugar and rice that were lifted in 2009 did not concern Niger.
[23] The Conference explicitly called for the signing of the Agreement and its ratification by all Member States. The main concerns are being raised by Nigeria. Niger should sign the agreement in all likelihood.

to the EU market. West African countries will keep the possibility of protecting their market for sensitive products by keeping current tariffs or by imposing safeguard measures when necessary. Finally, the agreement gives room for future negotiations on services and the EU has committed to support West African countries with €6.5 billion in development assistance during 2015-2020. As an LDC, Niger should be a key target for this fund. It is worth noting that most of the sensitive products for West African countries, including Niger, have been excluded from the liberalisation process. This is the case for onions, peas, beans, citrus fruit, rice, groundnuts and oil, preparations of meat, fish or crustaceans, cane or beet sugar, most vegetables prepared or preserved, some man-made filaments and staple fibres, cotton, and cigarettes.[24] On the export side, Niger's situation remains fundamentally the same in terms of market access but with more flexible rules of origin.

9.6 Agreements active for key trading partners

This section provides a brief description of Niger's relations with its key bilateral trading partners. Given the dozens of agreements that may be active in these partner countries, the most critical issue is the preference erosion for Niger when it manages to diversify its exports beyond minerals.

9.6.1 International partners

At the international level, Niger's key trading partners for exports are France, which accounts for more than 34% of Niger's total exports, and the USA, which receives 9% of Niger's exports (BCEAO, 2014). With regard to the EU, the Union has 33 active free trade agreements covering both goods and services (WTO, 2013) and all regions. Beyond these agreements it has also granted unilateral preferences to many developing and least developed countries and it is that component that is relevant for Niger. These preferences fall under the EU Generalized System of Preferences (GSP) scheme, which consists of three arrangements: the standard GSP, the GSP+ and the Everything But Arms (EBA) initiative. The standard GSP grants tariff preferences to eligible developing countries, while the GSP+ provides additional tariff reduction to the so-called 'vulnerable' countries provided that they implement international conventions in human rights, good governance and sustainable development. As mentioned earlier, the EBA initiative offers duty-free and quota-free access to EU markets for all products except arms and ammunitions from LDCs. This is the actual status for Niger.

Since Niger is part of the ACP group and France is a member of the EU, the relations between the two countries are governed by the Cotonou Agreement and will remain under the new EPAs that the West African Region is about to sign with the EU. It is now almost certain that this agreement will take place (see previous section). The EU is also negotiating with other regions (Table 9.7) and is about to sign an EPA with the South African Development Community (SADC) EPA

---

[24] This list is not exhaustive.

Table 9.7. Overview of regional EPA negotiations (EU DG Trade, 2018).

Regions	Status of the negotiations
West Africa	An agreement was concluded in June 2014 and the final document endorsed by ECOWAS Heads of States in July 2014 for signature.
South African Development Community (SADC) EPA Group	An agreement was concluded in July 2014 and the final document is under scrutiny for signature.
East African Community (EAC)	An agreement was concluded in October 2014 and is under scrutiny for signature.
Eastern and Southern Africa (ESA)	Negotiations are still ongoing. Mauritius, Seychelles, Zimbabwe and Madagascar signed an interim agreement in 2009 which has been provisionally applied since 2012.
Central Africa	The negotiations are still ongoing. Cameroon is the only country of the region to sign an interim agreement in 2009 and to ratify it in 2014.
Pacific	Talks are still ongoing. Papua New Guinea signed an interim agreement in July and Fiji in December 2009. Papua New Guinea ratified in May 2011 and Fiji is provisionally applying the agreement since July 2014.
Caribbean	An EPA between EU and CARIFORUM (including trade in services) was signed in October 2008.

Group[25] and the East African Community (EAC).[26] However, this may not fundamentally change Niger's position in EU market as most of these countries already benefit from preferences or will enter an EPA. The other developing countries that do not have an EPA will automatically fall under the GSP. According to the new EU GSP scheme, trade preferences will be removed for middle income countries in 2016. Indeed, the new GSP scheme will concentrate the preferences on a few countries, since among the 176 beneficiaries, 34 have better preferential access under other trade arrangements and 20 were classified as high or upper-middle income countries by the World Bank.

Regarding the United States, most of Niger's trade is governed by the MFN regime and unilateral preferences that are declining. To date, the USA has 14 active bilateral or regional free trade arrangements (WTO, 2014). The developing and middle-income countries covered by these agreements are Colombia, Costa Rica, the Dominican Republic, El Salvador, Guatemala, Honduras and Nicaragua (CAFTA). The USA also continues to grant unilateral preferences to a number of developing and least developed countries under the GSP scheme and AGOA, with the least preferential coverage given for textiles and apparel. The US GSP has been USA's main global program for preferences granted to developing and least developed countries. However, the program expired in July 2013, leaving imports that used to benefit from GSP provisions subject to MFN tariffs starting in August 2013 with the exception of GSP-eligible imports from

---

[25] Botswana, Lesotho, Mozambique, Namibia, South Africa and Swaziland.
[26] Burundi, Kenya, Rwanda, Tanzania, and Uganda.

AGOA beneficiary countries that continue to receive eligible GSP duty-free treatment. The other unilateral preferences mainly concern the Caribbean Basin Economic Recovery Act (CBERA) and the US-Caribbean Basin Trade Partnership Act (CBTPA) that provide duty-free access to the US market for a limited number of goods from certain countries in the Caribbean and Central America, including now textiles from Haiti.

For Niger, its relations with the USA are governed by AGOA which is expected to be renewed this year. It remains to be seen whether or not the USA will bilaterally or multilaterally give additional preferences to other competing countries (besides Niger) which would result in a preference erosion for Niger. However, most of Niger's potential competitors are already under AGOA or another preferential agreement. Thus, these competitors will not benefit from more preferences in the future which would yield an erosion of preferences for Niger.

9.6.2 Regional partners

At the regional level, Nigeria, Benin, and Côte d'Ivoire are Niger's main trading partners, which respectively make up 4.1, 2.3 and 1.0% of Niger's total exports. It is worth noting that these shares should be taken with caution as there is a high level of informal trade between West African countries. Like Niger, both Benin and Côte d'Ivoire are members of WAEMU and ECOWAS. Therefore, their trade policies are fully aligned with Niger's in terms of both tariffs and non-tariffs measures. Although Nigeria is not a WAEMU member, it now shares the same trade policy with Niger under the new ECOWAS (customs union) pattern. It is worth noting that most of the rules active in ECOWAS (including the CET) are previous WAEMU rules. Also, for all West African countries, all previous bilateral trade agreements will be gradually replaced by agreements between either WAEMU or ECOWAS and third countries.

9.7 Niger's capacity to implement trade commitments and to take advantage of trade opportunities

9.7.1 Implementation record

Niger's record on implementing its various trade agreements has been mixed. Regarding tariff measures, at the sub-regional level, Niger started applying the WAEMU CET in 2001, and the ECOWAS CET that should have been applied in January 1, 2015 has been effective since April 2015. At the multilateral level, Niger has bound most of its tariff lines and had not violated these commitments until the introduction of the ECOWAS CET. The ECOWAS CET resulted in a violation of 10% of Niger's bound tariffs and thus the country has started fixing this issue by negotiating at the WTO. With regards to non-tariff measures, the results are mixed. One important thing to note is that for non-tariff measures, most of the regulations adopted at the sub-regional level are designed to comply with international standards recommended by WTO agreements. This is particularly the case for custom valuation, TBT and SPS measures. On customs valuation, Niger applies 'the transaction value' for most of its procedures. For some small operations at the border offices, it applies WAEMU reference values. So there is still some work to be done before the custom valuation agreement is fully implemented.

In terms of standardisation, technical regulations, and SPS measures, Niger has also made considerable progress. A National Standardization Council (CNN) as well as a National Committee on SPS Measures have been created and the AVCN has been in place since April 2015. This board grants certificates for both technical quality standards and SPS related issues. The country has also adapted its legislation to comply with international standards such as the *Codex Alimentarius* and the norms of the International Plant Protection Convention.

One of the main challenges ahead of Niger, in addition to the full implementation of previous agreements, will be in implementing the new TFA which will enter into force once it has been ratified by two-thirds of WTO members. The implementation of the TFA will require a lot of effort by Niger and thus the country will need assistance to fully implement the agreement.

9.7.2 Main obstacles to implementation

As the previous subsections have highlighted, there is still some work to be done before Niger fully implements all its trade commitments. Several factors are holding the country back while many factors are preventing it from fully taking advantage of the preferences granted to it. Very often these two aspects are interrelated.[27]

Lack of internal capacity

The main obstacle that Niger faces in fully implementing its various commitments is the lack of internal capacity in terms of human resources, equipment, and financial resources. The lack of human resources (both in terms of number of people and in terms of technically qualified people) is pervasive at all levels. A key challenge is the country's inability to follow and to participate in all WTO trade negotiations in Geneva. Even if representatives of Niger are able to travel to Geneva, it lacks the resources, like many other developing countries, to fully participate in trade negotiations. Before ECOWAS and WAEMU received the mandate to negotiate as a group on behalf of their member countries, inadequate human capacity was a particularly major shortcoming. The lack of human resources also affects the implementation of trade agreements by executing agencies. At the Ministry of Trade level, there is need to build human capacity for trade negotiation, economic policy formulation, and analysis and in English language communication skills. The TFA will require experts in electronic trade, who would help establish a legal framework for electronic trade. Capacity will also need to be developed in the line of customs which will be highly impacted by the agreement. Within the AVCN, there is need to build internal capacity for conducting inspections which is currently lacking in

---

[27] For instance, the lack of an up-to-date legislation and of good reference laboratories to comply with SPS measures may prevent the country from exporting to EU or US markets even if Niger has a preferential access to these markets.

both quantitative and qualitative terms. The agency needs more inspectors that are technically qualified to conduct inspections that are currently carried out by subcontractors.

The low levels of investment in trade equipment are a major hindrance to the implementation of trade agreements within both the private and public sectors. Within the public sector, the lack of appropriate equipment for inspections is impacting the work of Niger's AVCN, the customs agency, and the Ministry of Trade. The AVCN does not have the equipment for sampling and analysing imports and exports and therefore relies on subcontractors. In addition to not having the needed laboratory equipment, the AVCN lacks physical infrastructure (buildings). Moreover, with no regional offices across Niger, AVCN needs vehicles to go around the country conducting inspections. The Customs Administration at the border needs telecommunications equipment to connect to their central database at the headquarters to apply the transaction value and to comply with the WTO Customs Value Agreement. This need will be exacerbated by most provisions of the TFA that demand telecommunications and in particular those relating to electronic payments (see Appendix Table 9.A2). For the TFA to be implemented effectively, good road and transport infrastructure will also be required. Niger's Ministry of Trade will also need improvements in its information and communication technology infrastructure to comply with the TFA. For instance, the agreement requires that a large amount of information be made available through the internet; this infrastructure is not available at present. Niger's private sector lacks certified laboratories and companies that are needed by economic actors. For most certifications required by EU and USA importers, Niger's exporters must rely on private laboratories outside Niger to certify their goods, which is costly and results in higher priced goods.

Lack of trade related information

Most of trade agreements and the preferential market access granted to Niger are not well known or well understood at the local level by economic actors. The CCIAN, which serves as an interface between authorities and economic actors and delivers certificates of origin, does not always manage to communicate with all importers and exporters across Niger. This has resulted in limited communications between CCIAN and Nigerien importers' and exporters' union. The latter are not always aware of trade related legislation and only have broad knowledge of the required standards for export markets. Also, the AVCN is not well known and often has conflicts with importers and exporters on the pricing of inspections. The importers' and exporters' union lacks the financial resources required to disseminate among its members information about trade regulations and standards.

Supply side constraints

Like many developing countries, Niger faces supply side constraints that affect its capacity to address challenges associated with implementing trade agreements. A 2008 diagnostic trade integration study and the last trade policy review by the WTO in 2009 highlighted some of these challenges, such as the poor quality of the infrastructure (road and transport) needed to transport goods to markets and export centres, which is particularly harmful for a landlocked country like Niger. The high cost and intermittence of the energy supply and poor telecommunications also hinder production of goods and services, which results in higher prices of goods and undermines the country's competitiveness. Lack of access to credit is another challenge faced by Nigerien economic operators especially given high interest rates for borrowing money. Moreover, most operators still work on an informal basis even with respect to access to finance.

9.7.3 Political will and risks to meet trade liberalisation commitments in key trading partner countries

Niger does not present a high political risk in not meeting the trade liberalisation commitments it has made with its trading partners. As highlighted in the section about the WTO, regarding disputes at the WTO, no cases involved Niger as complainant, respondent or third party. The authorities have put in place the legislation and the institutional framework to meet most of the commitments and the main issue is related to the lack of resources not the political will of Nigerien authorities. During the review process, none of the trade agreements were condemned by current authorities. The EPAs with the EU were the only agreement that could have been an issue. However, since this agreement has been signed at the ECOWAS level, its enforcement is easier. Niger does not face high political risks either in its main trading partner countries. This is true at both the global and the regional levels and in particular in the case of AGOA.

9.7.4 Multilateral and plurilateral level

If a WTO member state does not comply with its commitments and discriminates against Niger's products, Niger has legal recourse it can take. Nonetheless, such a scenario has not arisen as there have been no dispute cases involving Niger as complainant, respondent, or third party. Niger's relationships with the EU will now be governed by the EPA. The risk that the EU will not meet its commitments is small and it has already granted Niger the 'Everything But Arms' preferences that were more generous than the EPA. As with the former EBA mechanism, the main issue here relates to the rules of origin and standards that Niger will have to fulfil in order to have duty-free, quota-free access to the EU markets.

In the case of AGOA, the risk that the US does not implement its commitments is rather low despite the legislation regarding AGOA needing to be renewed every year. However, its need for renewal can create uncertainty and hinder investment by economic agents. The fact that apparel is not covered is detrimental to Niger, whose traditional apparel sector is claiming to be a part of the agreement, but not a risk per se. This is just a point of discussion between the parties. Niger also faces the risk of becoming ineligible under AGOA if there is for example a non-constitutional regime change in the country.

9.7.5 Regional level

At the regional level, Niger's main trading partners are all members of WAEMU or ECOWAS and thus Niger is in a customs union with its main trading partners. The countries share the same trade regulations, rules and norms. Theoretically, there is no risk that WAEMU or ECOWAS will go back to pre-union statuses with trade barriers between countries. A more likely scenario is that of WAEMU disappearing into ECOWAS, the larger economic block, and all WAEMU countries giving ECOWAS the mandate over their trade policy.

Within the West Africa sub-region there are several factors that hinder trade. For example, economic agents, including those from Niger, are often faced with cross border harassment especially at customs agencies. The harassment is an obstacle to trade that needs to be tackled. Nigerien traders have in the past questioned customs procedures imposed on its goods by port authorities in its neighbouring countries. For example, in the case of Benin, Nigerien importers have reported that authorities at the Cotonou Port tax their products as if their final destination was Benin when in fact they were only transiting through Benin. Nigerien importers are therefore asking to be refunded their costs due to the higher taxation, claiming that Benin's port has violated international and WAEMU agreements. As Benin has in the past justified its taxation practices, the two countries are still trying to find a resolution to the matter.

9.8 Conclusions and recommendations for international support

Niger is a poor landlocked country which has gone through major economic changes over recent years. Despite unstable economic growth, its GDP almost tripled over the last fifteen years. Niger's international trade remains concentrated in a few commodities and the recent discovery of oil has not fundamentally changed the landscape.

An assessment of Niger's commitments under the various trade agreements it has signed shows mixed results. Regarding tariff commitments, with the exception of the recent introduction of the ECOWAS CET, the country has not violated any commitments, particularly in terms of MFN treatment. Niger has also made progress in the case of its non-tariff commitments by changing its legislation and putting in place the institutions need to implement the commitments. There is still some work to be done as not all the agreements have been fully implemented. Inadequate human capacity, poor infrastructure, telecommunications, and trade equipment as well as supply side constraints are the main obstacles to implementing commitments in trade agreements. Niger is need of international technical support in these areas to help it achieve the objectives of its various agreements.

The capacity of the AVCN needs to be enhanced particularly in addressing TBT and meeting SPS measures. The AVCN has been operating with support from the EU which is due to end in 2016. The AVCN plays a key role in guaranteeing the conformity of Niger's imports and exports with international agreements. By applying international standards to the country's exports, AVCN helps to protect Niger from any legal action by other WTO members. It also facilitates trade and helps exporters to comply with international standards. The agency will need vehicles, improvements in its telecommunications equipment, and a strengthening of its human and institutional capacities to enable it to take over the quality control and sanitary inspections currently done by international subcontractors. The AVCN would benefit greatly from the establishment of regional offices in order to reduce transaction costs for importers and exporters. The capacity of the private sector and private laboratories involved in the certification of goods could be strengthened to ensure conformity of their procedures with ISO norms. The capacity of producers to meet norms, grades and standards also need to be strengthened through trainings and information campaigns about the standards in Niger's main trading partners.

Niger's customs will also need be improved/strengthened to better comply with the custom valuation agreement and to implement all the incoming measures associated with the TFA. This will require improvements in equipment (including information and telecommunications) as well as human resources capacity with the necessary technical qualifications (see Appendix Table 9.A2 for a detailed analysis of the needs).

Niger's Ministry of Trade will be strongly involved in the implementation of the TFA. Therefore, the ministry's human capacity needs to be strengthened to ensure it has highly qualified trade experts to support the TFA, as well as the formulation of trade policies and negotiations. The one expert that has been appointed by the International Organization of La Francophonie to help Niger in designing its trade policy will need to be supported by one or two other trade experts within the ministry. The ministry will also need experts in electronic commerce to set up the legal framework for the electronic commerce component. The ministry need to set up an internet infrastructure to make publicly available the measures covered by the TFA so that domestic and foreign economic actors have the same information in a non-discriminatory basis.

Although this chapter did not cover supply side constraints such as those due to poor road and transport infrastructure in detail, they need to be addressed to enable Niger to take advantage of its various agreements. They may very well be a key condition for the implementation success of some of Niger's agreements and in particular the TFA. Table 9.8 summarises the main weaknesses that were found during the study and lists recommendable actions to address them.

Table 9.8. List of recommendations.

Institutions/agents	Weaknesses	Recommendations
AVCN	• Lack of human resources both quantitatively and qualitatively • Lack of appropriate equipment (vehicles and laboratory infrastructure) to proceed to the controls • Misunderstandings between the Agency and economic agents, especially importers, about the procedures • Limited number of international subcontractors	Build a program that will strengthen the capacities of the AVCN in implementing the TBT and SPS measures by: • Increasing the number of inspectors • Training inspectors to conduct the controls • Providing more vehicles and inspection equipment • Building regional offices throughout the country • Encouraging partnership between AVCN and foreign firms • In the very short term: open access for more providers to offer inspection services
Ministry of trade	• Lack of human resources (experts) in trade policy formulation and analysis • Absence of the electronic infrastructure to fully implement all the provisions of the TFA	Build a program that will: • Provide assistance to the Ministry in designing trade policies and trade negotiations through training programs and hiring of international experts • Help the Ministry define a legal framework for electronic commerce with the assistance of an international expert • Help the Ministry set up a platform to make publicly available the measures covered by the TFA
Customs	• Lack of telecommunication equipment in border offices • Lack of ICT equipment to fully implement the TFA • Training needs to fully implement the provisions of the TFA	Build a program that will support the institution in: • Providing telecommunications equipment to connect border offices to the headquarters • Providing assistance in infrastructure and equipment (including ICT) in the topics covered by the TFA • Providing trainings in all the topics covered by the TFA
Private sector	• Misunderstandings of the formal procedures for importing or exporting goods • Limited knowledge of the quality and sanitary standards in force in key trading countries • Difficulty in complying with quality and sanitary standards	• Help the CCIAN build information and communications infrastructure to make economic actors and unions aware of the legislation • Support private sector (particularly traders' unions) capacities to comply with SPS measures through trainings • Help the CCIAN and AVCN through trust building activities between them • Support private companies to set up traceability processes
Private laboratories	• Lack of capacity (equipment and certification) to do for Niger's exporters the tests required to fulfil the SPS and technical measures in force in Niger's trading partners' markets	• Help private laboratories involved in the certification process with accreditation in accordance with ISO norms

References

African Statistical Yearbook (ASY), 2014. African Statistical Yearbook 2014. African Development Bank, the African Union and the United Nations Economic Commission for Africa. Available at: http://tinyurl.com/ycmkjl23.

African Union, 1991. Treaty Establishing The African Economic Community, Addis Ababa, Ethiopia. Available at: http://tinyurl.com/y9wzjfu8.

BCEAO, 2012. Annuaire Statistique 2012, Dakar, Senegal.

BCEAO, 2013. Balance des Paiements et Position Extérieure Globale. Niger 2013. Dakar, Senegal.

ECOWAS, 2006. Decision A/Dec.17/1/O6 Adopting The ECOWAS Common External Tariff. ECOWAS Official Journal 48.

ECOWAS, 2009. Supplementary Act A/SA 1/06/09 Amending Decision A/Dec.17/04/06 Adopting The ECOWAS Common External Tariff', ECOWAS Official Journal 55.

ECOWAS, 2013. Special Protection Measures (SPM) Regulation C/REG 1/09/13.

ECOWAS, 2014a. Final Communique: Forty-Fifth Ordinary Session of the Authority of ECOWAS Heads of State and Government. No. 134/2014, Accra, Ghana. Available at: http://tinyurl.com/ycw5kevh.

ECOWAS, 2014b. Final Communique: Forty-Sixth Ordinary Session of the Authority of ECOWAS Heads of State and Government. No. 248/2014, Abuja, Nigeria. Available at: http://tinyurl.com/y9yecodq.

EU DG Trade, 2018. Overview of economic partnership agreements. European Commission, Brussels, Belgium. Available at: http://tinyurl.com/y7ktof3y.

European Commission, 2014. Economic Partnership Agreement with West Africa. Facts and figures. tradoc_152694. Available at: http://tinyurl.com/y98enfr3.

Office of the United States Trade Representative, undated. The African Growth and Opportunity Act. Available at: http://tinyurl.com/y7c4abbc.

UEMOA, 1994. Traite Modifie De L'union Economique et Monetaire Ouest Africaine, Ouagadougou, Burkina Faso. Available at: http://tinyurl.com/y9gbvnmj.

UEMOA, 1999. Règlement N° 05/1999/CM/UEMOA portant valeur en douane des marchandises, Ouagadougou, Burkina Faso. Available at: http://tinyurl.com/ycb8quby.

UEMOA, 2007. Rapport annuel de la Commission sur le fonctionnement et l'évolution de l'Union, Ouagadougou.

WTO, 1994. General Agreement on Trade in Services. Niger: Schedule of Specific Commitments. WTO, Geneva, Switzerland.

WTO, 2003. Trade Policy Review. Report by the Secretariat. Niger. WTO, Geneva, Switzerland.

WTO, 2009. Trade Policy Review. Report by the Secretariat. Niger and Senegal. WTO, Geneva, Switzerland.

WTO, undated. Situation of schedules of concessions in goods. Available at: http://tinyurl.com/yae7sx35.

World Bank, 2015. World Development Indicators 2015. World Bank, Washington, DC, USA. Available at: http://tinyurl.com/oejaw9t.

Appendix 9.

Table A9.1. List of institutions visited and persons interviewed.

Agence de Vérification et de Conformité aux Normes (AVCN)
Mr. Bako Illiassou, Directeur Général

Chambre de Commerce d'industrie et d'artisanat du Niger (CCIAN)
Mr. Oumarou Mamoudou, Chef Service Guichet Unique des formalités du commerce extérieur Mr. Mani Chaibou, Chef
    du département Promotion des échanges

Syndicat des importateurs et exportateurs du Niger
Mr. Chaïbou Tchiombiano, secrétaire général

Direction Générale des Douanes
Colonel Attaher Baba, Directeur de la règlementation et des relations internationales

Ministère du commerce et de la promotion du secteur prive
Ms. Aichatou Mamadou, Directrice Générale du Commerce
Mr. Hamadou Karidio, Directeur du commerce extérieur et du partenariat économique
Mr. Basile AWASSI, Conseiller national pour les négociations commerciales internationales

Direction Générale de la Protection des Végétaux
Ms. Alimatou Douki, Directrice de la Règlementation

Direction de la sécurité sanitaire des produits d'origine animale
Mr. Mahamane Majitaba, Chef de la Division inspection et contrôle qualité

Table A9.2. Classification of measures and assistance needed under the Trade Facilitation Agreement (Ministry of Trade).

Article	Title	Category	Timing/transitional period[1]	Assistance in capacity building (human resources)	Assistance in infrastructure and equipment (including ICT)
1.1	Publication	C	3 years	-	-
1.2	Information available through internet	C	3 years	Yes	-
1.3	Enquiry Points	C	1 year	Yes	-
1.4	Notification	C	1 year	Yes	
2.1	Opportunity to Comment and Information before Entry into Force	C	1 year	-	-
2.2	Consultations	A	-	-	-
3.1	Advance Rulings	B	3 years	Yes	
4.1	Procedures For Appeal Or Review	A	-		
5.1	Notifications for enhanced controls or inspections	C	5 years	Yes	Yes
5.2	Detention	B	3 years	Yes	Yes
5.3	Test Procedures	C	5 years	Yes	Yes
6.1	General Disciplines on Fees and Charges Imposed on or in Connection with Importation and Exportation	A	-	-	-
6.2	Specific disciplines on Fees and Charges for Customs Processing Imposed on or in Connection with Importation and Exportation	A	-	Yes	
6.3	Penalty Disciplines	B	3 years	Yes	Yes
7.1	Pre-arrival Processing	C	3 years	Yes	Yes
7.2	Electronic Payment	C	-	-	-
7.3	Separation of Release from Final Determination of Customs Duties, Taxes, Fees and Charges	A	-	-	Yes
7.4	Risk Management	C	5 years	Yes	-
7.5	Post-clearance Audit	B	3 years	Yes	Yes
7.6	Establishment and Publication of Average Release Times	C	3 years	Yes	Yes
7.7	Trade Facilitation Measures for Authorized Operators	C	5 years	-	Yes
7.8	Expedited Shipments	B	3 years	-	Yes
7.9	Perishable Goods	B	3 years	-	-
8	Border Agency Cooperation	C	3 years	Yes	Yes
9	Movement of Goods Intended for Import under Customs Control	B	3 years	-	Yes
10.1	Formalities and Documentation Requirements	B	3 years	Yes	-
10.2	Acceptance of Copies	C	3 years	-	-

Table A9.2. Continued.

Article	Title	Category	Timing/transitional period[1]	Assistance in capacity building (human resources)	Assistance in infrastructure and equipment (including ICT)
10.3	Use of International Standards	C	3 years	Yes	-
10.4	Single Window	C	5 years	-	-
10.5	Preshipment Inspection	C	5 years	Yes	Yes
10.6	Use of Customs Brokers	B	3 years	-	Yes
10.7	Common Border Procedures and Uniform Documentation Requirements	C	3 years	Yes	Yes
10.8	Rejected Goods	B	3 years	-	Yes
10.9	Temporary Admission of Goods and Inward and Outward Processing	A	-	-	-
11.1-3	Regulations and formalities regarding transit	C	3 years	-	Yes
11.4	Enhancement of non-discrimination	A	-	-	-
11.5-10	Procedures and controls regarding transit	C	3 years	Yes	Yes
11.11.1-5	Guarantees	C	5 years	Yes	Yes
11.12-13	Cooperation and coordination	C	5 years	-	Yes
12	Customs Cooperation	C	3 years	Yes	Yes
13.2	National Trade Facilitation Committee	A	-	-	Yes

[1] Only B and C categories require a delay/transitional period.

Chapter 10.
Assessing the socioeconomic impact of ECOWAS CET implementation in Niger

Ismaël Fofana

IFPRI-Dakar, Titre 3396, Lot #2, BP 24063 Dakar Almadies, Senegal; i.fofana@cgiar.org

Abstract

The fifteen Member States of the Economic Community of the West African States (ECOWAS) adopted on October 2013 a Common External Tariff (CET) with the aim of strengthening and accelerating regional integration. Niger is among the first countries to implement the ECOWAS CET scheme on April 2015. This study assesses the ex-ante economic impact for Niger of a successful implementation of the CET scheme by the fifteen Member States. It uses fifteen single-country computable general equilibrium models interconnected through the trading of commodities and the mobility of labor and capital. A welfare improving impact is simulated for Niger. Custom union is welfare improving if the benefits of trade creation overcome the costs of diverting trade. Indeed, Niger expands its trade with both ECOWAS and non-ECOWAS partners more rapidly under the CET compared to the continuity, i.e. CET scheme not implemented.

Keywords: CET, trade, welfare, economic, modelling

10.1 Introduction

Regional integration is a dynamic process of establishing a unified larger entity from individual countries. There are different steps in the process (preferential trade agreement, free trade area, customs union, common market, economic and monetary union, etc.) and the establishment of a Common External Tariff (CET) is a crucial step towards further regional integration. There are benefits and costs of joining a custom union through the establishment of a CET.

Trade creation and trade diversion effects of a custom union have been extensively studied since the pioneering work of Viner (1950).[1] Trade creation is welfare improving while trade diversion has a negative effect on welfare. Trade diversion and trade creation effects are considered as static effects of a customs union compared to the dynamic effects as introduced by Balassa (1961). The latter include, among others, increased competition among member countries, economies of scale, and increased productivity through the spread of new technology. A customs union is welfare improving for a given country if the benefits of trade creation overcome the costs of diverting trade.

---

[1] Meade (1955), Lipsey (1957), Bhagwati (1970), and Michalopolou and Tarr (1997), among others, have also investigated the welfare impact of custom union.

This chapter assesses the benefits and costs of a successful implementation of the Economic Community of West African States (ECOWAS) CET by its fifteen Member States, with a focus on Niger. A review of Niger's existing global and regional trade agreements indicates an implementation of the ECOWAS CET by Niger in April 2015. Moreover, Niger and other West African countries are about to establish an Economic Partnership Agreements with the European Union and are discussing other free trade agreements with other trading partners. The West Africa region is also involved in multilateral trade discussions and agreements under the World Trade Organization.

The analysis uses the ECOWAS Simulation Model (ECOSIM) to assess the implementation of the ECOWAS CET scheme in its fifteen Members States. ECOSIM is a multi-country computable general equilibrium (CGE) model developed by the International Food Policy Research Institute (IFPRI) for the ECOWAS member states. The model interconnects the fifteen ECOWAS economies through the trading of commodities and the mobility of production factors, i.e. labour and capital.

This chapter gives an overview of ECOWAS countries' intra- and extra-regional trade features. The results of a ten-year projection of regional trade under CET is presented and discussed. The CET simulation scenarios are built country-by-country with a special focus on Niger. The direct fiscal impact is measured for the fifteen ECOWAS countries. The economywide simulations of the CET allow the economy to adjust to the trade shock and provide useful insights regarding the direct and indirect impact of the trade reform on the ECOWAS countries with a focus on Niger.

10.2 ECOWAS trade profile

The ECOWAS economies are classified into four groups according to their contribution to intra-regional trade. The latter is measured as the share of the country's intra-ECOWAS trade in the total ECOWAS trade flows. Countries that trade the least, including Nigeria, Cote d'Ivoire, Ghana and Liberia, have 4 to 6% of trade with the region. Countries that trade moderately, including Burkina Faso, Guinea, Benin, Cape Verde, and Togo, have around 20% of trade with the region. Countries that trade the most, including Sierra Leone, Gambia, Guinea Bissau, Mali, Senegal, and Niger, have 25-35% of trade with the region.

ECOWAS countries, in particular Togo, Burkina Faso, Ghana, Niger and Cote d'Ivoire, trade more agricultural than non-agricultural products. Agricultural goods are less traded by Sierra Leone, Gambia, Senegal, and Benin. Niger shows the highest share of intra-regional trade in total trade flows, 35% for all traded products with other ECOWAS countries and 46% for agricultural products. Thus, Niger appears to be the most trade-integrated country in West Africa in terms of share of intra-regional trade in countries total trade flows. However, Niger accounts for 3% in the total imports into the region and 6% of regional food imports according to a report by ENDA – CACID in 2012. In addition to fuel which is the most important imported product, Niger buys fruits from Nigeria, Ghana, Cote d'Ivoire and Burkina-Faso, cereals from Benin,

Nigeria, Burkina Faso, Mali, Togo, Ghana and Cote d'Ivoire and manufactured food products from Benin, Nigeria, Togo Cote d'Ivoire and Senegal. The share of Niger exports represents 2% of the intra-regional exports. It rises to 6% if one takes account of re-exports (ENDA-CACID, 2012). The country exports mainly live animals, 69% of its regional exports, primarily to Nigeria and Benin and re-exports roots and tubers derivatives and some seeds and fruits to Nigeria according to the same report.

10.3 Analytical framework

A multi-country simulation model is built up for the fifteen ECOWAS member States to assess the impact of the ECOWAS CET. The ECOWAS simulation model (ECOSIM) follows the tradition of multi-country CGE models developed to assess regional integration policies. Similar models have been developed by, among others, Hinojosa-Ojeda *et al.* (1995) for the analysis of the North America Free Trade Agreement (NAFTA) and Lewis and Robinson (1996) to assess the impact of regional trade liberalisation in Indonesia. Following this tradition, ECOSIM is organised in two components: the country models which follows the standard single-country CGE archetype, and the regional modules that specify the interactions among country models.

ECOSIM integrates two blocks of countries with different degrees of integration: The West African Economic and Monetary Union (WAEMU) consisting of eight countries and the ECOWAS grouping fifteen countries, including the eight WAEMU countries. WAEMU member countries have abolished internal tariffs on goods and services (free trade area), adopted a CET against the rest of the world (customs union), extended the free movement of goods and services to labour and capital (common market), and adopted one single currency and a set of fiscal and monetary rules (economic and monetary union). ECOWAS is a free trade area and has recently adopted a customs union which is an extension of the WAEMU CET.

Although country models are the cornerstone of the ECOSIM framework, the relationships among the fifteen ECOWAS economies, on the one hand, and the eight WAEMU economies, on the other, are captured trough additional features. Regional specificities that apply to the ECOWAS region include the following. The existence of multiple trading partners; these partners exchange goods and services among themselves through import and export flows. The standard small country assumption does not apply to the regional trade of goods and services and the openness of countries to regional trade is lower than their openness to trade with non-ECOWAS countries due to multiple cross-country barriers. Labour mobility is greater within a country than between countries and there is a mismatch between the location of factor employment and the location of expenditure of factor income.

The WAEMU countries, as well as being member states of ECOWAS, have succeeded in promoting economic integration through the adoption of a CET and customs union and joint regulatory measures and policies. One interesting feature of the WAEMU common currency is the pooling of 6% of the member states reserves and an overdraft facility on the central bank operations account maintained with the French treasury (Zafar, 2005). This has major implications for the current account constraint of the economies of the union. Domestic savings and investments are less likely to move across countries than within countries, and there is a positive relationship between flows of foreign investment and economic performance. The following section discusses further the above-mentioned features of the regional integration processes in West Africa within the ECOSIM framework.

10.3.1 ECOWAS trade

ECOSIM establishes trading relationships among the ECOWAS economies (country models) at two levels. It distinguishes two categories of partners: other ECOWAS countries (ECOWAS) and non-ECOWAS countries (ROW). The small country assumption is subsequently relaxed for goods and services traded within the ECOWAS region. The regional trade module allows for determining regional prices of goods and services traded among countries by linking export demand addressed to the region to imports from the region.

10.3.2 ECOWAS labour mobility

The model does not specify intraregional flows of labour across countries. It considers various categories of labour face demand constraints in every country. Thus, the excess supply of labour makes the analysis of intraregional mobility of labour less relevant. The assumption is that newcomers add to the large pool of unemployed and underemployed individuals in the host country. The probability of newcomers finding employment is relatively low compared to the local population. The macroeconomic consequences of the intraregional mobility of labour are thus relatively weak. However, labour mobility across the region can be interesting with further disaggregation of labour categories and labour markets by country and the integration of different skill-level markets.

10.3.3 WAEMU external current account

By pooling part of their reserves, the eight WAEMU countries are partially interconnected through their external current account and real exchange rate. Current accounts of WAEMU countries exhibit extra-transfers of capital with other member States. Transfers revenues to and payments of individual countries are equal to the difference between endogenous balances generated from the WAEMU aggregate external account balance and the external account balance of individual countries.

10.3.4 WAEMU saving-investment constraint

WEAMU countries have adopted a common monetary policy and, consequently, a common interest rate policy. Therefore, a single interest rate that reconciles the aggregate supply of investment (savings) and the aggregate demand for investment applies within the WAEMU region. Domestic savings and investments are less likely to move across countries compared to within countries. Capital transfers are reflected in individual country models through the aggregate savings-investment closure rule. Capital transfers among countries are given by the differences between national supply and regional supply.

10.4 ECOWAS trade outlook

The projection of the ECOWAS countries' economic growth and external trade are discussed in this section. It serves as the reference or baseline scenario also known as the business as usual scenario. In the reference scenario, real income growth is the main driver of the change in aggregate demand and, therefore, the change in intra-ECOWAS trade pattern. The analysis uses the ECOWAS Simulation (ECOSIM) model. The baseline scenario provides a projection of the gross domestic product (GDP) growth rates for the fifteen ECOWAS economies over the period 2015-2025 (Table 10.1). Niger appears to be among the high-performing group of economies with an average annual growth rate close to 6%. Changes in a country's GDP level are driven by capital accumulation and labour force growth (Table 10.1). The country-specific labour force

Table 10.1. Average annual increase of capital and gross domestic product (GDP) 2015-2025, reference scenario (%) (simulation results).

	Capital	GDP
Benin	7.5	5.0
Burkina Faso	6.6	4.5
Cape Verde	6.1	5.4
Gambia	4.8	3.4
Cote d'Ivoire	6.3	5.2
Ghana	6.8	5.6
Guinea	5.9	3.9
Guinea Bissau	7.3	2.6
Liberia	4.3	3.5
Mali	4.1	4.1
Niger	10.0	5.8
Nigeria	8.9	7.0
Senegal	9.2	5.2
Sierra Leone	7.5	4.0
Togo	6.8	3.9

grows at an exogenous rate.[2] Capital accumulation is closely linked to the initial investment level given by the social accounting matrices[3] and the past GDP growth rates.

Table 10.2 shows baseline projections of household gross income, consumption price index (relative)[4], and public and private consumption for Niger. The latter are the main drivers of the demand for goods and services and, thus, the external trade pattern. Declining price index and rising gross income boost real incomes and rapid increase in private final consumption. Public consumption is assumed to grow at the population growth rate, i.e. it is constant in per capita terms.[5]

Niger's trade performance improves under the reference scenario. The country trade openness increases with the non-ECOWAS countries while it stagnates with the ECOWAS countries (Figure 10.1). Non-ECOWAS imports and export prices are fixed, i.e. the small country assumption. In contrast, prices in Niger and within the fifteen ECOWAS countries are determined through the market clearance mechanisms. Under the reference scenario, domestic prices fall compared to non-ECOWAS prices making Niger's economy more competitive vis a vis non-ECOWAS partners (Figure 10.2). However, Niger becomes less competitive vis-à-vis the ECOWAS partners as its domestic prices fall less than the ECOWAS average prices. Therefore, exports by Niger towards non-ECOWAS partners increase substantially while its exports towards ECOWAS partners decline slightly (Table 10.3). However, ECOWAS imports by Niger increase faster than non-ECOWAS imports.

---

[2] The labour force growth rate is estimated using the World Development Indicators database.
[3] The SAM for Niger is built for year 2004 and updated to 2009. Data from the World Development Indicator (World Bank, 2017) and the Africa Statistical Yearbook (Anonymous, 2017) show not significant change in the structure of the economy between the 2009 SAM and the average of 2004-2014 period).
[4] Changes in consumption price index are measured against fixed international price index which serve as the 'numeraire' in the model.
[5] This closure rule is desirable as the analysis does not measure the welfare impact of variation in public expenses.

Table 10.2. Annual variation of income and consumption in Niger, reference scenario (%) (simulation results).

	2016	2017	2018	2019	2020	2021	2022	2023	2024	2025
Gross income	1.8	2.9	3.7	4.2	4.7	5.0	5.4	5.7	6.1	6.4
Consumption price index	-2.2	-1.5	-1.1	-1.1	-0.7	-0.7	-0.6	-0.7	-0.5	-0.4
Private consumption	3.5	4.1	4.6	5.0	5.3	5.6	5.9	6.2	6.5	6.8
Public consumption	3.5	3.5	3.5	3.5	3.5	3.5	3.5	3.5	3.5	3.5

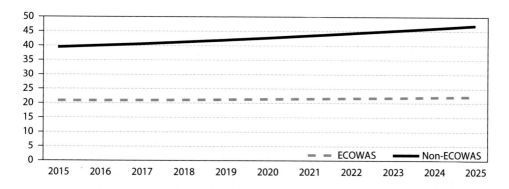

Figure 10.1. Niger trade openness, variation 2015-2025 under the reference scenario (%) (simulation results). Trade openness is measured by the ratio of imports and exports to GDP.

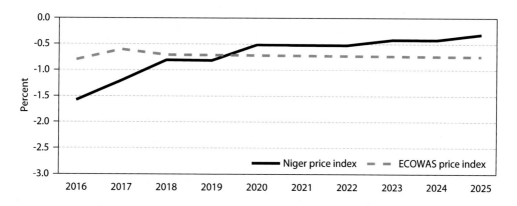

Figure 10.2. Price indices, variation 2015-2025 under the reference scenario (%) (simulation results). The price indexes are the average weighted market clearance price in Niger, and the average weighted market clearance prices in the fifteen ECOWAS countries.

Table 10.3. Niger imports and exports with ECOWAS and non-ECOWAS partners, variation 2015-2025 under the reference scenario (%) (simulation results).

	2015	2016	2017	2018	2019	2020	2021	2022	2023	2024	2025
ECOWAS											
imports	9.8	10.0	10.1	10.3	10.4	10.6	10.8	11.0	11.2	11.4	11.6
exports	11.0	10.9	10.9	10.8	10.8	10.8	10.7	10.7	10.7	10.6	10.6
Non-ECOWAS											
imports	30.6	30.3	30.2	30.3	30.4	30.5	30.7	30.9	31.1	31.3	31.6
exports	8.9	9.7	10.4	11.0	11.6	12.2	12.8	13.4	14.1	14.7	15.4

10.5 ECOWAS CET impact simulation

The trade data (prices and trade flows) used in the study are extracted from WITS (World Integrated Trade Solution) database.[6] The computation of the tariff rates before and after the implementation of the ECOWAS CET by product and country is undertaken at a disaggregated level (6 digits of the Harmonized System, HS6 for pre-CET tariffs and tariff line level[7] for the CET) before their aggregation into seven categories of products[8] that are of interest to the simulations.[9] Tariff rates used by the analysis are actual applied rates (most favoured nation or preferential if there is a trade agreement between the two partners). The aggregate rates correspond to the average rates weighted by volume. However, aggregate tariff revenues (aggregated value duty) are calculated by summing individual tariff lines (and not through the computed aggregated rates). Thus, tariff revenues do not include the community solidarity levy nor the statistical tax levied on various products. The most recent year of tariffs and trade data available for 2012 for most countries are used. In some cases, the trade year is different from the tariff year in which case the nearest tariff year (before or after) is used.

Under the CET scenario, the ECOWAS average tariff rate remains slightly unchanged (Figure 10.3). Including Niger, tariff rates decline in all countries except Ghana, Cape Verde, and Togo. The average tariff rates decline by 2.5% in Niger.

---

[6] The WITS database is developed by the World Bank in collaboration with the International Trade Centre, the United Nations Statistics Division and the World Trade Organization. It includes bilateral trade and tariff information for over 170 countries.
[7] The tariff line for the CET uses 10 digits.
[8] Rice, staple crop, cash crop, livestock and fish, silviculture, mining and quarrying, and manufacturing.
[9] The average changes computed for the seven categories of products are applied to products included in these categories and highlighted by the ECOWAS countries' SAMs. This version of ECOSIM is calibrated on fifteen SAMs which dimensions range from 6 to 12 categories of industries and the same number of products.

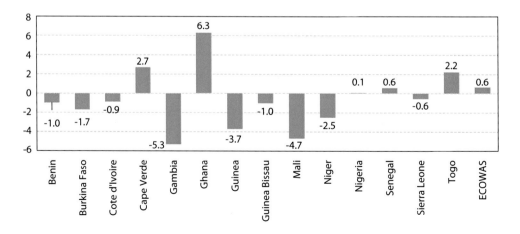

Figure 10.3. Average import tariff rates, variation before and after CET (%) (WITS, 2014).

Table 10.4 shows that the implementation of the ECOWAS CET in Niger translates into: increasing tariff rates for rice and cash crops and decreasing tariff rates for other staples products, and forestry and silviculture products and mining and quarrying products. There is no substantial change in tariff rates for livestock and fishery products and manufactured products.

Manufacturing products contribute for 58.3% of total imports by Niger. The contribution reaches 92.3% when mining and quarrying products are added up. Niger primarily imports crude oil from Nigeria which is exempt from tariff payment. Thus, with the decline of the average tariff rate for manufacturing goods, a decline in tariff revenues is expected in Niger under the CET scenario. Indeed, Niger is among the four countries (including Mali, Gambia and Guinea) expecting a decline in tariff revenues as depicted by Figure 10.4. On the other hand, custom

Table 10.4. Effective tariff rates for Niger, variation before and after CET (WITS, 2014).

	Change in average tariff rates (%)	Imports share in 2012 (%)
Rice	20.6	2.4
Other staples	-3.9	1.1
Cash crops	11.8	1.7
Livestock and fishery	0.5	1.8
Silviculture and forestry	-7.2	0.7
Mining and quarrying	-5.8	34.0
Manufacturing	-2.0	58.3
All	-2.5	100.0

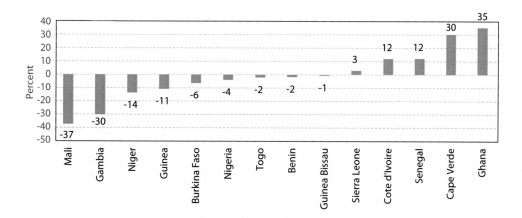

Figure 10.4. Tariff revenues, variation in aggregated duty value, before and after CET (WITS, 2014). Change in tariff revenues as share of initial tariff revenues.

revenues are expected to increase in Ghana, Cape Verde, Senegal, and Cote d'Ivoire. Slight changes in tariff revenues are recorded for Burkina Faso, Nigeria, Togo, Guinea Bissau and Sierra Leone.

As manufacturing goods represent more than half of Niger's imports and given the small variation in their tariff rates for manufactured goods (average -2.0%) the study does not go into analyses and discussions of trade diversion and trade creation and related welfare effects The study rather focuses on the induced fiscal effect and government response and, thus the impact on the Niger's economy.

10.5.1 Trade effects

Figure 10.5 shows a gradual acceleration of the intra-ECOWAS trade under the implementation of the CET as compared to the reference scenario (i.e. absence of CET) over a ten-year period. The expansion is more pronounced for agricultural products compared to non-agricultural products. In contrast, agricultural trade (imports and exports) with non-ECOWAS decelerates under the CET scenario as compared to the reference scenario.

Niger expands its trade with both ECOWAS and non-ECOWAS partners more rapidly under the CET scenario compared to the reference scenario (Figure 10.6). Although Niger trade with ECOWAS and non-ECOWAS partners accelerates under the CET implementation, the trend between the intra and extra ECOWAS trade remains the same as in the reference scenario. Indeed, trade with non-ECOWAS partners increases at a faster pace than the intra-ECOWAS trade for all goods, including agriculture. One can explain the latter results by the small variations in ECOWAS prices under the CET scenario as compared to the reference scenario (Figure 10.7).

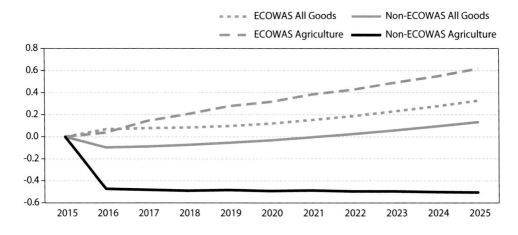

Figure 10.5. ECOWAS intra and extra trade, variation between CET and reference scenarios (%) (simulation results).

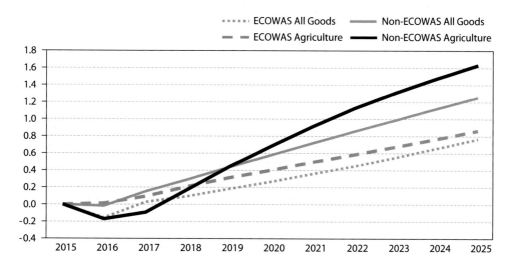

Figure 10.6. Niger's trade with ECOWAS and non-ECOWAS partners, variation 2015-2025 between CET and reference scenarios (%) (simulation results).

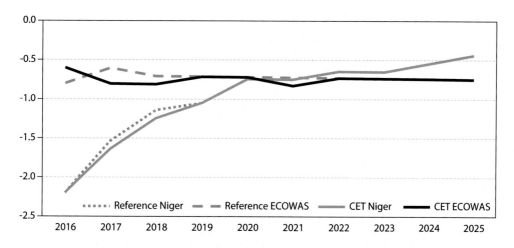

Figure 10.7. Prices indices, variation under the CET and reference scenarios (%)(simulation results). The price indexes are the average weighted market clearance price in Niger, and the average weighted market clearance prices in the fifteen ECOWAS countries.

The modest decline in tariff rates for manufacturing goods explains the slower acceleration of imports from non-ECOWAS countries compared to the rapid acceleration from ECOWAS countries (Figure 10.8). Furthermore, imports by Niger from ECOWAS countries increase much faster than its exports to the region. Thus, Niger's trade balance with ECOWAS countries tends

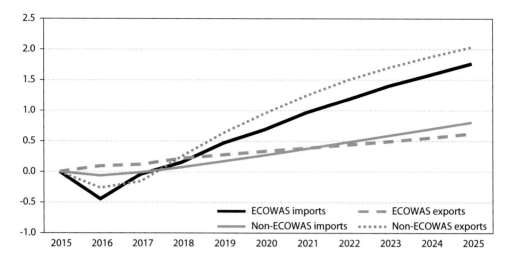

Figure 10.8. Changes in agricultural trade growth under CET compared to baseline, Niger (simulation results).

to deteriorate gradually under the CET as compared to the baseline. On the other hand, Niger's trade balance with non-ECOWAS partners improves as the increase of its exports to the latter group of countries accelerates faster than its imports from the same group of countries.

10.5.2 Fiscal and welfare impact

The major concern of governments with respect to the CET is the possible fiscal implications. The study shows a loss of fiscal revenues as compared to the reference for Niger during the first years of the CET implementation (Table 10.5). However, the losses decrease gradually and turn into fiscal gain in the medium run as the GDP growth accelerates and imports from non-ECOWAS countries restart.

Niger's overall GDP as well as its agricultural GDP increase faster with the implementation of the ECOWAS CET as compared to the reference (Table 10.5). Growth in the agricultural sector accelerates faster compared to the non-agricultural sector under the CET reform. Although relatively small, consumption of agricultural and non-agricultural products also expands faster compared to the reference; the increase reaches 0.3 to 0.4% at the end of the ten-year period (Table 10.5). A successful implementation of the CET by the fifteen ECOWAS member states is welfare improving in Niger as the country's GDP and household real consumption both improve compared to the reference.

Table 10.5. GDP, household consumption and government earnings in Niger, change between CET and reference scenarios (%) (simulation results).[1]

	GDP		Household consumption		Government
	National economy	Agriculture	All products	Agricultural products	earnings
2016	0.0	0.0	0.0	0.0	-0.8
2017	0.1	0.1	0.1	0.1	-0.2
2018	0.2	0.2	0.1	0.1	-0.1
2019	0.3	0.3	0.2	0.1	-0.1
2020	0.3	0.4	0.3	0.2	0.0
2021	0.4	0.5	0.3	0.2	0.1
2022	0.5	0.6	0.4	0.3	0.1
2023	0.6	0.7	0.5	0.4	0.2
2024	0.7	0.8	0.5	0.4	0.3
2025	0.8	0.9	0.6	0.5	0.4

[1] Change in government revenue between the CET and reference scenarios as share of government initial revenue (2015).

10.6 Conclusions

A customs union is welfare improving if the benefits of trade creation exceed the costs of diverting trade. Niger has implemented the ECOWAS CET in April 2015. This chapter assesses the economic impact of a successful implementation of the ECOWAS CET by the fifteen member states with a focus on Niger. The chapter used the ECOWAS Simulation model, a multi-country CGE model developed by IFPRI for the ECOWAS member states. The model interconnects fifteen economies through the trading of commodities and the mobility of production factors, i.e. labour and capital.

Under the CET reform, the ECOWAS tariff rate applied to non-ECOWAS commodities remains slightly unchanged on average. However, a small decline (-2.5%) in tariff rates is observed for Niger with the implementation of the ECOWAS CET. Manufactured goods representing 58.3% of the country's imports also face a small decline (-2.0%) in tariff rates on average. Under the CET, Niger more rapidly expands its trade with both ECOWAS and non-ECOWAS partners compared to the reference, i.e. CET scheme not implemented. Trading of agricultural goods accelerates much faster than trading of non-agricultural products, particularly with non-ECOWAS countries. Niger's trade balance with ECOWAS countries deteriorates under the CET as compared to the reference. In contrast, Niger's trade balance with non-ECOWAS partners improves as its exports to the latter group of countries accelerates faster than its imports from the same group of countries.

The CET implementation increases the pressure on government fiscal revenue during the first years. However, the fiscal losses decrease gradually and turn into a gain in the medium run as GDP growth accelerates and imports from non-ECOWAS countries pick-up. A successful implementation of the CET by the fifteen ECOWAS member States is welfare improving in Niger, as the country's GDP and household real consumption improve compared to the reference.

References

Anonymous, 2017. Africa statistical yearbook 2017. Available at: http://tinyurl.com/y92b3zrt.

Balassa, B., 1961. The theory of economic integration. R.D. Irwin, Inc., Homewood, IL, USA.

Bhagwati, J.N., 1970. Trade diverting customs unions and welfare improvement: a clarification. Working Paper Number 56, Department of Economics, MIT, July 1970.

ENDA-CACID (Centre Africain pour le Commerce, l'Intégration et le Développement), 2012. L'état du commerce en Afrique de l'Ouest. Annual Report. Dakar, Senegal.

Hinosjosa-Ojeda, Lewis, J.D. and Robinson, S., 1995. Regional integration options for Central America and the Caribbean after NAFTA. North American Journal of Economics and Finance 6: 121-148.

Lewis, J.D. and Robinson, S., 1996. Partners or predators? The impact of regional trade liberalization on Indonesia. Policy Research Working Paper 1626. World Bank, Washington, DC, USA.

Lipsey, R., 1957. The theory of customs unions: trade diversion and welfare. Economica 24: 40-46.

Meade, J., 1955. The theory of customs unions. North-Holland Publishing Co., Amsterdam, the Netherlands.

Michalopolous, C. and Tarr, D., 1997. The economics of customs unions in the commonwealth of independent states. Policy, Research working paper no. WPS 1786. World Bank, Washington, DC, USA. Available at: http://tinyurl.com/ycfvu434.

Viner, J., 1950. The customs union issue. Studies in the administration of international law and organization, no. 10. The Carnegie Endowment for International Peace, New York, NY, USA.

World Bank, 2017. World Development Indicators 2017. Available at: http://hdl.handle.net/10986/26447.

World Integrated Trade Solution (WITS), 2014. Trade database. Available at: https://wits.worldbank.org/Default. aspx?lang=en.

Zafar, A., 2005. The impact of the strong euro on the real effective exchange rates of the two Francophone African CFA Zones. Policy, Research working paper no. WPS 3751. World Bank, Washington, DC, USA. Available at: http://tinyurl.com/y7ga9mbo.

Chapter 11.
Summary and conclusion

Fleur Wouterse

IFPRI c/o ISS, Kortenaerkade 12, 2518 AX, The Hague, the Netherlands; f.wouterse@cgiar.org

For Niger, the development of agriculture is essential to strategies to raise incomes and eradicate poverty in a sustainable manner, that is without further depleting its natural resource base. Africa is increasingly emphasising the role of innovation in development. The Science, Technology and Innovation Strategy for Africa 2024, for example, takes into consideration the social, economic, and technological progress Africa has made over the last decade. Innovation for sustainable agricultural growth forms an important part of this ambition. Traditional approaches to agricultural development have emphasised food security and have been rather technology focused – helping farmers to grow enough to feed themselves and their families, and perhaps a surplus to sell. However, reducing rural poverty across the board requires more than a green revolution. More recently, concern with markets has become prominent. Even subsistence farmers need cash, goes the reasoning; they need to be able to grow things they can sell. And if they have a market for their produce, they have an incentive to grow more to earn more. This ushers in a virtuous cycle of higher yields and production, greater incomes, higher living standards, and more investment in production. The agricultural value chain perspective provides a reference point for improvements in supporting services and the business environment and can contribute to pro-poor initiatives and better linking of smallholders to markets.

In the current publication, we have sought to contribute to the understanding of potential innovations that can sustainably transform the agriculture sector in Niger and the role of the market and institutional environment. The first six chapters have looked at various innovations, factors promoting their adoption and impacts on smallholders. Chapter 1 reveals that farmer-managed natural regeneration, which entails the protection of sprouting seedlings and the selection and pruning of stems regenerating from stumps of felled trees that are still living, has produced multiple, long-term benefits and because it is managed and maintained by land users there are no recurring costs to governments or donor agencies. The authors suggest that there is considerable scope for building on the existing successes of farmer-managed natural regeneration in Niger. They also highlight several important lessons about effective partnerships for agricultural development. First, they point out that from a technical perspective, both 'barefoot science' and cutting-edge science are important, particularly in difficult environments such as the West African Sahel and that the most successful innovations tend to be low-cost technical improvements on local practices. Second, the authors suggest that a single technique or practice alone, while generally insufficient to achieve meaningful environmental and economic impacts alone, can act as a trigger for other innovations. Third, the authors point out that a single 'menu' of technical options can be adopted on a large scale but that it must be flexible, adaptable, and testable by farmers under their own social, economic, and environmental conditions.

Chapter 2 points to the need for the Nigerien government to find cost-effective methods for providing incentives for tree planting and protection and other land management practices which have large off-farm benefits. The authors suggest that it is possible to develop a payment for ecosystem services (PES) in which the government – in collaboration with international carbon and biodiversity programs – could establish an effective mechanism for rewarding farmers. The authors also mention that proximity to roads and higher education enhance adoption of sustainable land and water management and that these two factors also enhance household food and nutrition. Additionally, access to extension services play a key role in enhancing adoption. These rural services thus need to be enhanced significantly as part of Niger's efforts to reduce poverty and improvement of other human welfare aspects.

Chapter 3 has analysed smallholder behaviour and adaptation to climate change through the construction of zaï pits using recent household level data for the Tahoua region. The chapter shows that households that perceived increased drought were more likely to have employed zaï pits but that important human capital-related obstacles to adaptation exist. Inadequacy in empowerment (measured using the Women's Empowerment in Agriculture Index) was, for example, shown to hamper zaï pit adoption. Estimation results revealed that productivity was higher in households that had implemented zaï pits, underlining the conclusion of Chapter 1 that the most successful innovations tend to be low-cost technical improvements on local practices. These findings are particularly pertinent because they point to the importance of bare foot science and highlight the success of grassroots innovations, suggesting that rather than planning climate change adaptation strategies, programs and interventions could more usefully focus on alleviating barriers to adaptation. The findings also speak to the importance of empowerment as a development goal, both for its intrinsic value and for its instrumental value in promoting adaptation and its productivity effects, particularly for vulnerable households. It is therefore important for policy makers aiming to enhance agricultural productivity of those households to consider empowerment-augmenting programs and interventions.

Using recent household data from the Tahoua and Dosso regions, Chapter 4 has highlighted the role that gender parity – which holds when women are at least as empowered as the men in their households – plays in the adoption of inorganic fertiliser in farm households. The author finds that increased power of women vis-à-vis men does not induce the adoption of inorganic fertiliser. The author suggests that this is so because with gender parity, the decision and negotiation power of a woman in the household determines the degree to which her unobserved characteristics like risk aversion or time preference may affect technology choice. Literacy and education of women seem to play an important role as a potential encouraging factor for technology adoption. The findings presented here are important because they point to a range of factors that may affect agriculture decision-making of men and women in rural households differently.

Chapter 5 has assessed *ex-ante* impacts of a small irrigation scheme (SPIN) on the livelihoods and food security of smallholder farmers in Niger using a micro-simulation model and data from the 2011 Living Standard Measurement Survey – Integrated Survey of Agriculture (LSMS-ISA).

The authors uncover a large effect of small-scale irrigation on crop allocation, production and farm income. Their estimates suggest that the total cropped area would increase by 5% in Niger, representing a positive impact for the availability of food and food security. The cultivated areas of paddy rice and cassava, two staple crops that play a key role in the diet of farm households, would see dramatic increases. Because irrigation smooths the potential dramatic impacts of drought and rainfall variability on yields, an important contribution of irrigation to food security is the stabilisation of crop yields. Despite some of its limitations of the model such as the fact that output prices are taken as exogenously given and that other constraints to the extensions of irrigated production are not treated, results pointing to high returns are useful to policy makers who are currently developing small irrigation support programs in Sub-Saharan countries.

Chapter 6 reviews the evidence of links between information and communication technologies (ICTs) and outcomes of farm households and concludes that ICTs can have a substantial effect on agricultural price dispersion, prices, and crop choice and have the potential to play a role in poverty reduction. An important finding that emerges for Niger is that farmers who receive access to a joint mobile phone and learn how to use it, increase the number of types of crops grown, primarily by increasing their production of marginal cash crops. However, the authors point out that the results vary by setting and that studies on the effects of ICTs on agricultural outcomes do not point to a unique, most effective approach. Instead, the evidence suggests that the approach to be used will depend on the constraint that will be addressed, the population experiencing the constraint and the ability to tailor the system to address the needs of the specific population. This conclusion also resonates Chapter 1 in that it suggests that for innovations to be successful they need to be flexible, adaptable, and testable by farmers under their own social, economic, and environmental conditions.

Chapters 7 to 10 have analysed price formation and the integration of cereal markets, trade and the agreements governing trade and have formulated suggestions for policy that could foster a sustainable agricultural transformation. Chapter 7 has used spatial econometrics and monthly cereal price data for Niger's eight regions from January 2000 to December 2012 collected by the System of Agricultural Market Information (SIMA) to study market integration of cereals in Niger with a special focus on the millet market. The authors find that price transmission is stable but that markets are not cointegrated. Results reveal a relationship between locally traded commodities such as millet and sorghum but no linkage between locally, regionally or internationally traded products such as millet, rice, or maize. These findings have some policy implications. First, the absence of inter-region price transmission reveals that a unique market-based price policy in Niger might not be effective in terms of mitigating the impact of a food crisis. To be effective, the government must design region-specific interventions. However, such options come at an elevated cost. Therefore, strategic investments are required to create conditions for price transmission between regions and ensure market integration. For example, investments in road infrastructure, which are essential for transport costs reduction, could be a good starting point. Second, since there is price transmission only between locally produced and consumed cereals (millet and sorghum), it would be important for the government to promote growth in their production, which may be a good resilience strategy for consumers.

Chapter 8 has assessed the structure, past trends and prospects of agricultural trade between Niger and the rest of the region and projects changes in traded quantities, both imports and exports, assuming a continuation of current trends in production, population and non-agricultural income. The chapter has demonstrated that Niger continues to play a key role in regional agricultural trade in West Africa and that the country's participation in regional trade will continue to expand both in terms of net imports and exports. The authors suggest that the level of participation in the future could be affected considerably by potential changes in policy and productivity. For instance, the simulation results presented in this chapter suggest that a modest reduction in general trading costs, the removal of cross-border trade obstacles, or a slight increase in yields, all realistic changes, would increase cross-border trade between Niger and its neighbours. A modest reduction in trade costs or a removal of cross-border trade barriers will increase not only net imports of cereals and other staple food products but also the net-exports of live animals. Moreover, a modest improvement in crops yield will reduce the levels of the country's net imports of food products and enhance the potential for net-exporting vegetables and spices to the regional market. Policy changes along the lines of the scenarios that are simulated would have important implications not just for the country's trade with the rest of the region but also for its ability to improve food security for its population. This would happen through improved and more stable domestic food supplies as well as higher incomes.

Chapter 9 gives an overview of the trade patterns in terms of commodities, geographical orientation and nature and provides a description of the institutional framework governing Niger's trade policy. Despite unstable economic growth, the country's gross domestic product (GDP) almost tripled over the last fifteen years but its international trade remains concentrated in a few commodities and the recent discovery of oil has not fundamentally changed the landscape. The author finds that regarding tariff commitments, except for the recent introduction of the Economic Community of West African States (ECOWAS) Common External Tariff (CET), the country has not violated any commitments, particularly in terms of most favoured nation (MFN) treatment. Niger is also found to have made progress in the case of its non-tariff commitments by changing its legislation and putting in place the institutions needed to implement the commitments. The author concludes though that inadequate human capacity, poor infrastructure, telecommunications, and trade equipment as well as supply side constraints are the main obstacles to implementing commitments in trade agreements.

The importance of implementing commitments in trade agreements is underlined by Chapter 10, which delves into one arrangement governing regional trade, the ECOWAS CET and has used the ECOWAS Simulation Model (ECOSIM) to assess the implementation of the ECOWAS CET scheme in its fifteen Members States. Results reveal that under the CET, Niger would more rapidly expands its trade with both ECOWAS and non-ECOWAS partners compared to the reference and that trading of agricultural goods would accelerate much faster than trading of non-agricultural products, particularly with non-ECOWAS countries. The country's GDP and household real consumption would also improve compared to the reference implying that a successful implementation of the CET by the fifteen ECOWAS member States is welfare improving in Niger.

In summary, this volume has shed light on several interesting innovations that could contribute to enhancing agricultural productivity. Particularly interesting is the emphasis on the grassroots nature of some of these innovations. At the same time, the chapters also highlight changes to the institutional environmental that could further enhance Niger's sustainable agricultural transformation.

Printed in the United States
by Baker & Taylor Publisher Services